Nature-Based Play Therapy

Nature-Based Play Therapy brings a theoretical basis to arguments for including nature in play therapy and provides tools for that inclusion with a prescriptive model. Throughout this book, play therapists are introduced to the histories of nature and play across cultures and cultural expectations and are then guided into an understanding of how nature and play intersect with current trends in society and psychotherapy. Readers will learn about how the therapeutic powers of play are activated and facilitated by the inclusion of nature in play therapy, and they will be taken step-by-step through a prescriptive case conceptualization model. They'll also find case studies that link theoretical tenets, the therapeutic powers and play and nature, and intended treatment outcomes.

Nature-Based Play Therapy is an excellent introduction to a vital and growing area of the field, one that gives a well-rounded summary to a theoretically based model of treatment.

Julie Blundon Nash, PhD, RPT-S, is a clinical psychologist and registered play therapist-supervisor. She works with individual clients, supervises prospective play therapists, and provides continuing education trainings to share play therapy.

Nature-Based Play Therapy

A Prescriptive Approach to Integrating the Therapeutic Powers of Nature and Play

Julie Blundon Nash

Routledge
Taylor & Francis Group

NEW YORK AND LONDON

Cover image by Julie Powell of Rockland Studios Photography

First published 2024
by Routledge
605 Third Avenue, New York, NY 10158

and by Routledge
4 Park Square, Milton Park, Abingdon, Oxon, OX14 4RN

Routledge is an imprint of the Taylor & Francis Group, an informa business

© 2024 Julie Blundon Nash

The right of Julie Blundon Nash to be identified as author of this work has been asserted in accordance with sections 77 and 78 of the Copyright, Designs and Patents Act 1988.

Library of Congress Cataloging-in-Publication Data
Names: Nash, Julie Blundon, author.
Title: Nature-based play therapy: a prescriptive approach to integrating
the therapeutic powers of nature and play / Julie Blundon Nash.
Description: New York, NY: Routledge, 2024. | Includes
bibliographical references and index. |
Identifiers: LCCN 2023024479 (print) | LCCN 2023024480
(ebook) | ISBN 9781032360607 (hardback) |
ISBN 9781032360584 (paperback) | ISBN 9781003332343 (ebook)
Subjects: LCSH: Play therapy. | Nature, Healing power of.
Classification: LCC RJ505.P6 N37 2024 (print) | LCC RJ505.P6
(ebook) | DDC 618.92/891653—dc23/eng/20230817
LC record available at https://lccn.loc.gov/2023024479
LC ebook record available at https://lccn.loc.gov/2023024480

ISBN: 978-1-032-36060-7 (hbk)
ISBN: 978-1-032-36058-4 (pbk)
ISBN: 978-1-003-33234-3 (ebk)

DOI: 10.4324/9781003332343

Typeset in Times New Roman
by codeMantra

This book is dedicated to my family. I'm so blessed to be living life with you.

GR, for always believing in me and loving me through it all.

Ben, for reminding me of the importance of play and nature as you grow.

Josh, for getting me in the woods so often and being willing to explore as you reach your goals.

Kelly, for always being up for an adventure and consistently showing true joy.

Contents

About the author

Julie Blundon Nash, PhD, is a clinical psychologist and Registered Play Therapist-Supervisor. She serves the Association for Play Therapy on various committees and the board of directors and served as president of the New England Association for Play Therapy. She owns Riverside Psychological Associates, LLC, a private practice through which she works with individual clients, supervises prospective play therapists, and provides continuing education training for those seeking play therapy credentials. Dr. Nash has published multiple book chapters on foundational principles of play therapy and enjoys teaching and encouraging play therapists to have a solid foundation in theoretical understanding and the powers of play. As a homeschooling family, Dr. Nash and her husband believe in the importance of both God and nature as integral parts of raising their three kids, and they can often be found exploring the woods.

Chapter 1

Introduction

"I like nature … but only when I get to PLAY in it!" said my then five-year-old daughter as were taking a family hike one beautiful, unseasonably perfect summer Saturday. As we explored the trails, found frogs, surprised a garter snake, and climbed rocks, I thought about her words and the point she made. Making the time to consistently explore and interact with nature on your own terms is key—or else it will become a chore. We hike a fair amount as a family. My middle son has a goal this year to reach twice the number of miles he hiked last year. As he is nine, and not allowed to do long hikes alone yet, his siblings and I tag along much of the time. This is often an opportunity for time in nature to become a chore, so long as we let it. Instead, we will often pick a rest stop location as our primary goal for the day and build in time to explore as an incentive to get his siblings motivated as well and to enjoy part of the day together. These times of exploration and adventure have revealed so much.

On one recent outing I was sitting on a rock in a swamp, watching my three kids explore cattails and experiment with how the seeds fly when the wind blows in different ways. They would take off to look in the water, racing sticks as the water flowed over the rocks and seeing if they could spot signs of beaver activity by examining the water itself. Tracks, bent grass, hidden hollows, and overturned rocks were all explored in turn. I watched them scamper across rocks through this swampy area, navigating clumps of grass as footholds, with no care for the muck and mud, but staying dry. They were able to correct their steps in the moment to gain a stronger foothold whenever they wobbled even slightly. One miscalculated and went down, only to hop right back up and continue on with no prolonged concern for a potential minor scrape. While one child was out that day hoping to log a good number of miles on his record, he and the others had no care during that moment for anything other than what was right in front of them. That was the true goal of the day. It struck me in that moment how different an hour spent outside in nature truly is compared to a "regular hour." An hour of nature is so much more than a regular hour spent indoors. As we have spent more time outdoors over the years, I have learned that 20 minutes is the magic number for me (and researchers agree with this amount of time, but more on that

DOI: 10.4324/9781003332343-1

later). Those 20 minutes could be hiking, as about a mile to a mile and a half into a hike is when I notice my thoughts clear enough to be able to see the solution to a challenge I have been working through at my desk. Or those minutes could be spent just walking around the house, observing what is happening outside of my head and my usual space. Twenty minutes is also enough for my kids to engage in free play outside, encouraging pretend play, challenging themselves, getting creative, and changing any negative attitudes almost immediately.

There are so many ways and reasons to experience nature, with so many lasting benefits. Nature and play have been linked since the earliest days of human experience. The freedoms the two allow form the basis for many an amazing discovery or community-changing innovation (have you read *The Boy Who Harnessed the Wind* by William Kamkwamba?). Perhaps most important, time in nature to play allows for the lazy summer day of a child busy from sunup to sundown. There can be something spiritual and almost magical about being surrounded by nature. That same something is present to some degree with any interaction with nature including just staring out a window or being able to view images of an outdoor scene. It gives a sense of being part of something so much bigger than yourself and lets you view your concerns as so much smaller than they once felt and part of an ongoing cycle or system, which helps regulate the human experience. That overarching, therapeutic benefit of interconnectedness impacts us all.

The importance of nature exposure, child-led free play, and nature exploration have been highlighted many times, and making this connection is a primary reason for including nature in play therapy. The focus of this book is to bring a theoretical basis to the inclusion of nature in play therapy and to provide a way in which to do so through a prescriptive model. Mental health clinicians are now utilizing nature-based techniques to provide play therapy, but the connection to a theory and way of understanding clients and their needs, while integrating the therapeutic powers of both play and nature, has not been made on a large scale.

Here, play therapists will be introduced to the history of play and the role of nature in children's development across cultures and religious beliefs, and be guided through an exploration of the intersection of these with current trends. Chapters will be devoted to the historical changes in time in nature and the importance of nature in societies, as well as children's play. These will be explored across geographical locations, cultural experiences, and religious understandings and teachings with the goal of understanding more deeply what cultural expectations and current trends of nature-based play and child-led free play time show us in terms of individual development across cultures and as societies. The increase in structured, adult-guided play and the decrease in child-led free play time, specifically in nature, are related to an increase in mental health conditions (Csikszentmihályi & Hunter, 2003; Gray, 2011, 2013; Luthar & Latendresse, 2005). For children, these referrals can increasingly be made to play therapists. Thus, play therapists should be grounded in a theoretical approach to utilizing nature in play therapy.

The ten seminal or historically significant play therapy theories and approaches as identified by the Association for Play Therapy will be briefly explored and more specifically linked to the impact of nature than have been done previously. These theories and approaches include Adlerian, child-centered, cognitive-behavioral, developmental (Viola Brody's approach), ecosystemic, filial, Gestalt, Jungian, object relations, and Theraplay (Association for Play Therapy, 2022). Any research published connecting outcomes and inclusion of nature with the approach or theory will be examined, as well as original writings by the founders or developers of the approaches to identify links to inclusion of nature into the theory. For example, Carl Jung's deep personal connections to nature will be explored to determine any impact nature may have had on the development of Jungian theory and the subsequent integration within Jungian play therapy. Another example would be how Violet Oaklander used to engage in therapeutic interactions on playgrounds with school children, so the importance of the outdoor world in her thinking and subsequent impact on the development of Gestalt play therapy will be explored through her writings.

The therapeutic powers of play will be introduced with a specific focus on how these change agents are activated and/or facilitated by the inclusion of nature in play therapy. The therapeutic powers of nature-based therapies will also be introduced, described, and connected to the therapeutic powers of play. A prescriptive approach will then be presented to allow play therapists to integrate theoretical knowledge based on an understanding of *"What* treatment, by *whom*, is most effective for *this* individual, with *that* specific problem, with *which* set of circumstances?" (Paul, 1967). A model outlining a prescriptive approach to linking theoretical tenets, therapeutic powers, and play and nature with intended outcome of treatment will be presented. Composite case examples and ethical considerations will round out the presentation of nature-based play therapy to give a solid introduction to a theoretically grounded model of treatment based in theory and facilitating change agents.

We intuitively know that nature-based play therapy is important. We may have seen changes in children we know or work with as they spent time outside, or watched their overall development flourish as they developed new skills, strengths, and interests through time spent in nature. We may have noticed differences in ourselves when we got some fresh air as part of our day instead of staying inside all day. Direct physical impacts are seen in scientific literature specifically linking time spent in sunshine to improved key neurotransmitter markers related to depression and anxiety. Research supports our observations, as studies are showing direct links between outdoor activities and decreases in symptoms of attention-deficit hyperactivity disorder, for example (Kuo & Taylor, 2004). Across the board, physical, social, and emotional developments are positively impacted by time spent in nature. Knowing that we need to include nature in children's lives and play, the purpose of this text will be to bring the "how" and "why" to the planning, treatment, and outcomes phases of nature-based play therapy.

There are inherent limitations to this book, specifically regarding the inability to be fully comprehensive in a review of religions and cultural identities and experiences, but an overview will be provided. In the historical perspectives Chapters 2 and 3, you will often see more of a full age-range, societal approach to understanding the roles of nature and play in development rather than only a focus on childhood. However, the designated focus of the play therapy aspects will be on children's experiences with nature and play, while understanding that nature-based play therapy is appropriate and effective for the entire age range (and is even a wonderful way to encourage teens and adults to engage in play!).

Before we jump into the history, scientific research, and theoretical processes of play and nature, I encourage you to spend a few minutes reflecting on your own past and current experiences with play and with nature. You are likely reading this book because you believe in the importance of both nature and play therapy, yet so much of our understanding of nature and play experiences is truly hard to verbally define. We have visceral reactions and memories, feelings, and responses blending with thoughts and reconstructions of early experiences. Exploring these reactions and memories, even the difficult, challenging, or downright horrible ones, can help you to understand your own definitions of play and nature more fully, and their importance in your own life. Perhaps you want no child to ever experience the same as you did, or maybe you strive to help many children enjoy free play because you did, and you see the ongoing impact that had across your life span. This may be a wonderful time of recollection for you, or it might be something you choose to skip. I hope that you can use the following questions to guide your reflections, and perhaps even grow in your understanding of your own worldview regarding the importance of nature and play in development. Part of this exercise is to help you get more comfortable asking questions about play development and nature-based experiences and be able to explore the answers more fully. Taking a solid play history including intergenerational views and experiences can be eye-opening in a therapeutic setting. Incorporating the same for nature experiences can be equally profound and give a stronger understanding of clients and families in the nature-based play therapy setting. So, let's get started!

- What are your earliest memories of play?
- Who was involved?
- What was involved (toward which materials did you gravitate)?
- Where were you?
- What emotional reactions do you have looking back on these experiences?
- Are you remembering specific experiences or more of a fluid memory across time?
- What were your parents' or caretakers' reactions to your play time and storytelling?
- Did they encourage you, interact with you, or reject your play?

- What about your grandparents, extended family, and neighbors?
- Did you prefer solitary play or being with others?
- How did these play experiences differ?
- How do you define "nature" and nature spaces?
- What constitutes "time in nature"?
- Are there any special books from your childhood or young adulthood that were set in nature?
- What experiences of nature were available to you as a child?
- Are there certain sights, sounds, or smells of nature that trigger pleasant memories?
- What about unpleasant?
- What was the value of your time in nature when you were growing up?
- How do you think your parents and grandparents viewed time in nature?
- What gives you this impression?
- What is the value you currently place on time in nature?
- What does time in nature look like for you today?
- Do you purposefully integrate time with nature in your own life?
- How do you encourage this for others?
- What nature spaces are available where you practice play therapy? What spaces are readily available for your clients?
- What are the obstacles to overcome before engaging in nature-based play therapy yourself or prescribing outdoor play to your clients?

References

Association for Play Therapy. (2022, July 1). *Credentialing standards for the Registered Play Therapist™*. https://cdn.ymaws.com/www.a4pt.org/resource/resmgr/credentials/RPT_Standards.pdf

Csikszentmihályi, M., & Hunter, J. (2003). Happiness in everyday life: The uses of experience sampling. *Journal of Happiness Studies, 4*, 185–199. https://doi.org/10.1023/A:1024409732742

Gray, P. (2011). The decline of play and the rise of psychopathology in children and adolescents. *American Journal of Play, 3*(4), 443–463.

Gray, P. (2013). *Free to learn*. Basic Books.

Kuo, F. E., & Taylor, A. F. (2004). A potential natural treatment for Attention-Deficit/Hyperactivity Disorder: Evidence from a national study. *American Journal of Public Health, 94*(9), 1580–1586. https://doi.org/10.1177/1087054708323000

Luthar, S. S., & Lantendresse, S. J. (2005). Children of the affluent: Challenges to well-being. *Current Directions in Psychological Science, 14*, 49–55. https://doi.org/10.1111/j.0963-7214.2005.00333.x

Paul, G. L. (1967). Strategy of outcome research in psychotherapy. *Journal of Consulting Psychology, 31*(2), 109–118. https://psycnet.apa.org/doi/10.1037/h0024436

Chapter 2

The history of children's experiences with nature

The history of children's time in nature includes many changes over the years in both quantity and quality of time and experiences. The perceived importance (or lack thereof) of time in nature related to children's development will now be explored across multiple cultural groups, as well as how various cultural groups view nature (or wilderness, or landscape, depending on the location). The definition of nature differs by location, and this will be explained to guide cultural awareness. Spirituality and religion are closely intertwined with nature and the experience of the outdoors and open spaces. Some religious cultures have positive, reverent approaches to nature, while others do not. These topics must be explored to gain a full perspective of the impact of both including and excluding nature within children's lives. This discussion will also tie into how nature has guided personal and societal development, including health and physical benefits to time in nature and the advances in understanding made there.

Before I get too far into this discussion, I offer you a disclaimer as to some limitations of Chapters 2 and 3. I do not profess myself to be an expert in any major cultural or religious groups, but I can report what the literature suggests about a multitude of communities. I am going to give a brief (and often lacking, to be perfectly honest, due to a dearth of available research) synopsis of what the literature suggests about the history of what various cultural groups, people in various locations, and communities have experienced over time. This leads to another limitation, as the coverage here must be brief and therefore cannot possibly cover enough material to cover every person's experience or historical perspective. I fully understand and respect the fact that different groups have had different experiences of the same events, and I do not want to ignore, minimize, or diminish those experiences in any way. I will have to generalize and apologize now for all that that entails. The research and literature sources are readily available for a handful of geographical, cultural, and religious groups including the United States (some immigrant, some indigenous), Canada, Japan, the United Kingdom (especially England and Wales), Finland, Norway, Denmark, the Religious Society of Friends (Quakers), Christianity, Buddhism,

DOI: 10.4324/9781003332343-2

Catholicism, Judaism, Muslim, and a few other religious entities. For some of these groups, the religious aspect of their culture is part of their discussion, while for others they are separate as many religious beliefs extend across geographical areas.

Along with this, there is a difference between religion and spirituality that should be outlined for the purpose of this writing. Following a specific religious group or doctrine does not necessarily make one spiritual, just as finding an interconnectedness with a higher power might not make one religious and interested in worshipping with a specific denomination. For the purposes of this chapter, the specific religious ideals, tenets, and principles of multiple established religious groups will be explored, as will the spiritual sense of belonging, particularly in relation to nature experiences. This sense of belonging is particularly important as the awareness and acceptance of a higher power connecting humans, nature, and living organisms in the natural world leads to interconnection (McDonald et al., 2009). This interconnectedness grows when one meaningfully interacts with nature and begins to become part of the greater whole (Naor & Mayseless, 2020). This will be explored in greater depth in terms of the impact of nature on the development of the self and society.

Nature itself means different things to different people depending upon their experiences, cultural identification, and location in the world (Coscieme et al., 2019). After scrutinizing the use of the term "nature" in 60 languages, researchers determined there are three main conceptualizations of nature across the world: inclusive, non-inclusive, and deifying. These include humans as being a significant part of nature, humans and nature as separate entities, and nature having a more spiritual dimension (Coscieme et al., 2019). This suggests that people from various geographical, cultural, and religious backgrounds have different conceptualizations of what "nature" is, the importance of nature in relation to human growth and development, and how humans should and do interact with the natural world. Nature includes so many aspects of our world including the wilderness, plains, dense forests, the landscape, urban parks and walking trails, formal and vegetable gardens, plants that are on indoor windowsills, and so on. Within this, there are differences seen in the value (or lack thereof) of children spending free play time in natural settings, and thus, the energy adults put in to encouraging children to play outside and creating the environment to support such time. This is really a key factor. especially in current society. What we choose to focus on and dedicate time to is what we end up doing and encouraging! It is much easier to focus on passive entertainments that do not necessitate the time and energy it takes to get and keep kids outside. The availability of safe natural spaces, family and community reactions to time in nature, and viewed importance of the natural world are three of the primary variables I have seen in my research and work in the United States in terms of why parents and caregivers do or do not actively create more outdoor time for children.

Religious and cultural views

As religious beliefs transcend geography, we will start with exploring the value and understanding of nature within various religions. Different religions have different views on time in nature as well as conservation compared to preservation. For our purposes, conservation deals with sustainably using and enjoying nature. This includes using natural resources, but making sure that enough is left for regrowth and sustaining an area. The focus of preservation is to keep an area as pristine and untouched as possible. The common idea of "leave nothing but footprints and take nothing but photos" fits more within a preservationist worldview, while enjoying and gathering natural materials for later use but being sure to leave enough intact for continued growth and development is a conservationist worldview. Both protect natural resources but in different ways. At the extreme, preservation encourages restrictions on use of nature, while conservation encourages limited and sustainable use of the world. These concepts fit within religious worldviews as well as routine and clinical applications of the natural world.

For example, in Bible-based Christianity and Catholicism we see the impact of one God as creator of all. Everything in nature is seen as divinely inspired and developed. Man is expected to work and live from the land. Thus, experiencing nature is seen as connecting with God through His creation, which He has given for humans' use, growth, and nourishment, encouraging a conservation and stewardship mindset. Nature viewed from a biblical standpoint includes the dichotomy of positive and negative impacts on people, with many illustrations given of God's sovereignty and goodness and destruction through nature-based events. In some passages, these opposites work together through nature, such as in the account of the Great Flood. Here we see nature being used to destroy most of creation to eliminate sinful behaviors, and at the same time used to bring hope through an olive branch from dry land carried back by a bird after the earth was cleansed.

Judaism views the human and nature relationship as symbiotic, with respect for both being prevalent in Judaic texts (Vogel, 2001). While there is a creationist understanding of how both humans and nature developed, there is also an understanding that the two must work together in a sense to balance ongoing needs, suggesting a conservation-guided understanding of nature's use. Judaism includes encouragement to enjoy the natural world while imposing restrictions on its use. For example, on the Sabbath, productive work is not allowed, which gives people time to rest and spiritually reflect, and time for the land to rest without human interference. Nature is seen as having both positive and negative qualities, as it can supply many needs and replenish a person but can also cause havoc and destruction. Another example of the duality of nature is the Garden of Eden where all good was provided and needs met, yet the serpent brought people to sinful behaviors (Vogel, 2001). As the Torah and Pentateuch accounts are similar between the Hebrew, Orthodox, Catholic, and Protestant Bibles, the stories and examples are similar across these religions.

In other religions, shifts have been seen over time in the understanding of and interaction with the natural world. For example, early Quakers (Religious Society of Friends) in Britain and Ireland viewed creation and the subsequent natural world as knowable only through revelations by God (Morries, 2010). By the nineteenth century, this view had changed to allow for more individualistic understandings of the natural world and humans' place therein. God is still seen as the Creator, but knowledge of the natural world could be gathered from the natural world itself and personal experience (Morries, 2010).

Islamic traditions and the Quran view a balance in the natural world that is important to respect and uphold (Faruqi, 2007). Through respecting the earth and studying natural phenomenon, humans can seek to understand God and are responsible for the earth and its resources as representatives of God (Faruqi, 2007). The study of the natural world to seek a deeper understanding of God suggests a strong connection to the earth and natural forces. It is of note that balance is sought between production and consumption of natural resources to maintain ecosystems and the understanding that all creation has a purpose (Alpay et al., 2013). Thus, Muslims are encouraged to utilize only the resources they need and to show responsibility for their usage (Alpay et al., 2013). It is particularly important for play therapists planning to utilize natural materials in sessions to be aware of this more preservationist approach and to understand the need to encourage respectful harvesting (if any is done at all) and utilization of materials.

Very early Buddhist understandings of the natural world related to Buddha making sense of the natural world around him in relation to his worldview and experiences. The natural world was obviously important for survival, and thus held an important place in his thoughts. He observed the struggles and strengths of animals, commenting on their sensitivities, rudimentary moral sense, and how they often fight, but also recognized their hierarchies, gratitude, and positive interactions. Buddha spoke of humans being able to be reborn into the animal kingdom realm and the need for love and compassion for all. With this idea of reincarnation, the concept of preservation takes on a new meaning and necessity for human survival. As Buddhism spread, people grew in their compassion for the natural world and would leave water for animals and nesting places for birds. Monks were allowed to strain their drinking water to capture and release tiny insects and would supervise farming operations to ensure the natural world was as protected as possible. Natural elements such as flowers were used in religious ceremonies, and natural materials specifically collected for hygiene practices and building home items (Dhammika, 2015). The mindfulness of the early Buddhist traditions carries on, along with mindful use of natural materials and a deep respect for the natural world.

Native Americans and other indigenous populations tend to have spiritual relationships with nature while incorporating an understanding of nature as providing for their physical needs. Nature is the source of food, water, medicine, and community growth. These groups also view children's time in nature as significantly important for early learning. Children are encouraged to play to practice adult skills as well as to learn mathematical and other concepts. On a large scale, children experience the world around themselves and thus understand the reality of their place in the world, community, and importance of nature for their personal and generational survival. The outdoor world is the scene of personal growth and maturity, as well as a connection to the Creator and an open space to connect with the past, present, and future.

Indigenous populations were quite familiar with the importance of nature and the land for their survival, both physical and spiritual. The two have always been importantly entwined. Erik Erikson (1950) wrote about spending time with Sioux, Dakota, and Yurok communities to learn about their views of development across the age span and the role of children. He spoke about the Sioux people following the buffalo across the plains to provide for their families and understanding spatial concepts and the like based on knowledge of the geography of the land and beginning to understand the importance of the connection to and with sand, wind, and sun (among other elements) in terms of holistic development and mind–body stability. Sioux teenagers would undertake vision quests which involved spending time alone and naked in the outdoors for days, fasting, and awaiting dreams that would guide them in their future paths. Being exposed to and part of the natural elements was a key component to this guidance, allowing for intimate connection with the universe as a whole and the influence of generational experiences. Erikson described the Yurok tribe as creating borders of their territory for themselves and utilizing these borders to completely shut out the rest of the world. The river, sky, and land created and sustained their way of life, and prayers were made to the horizons for sustenance and survival. Instead of buffalo of the Sioux population, the salmon maintained the community (Erikson, 1950).

In early US history, time outside was an important part of daily life for new immigrants. Families worked together to provide for their physical needs through farming and working with their hands. Leisure trips to visit friends and family were few and far between, but even those were guided by the forces of nature. The weather and seasons would impact when leisure trips or more permanent household moves could be planned, as well as the harvest schedule. In their effort to develop larger economies and understand the country, many men became explorers and traveled thousands of miles on horseback to map various regions. Thus, nature was seen as a space for nourishment and survival, exploration, and development. Children in these populations were most often along for the journey and part of the farming life of the family to provide for physical needs. Children would engage in farm chores as early as they were physically able to do so and were seen as capable of gathering eggs, keeping birds away from crops, and harvesting vegetables at very young ages, especially compared to today's standards (Hopkins, 1994).

Over time, communities grew, and national economies were developed. By the nineteenth century, socioeconomic status impacted the amount of time children and families spent outdoors. In nineteenth-century England in particular, class structure and where families fit in that system made a notable difference in terms of experiences of childhood, activities, learning, and leisure pursuits. This changed greatly over the course of the century for working-class families in particular, as the focus of the childhood years was not growing, developing, and having a fun-filled youth experience as we may consider it now, but shifted from full-time work as soon as the child was physically capable of so doing to compulsory education following multiple reforms and new laws by the end of the century (Hopkins, 1994). Children typically worked in agricultural settings, manufacturing facilities, or factories. Most of the agricultural work was completed outdoors, and it was noted that these children often fared a bit better than their peers as the open air of the fields was healthier for them than that of the factory (Hopkins, 1994). Consistent with this finding, children who attended workhouse schools in the first half of the nineteenth century were found to require less discipline than the adults who worked in these settings, which was attributed to the fact that the children were allowed to walk in the gardens during break times (Hopkins, 1994).

Historical developments

In considering the historical aspects of time in nature, especially as economies became more developed and social status began driving changes between classes of people, I cannot help but think about how various populations must have had very different views of nature and the benefits of time outside when nature was depended upon for one's livelihood and sustenance compared to an avenue for entertainment or leisure. In some areas of the world today, there are many populations who continue to depend on the land to provide for basic and ongoing needs, while in other areas, people do not make the connection between food growing from the ground and ending up in a grocery store or on their plates! Across the world people tend to be moving out of the agricultural field as tasks become more mechanized and fewer workers are needed, even though the need for food production grows. This has been documented in such places as Tanzania (Wineman, et al., 2020), Bangladesh (Sen et al., 2021), and Vietnam (McCaig & Pavcnik, 2013), among other nations. Innovations in technology and process improvements contribute to this change (Njuki, 2021). There has also been an interesting shift as production and process improvements are made as rural areas become more urbanized by aging and wealthier people who want to experience "rural" living without engaging in agricultural pursuits, and therefore continue to grow the urban population within rural settings (Satterthwaite et al., 2010). The biophilia theory posits that people are naturally drawn to nature and that we have an intrinsic motivation to be in natural settings (Wilson, 1984). This can be part of the explanation of why people are being drawn into more rural areas even when trying to maintain their more urban pursuits!

In the United States, there are initiatives building in popularity to get people outside more frequently, including encouraging green "prescriptions" by doctors to share the importance of time in nature through the Park RX America program (Robbins, 2020). Our local schools encourage teachers to use extra outdoor recess time as rewards and birthday celebrations. The "10-Minute Walk" program is also working to ensure all communities are no more than ten minutes away from an open green space, and to date over 85% of the United States has been mapped and researched to determine where more parklands are needed (Trust for Public Land, 2022). There is still a lot to be done to reach this goal! There are other programs encouraging outdoor play time, such as 1,000 Hours Outside, which encourages families to swap or at least match children's screen time with outside time, aiming for at least 1,000 hours outdoors each year (Yurich, 2022). That said, there has also been a societal shift in the United States away from child-led free play and toward adult-guided, structured activities. Children's school hours are filled with academics, with recess being the last thing to fit into the schedule and all too often the first to be removed when a child misbehaves or needs extra time to study. After-school activities are often extracurricular lessons, sports practices and games, and so on. Play dates are structured events that must be fit into various calendars. In non-rural America, it is often hard to find children running amuck outdoors unless parents intentionally create that time and space in which it can happen. Parents also often must intentionally change their thinking patterns about the acceptability of this time and choose to make their schedules accordingly to make consistent outdoor free play a reality. This can be one of the most challenging aspects of getting children outdoors.

Impact of nature on development

It has been suggested that when children are consistently exposed to nature (or really anything!) at young ages, they will become both more knowledgeable about and more open to such experiences as they age. I think about this in relation to digital natives and digital immigrants. Those who grow up with technological devices at their disposal are much more likely to be able to pick up a new device, figure it out quickly, and use it fluently, while those of us who learned about computers and cell phones in even the teenage years or later will always be at a slight technological disadvantage. The same is true of people who were encouraged to be in nature often as a young child compared to those who learn later in life. This difference is quite clear to me when looking at my own family. We have always enjoyed the outdoors but did not put a big emphasis on truly learning about what is around us and the benefits and impacts the trees and plants in our area can have in the last five to ten years. In looking just at our children's knowledge of plants, our youngest has the easiest time picking up information about new plants. She is now six, and thus learning about plants has always been her world, whereas our older boys are in a middle ground of being immersed in this new language in their formative years but still needing to put in a more serious effort than she.

There are many benefits to spending time in nature as a child or teenager. In a review of the relevant literature, Gill (2014) looked at the benefits children experience when they spend time in nature. He found multiple positive benefits ranging from improvements in physical health by simply living near green spaces, increases in emotional regulation and overall mental health, and long-term improved environmental knowledge, sense of space, and connectedness with nature (Gill, 2014). Children, teenagers, and parents who live in areas where green spaces are available to them rate the physical health of their children as very good, higher than that of peer groups living in other areas. This is a consistent finding across multiple geographical locations including Sweden, Canada, Finland, and Scotland (Chawla, 2015). Blood pressure levels have been found to be lower for children in areas higher in greenness in various countries including Austria and Germany (Chawla, 2015). Children are also more likely to be more physically active, thus leading to improved physical health, when they have consistent access to outdoor space in which to run, jump, and play. Chawla's (2015) review of the literature found this result to hold true in studies completed in the United States, the Netherlands, and Canada. Tillman et al. (2018) noted that specifically for children living in urban or suburban environments, the impact of exposure to green and blue spaces (parks, trees, grass, and water) was significantly related to improvements in health-related quality-of-life measures. These positive impacts on physical health are crucial for overall healthy child development, which leads to improved possibilities for lifelong health. This can easily lead to thoughts of how improving the physical health of our children can lead to improving society as a whole and reducing the strain on the medical system, but that is a larger conversation for a different setting!

To go one step further in physical health and development, specific to motor development, Fjørtoft (2001) noted that the natural topographical differences found in nature settings such as rocks, vegetation, slopes, and meadows lead to multiple ways to challenge the body to develop abilities to overcome obstacles. After simply being allowed to maneuver in forested areas for an hour or two a day during their kindergarten year, a group of children in Norway showed significant differences in their abilities with balance and cross coordination compared to their peers. These findings were later replicated with similar results (Fjørtoft, 2004). This finding fascinated me, and I started thinking about balance and coordination in myself and my children. They are much more willing than I am to take risks when crossing streams, walking on fallen trees, or climbing rocks, and truly do seem to have a better sense of where their bodies are in space as well as a stronger ability to self-correct balance as needed. Shortly after I read these studies, my husband came home from a Cub Scout hike complaining about how many of the children struggled with maintaining their balance, judging distances between rocks, and simply maintaining enough core strength to maneuver an easy terrain through the woods. It was of note that the same children spent much of the hike comparing notes on video games they loved to play. These children complained about how hard the hike was for them, while those who routinely spent time outdoors simply exploring and engaging in the environment were at the front of the pack, chattering away about nothing in particular while hopping from rock to rock instead of walking on the even ground, making their trek more challenging while keeping a faster pace.

Time spent in nature has also been linked to improvements in mood states. At the most basic level, people who report higher connections with nature also report being happier overall, resulting in more positive affect and greater life satisfaction (Capaldi et al., 2014). Time in nature has been linked to mental health benefits for all ages, with systematic reviews of the literature supporting the links for children and adolescents (Tillman, Tobin et al., 2018). At the brain level, research indicates that walking in a natural environment compared to an urban setting leads to decreases in rumination and subgenual prefrontal cortex activity, which is related to rumination (Bratman, Hamilton, et al., 2015). There are also many positive physical impacts from spending time in the sunshine noted on a neurological level. For example, spending time in the sun, especially at relatively higher light intensities, is related to an increase in serotonin-1A receptor binding (Spindelegger et al., 2012). This study noted the increase in the limbic areas of the brain (Spindelegger et al., 2012), which is important because serotonin has been specifically linked to mood and energy. The more serotonin a person produces and the more receptor sites that are available for this monoamine neurotransmitter are related to happier moods and feeling more energetic. Tsai and colleagues (2011) also found an increase in neurotransmitter activity after exposure to sunshine when they found that dopamine D_2/D_3 receptor availability increased. Dopamine is known for improving mood but also supporting memory processes, attention, and movement abilities. Taken together, findings like this suggest that being outside in the sunshine improves mood, attention, and concentration from the brain-based neurotransmitter level on up.

Harte and Eifert (1995) had research participants engage in running both indoors and outdoors and found similar effects. Their research suggested that people who ran outside simply enjoyed it more than people who ran inside! Outdoor participants reported an environmental focus of attention as opposed to an internal focus of attention (which was reported by those who ran inside), and as such outdoor runners felt fewer negative emotions like anxiety, depression, and hostility than did indoor runners. Indoor runners showed increases in cortisol secretions that the outdoor runners did not, suggesting that being inside for this activity led to physical stress (Harte & Eifert, 1995). We can extrapolate from these benefits that being outdoors, especially in the sunshine, improves mood, attention, and memory at the brain level, encouraging activity of neurotransmitters.

As all humans have these neurotransmitters, it is not a huge stretch to understand children's time in nature as being physically beneficial at this brain level for children as well.

Multiple studies highlight the moderating effect of nature on the impact of stressful life events through both biological and self-report results. Hunter and colleagues (2019) noted that adults who spent at least ten minutes in nature measured almost twice the expected diurnal drop in salivary cortisol levels. This suggests that nature time reduced physical stress-level markers. Alvarsson and colleagues (2010) found that listening to nature sounds after a stressor was applied led to faster recovery of the sympathetic nervous system, as measured by skin conductance tests and in contrast to environmental noises being played. This research correlates to a study performed in Sweden in which amount of environmental noise and availability of green space were compared to experienced stress symptoms, in which it was found that increased availability of green space acted as a buffer to reduce stress symptoms (Gidlöf-Gunnarsson & Öhrström, 2007). In a national study based in the Netherlands, the number of health complaints and mental health self-ratings were compared in relation to stressful life events. Van den Berg and colleagues (2010) found that the amount of green space moderated the impact of stressful life events in that having a high level of green space nearby was related to lower levels of perceived stress. These results were similar to a study conducted with a population of children living in rural areas of New York in which higher amounts of nearby green space were correlated with lower impacts of stressful life events (Wells & Evans, 2003). Other research suggests that simply viewing green spaces or natural views from a window helps students recover from mental fatigue and perceived stress (Li & Sullivan, 2015)! Taken together, these studies suggest that time spent in nature not only improves physical functions but works to reduce the impact of perceived and real stressors on the body and mind.

These findings lead to the impact of time in nature on cognitive tasks and development. In particular, nature walks have been correlated with improvements on memory span tasks. Berman and colleagues (2012) found that adults who took a 50-minute nature walk were able to show significant increases in short-term memory tasks compared to those who did not walk or go outside. Bratman, Daily, and colleagues (2015) later found similar results when they asked adults to take 50-minute nature walks. Those participants also showed significant improvements in working memory tasks. Studies with children as participants have shown improvements on concentration tasks when nature views were seen from windows rather than more urban views (Taylor et al., 2002). Math and English Language Arts test scores were found to be higher for students who had views of trees and plants (Wu et al., 2014), and views like these were also found to be correlated with working memory and attention (Dadvand et al., 2015) and overall success in educational careers (Matsuoka, 2010). Those schools creating outdoor learning spaces will be able to reap the benefits of improved academic performance for their students!

There is a burgeoning field of research looking at the impact of nature time on the development and improvement of creativity. One group of researchers examined responses of backpackers participating in Outward Bound excursions who immersed themselves in nature, away from technology, for four days. Results indicated that creativity on a problem-solving task increased by 50% for these groups (Atchley et al., 2012). While this type of excursion and complete separation from technology is not achievable by all, the results suggest that reducing dependence on technology and increasing nature time can improve creativity. Increases in creativity are also seen through self-report measures as adults who relied on creativity for their professional work were asked to describe their relationships with nature and the impact they see nature as having on their creative processes. Results of the interviews indicated that nature tended to encourage flexible thinking and new ways of looking at stimuli (Plambech & Konijnendijk van den Bosch, 2015). Williams and colleagues (2018) hypothesize that this type of improvement in creativity is likely related to mind-wandering and attention control, as the mind is more capable of wandering in natural settings than more urban and busy settings, and natural settings allow for shifts between external and internal focus. These shifts and episodes of mind-wandering are vital as they allow for and encourage flexible thinking. Gould van Praag and colleagues (2017) found changes in brain activity and increases in parasympathetic nervous system activity, while adults listened to nature-based sounds as part of mind-wandering exercises. Results like these suggest that there is a full-body response to nature sounds and stimuli that leads to positive results in terms of the development of creativity and flexible thinking.

The attention restoration theory incorporates results like these to suggest that time in nature helps people restore their attentional abilities because directed attention needs are lower in nature settings. Directed attention is important for resolving conflict between stimuli and helps one choose which stimulus to focus on at any given time while directing attention away from other stimuli. This ability is restored by time in nature according to this theory. The component of attention that gets more use in natural settings is involuntary attention, which is captured by stimuli that is either inherently important or inherently intriguing. The suppression of competing stimuli does not carry nearly as much of a role in the involuntary attention aspect compared to directed attention. Especially when compared to urban settings, natural environments are less taxing on attentional abilities as these environments encourage bottom-up attention (notice what is pleasing and intriguing) rather than constant top-down competing stimuli (which is the directed attention aspect; Berman et al., 2008). Research indicates that directed attention can be replenished by time spent either walking in nature or looking at pictures of natural environments (Berman et al., 2008). This is particularly important in the research regarding nature and treating attention-deficit hyperactivity disorder, which will be discussed further in Chapter 4.

On the whole, these findings are significant for multiple reasons. As a society, time spent in nature has decreased over time. Not only is increasing time spent in nature going to benefit children's physical health, and mental health by improving mood, creativity, the ability to heal from stressful life situations, and recovery from mental fatigue, but helping children become connected with nature leads to stronger positive environmental attitudes and behaviors as an adult. Specifically, the more involved the physical interactions, the stronger the positive environmental understanding and ongoing behaviors of environmentalism will be over time (Wells & Lekies, 2006). This concept is crucial in terms of the development of society as a whole and maintenance of environmental resources. Chapter 3 will include discussion of the role of children's play from a historical perspective, and Chapter 4 will include discussion of the intersection of nature and play in terms of children's development. The idea of exposing children to positive experiences in nature and the impact that can have on lifelong development, not just of the person but of society, will be important to bear in mind.

References

Alpay, S., Özdemir, İ., & Demirbaş, D. (2013). Environment and Islam. *Journal of Economic Cooperation and Development*, *34*(4), 1–22.

Alvarsson, J. J., Wiens, S., & Nilsson, M. E. (2010). Stress recovery during exposure to nature sound and environmental noise. *International Journal of Environmental Research and Public Health*, *7*, 1036–1046. https://doi.org/10.3390/ijerph7031036

Atchley, R. A., Strayer, D. L., & Atchley, P. (2012). Creativity in the wild: Improving creative reasoning through immersion in natural settings. *PLoS one*, *7*(12), e51474. https://doi.org/10.1371/journal.pone.0051474

Berman, M. G., Jonides, J., & Kaplan, S. (2008). The cognitive benefits of interacting with nature. *Psychological Science*, *19*(12), 1207–1212. https://doi.org/10.1111/j.1467-9280.2008.02225.x

Berman, M. G., Kross, E., Krpan, K. M, Askren, M. K., Burson, A., Deldin, P. J., Kaplan, S., Sherdell, L., Gotlib, I. H., & Jonides, J. (2012). Interacting with nature improves cognition and affect for individuals with depression. *Journal of Affective Disorders*, *140*(3), 300–305. https://doi.org/10.1016/j.jad.2012.03.012

Bratman, G. N., Daily, G. C., Levy, B. J., & Gross, J. J. (2015). The benefits of nature experience: Improved affect and cognition. *Landscape and Urban Planning*, *138*, 41–50. https://doi.org/10.1016/j.landurbplan.2015.02.005

Bratman, G. N., Hamilton, J. P., Hahn, K. S., Daily, G. C., & Gross, J. J. (2015). Nature experience reduces rumination and subgenual prefrontal cortex activation. *Proceedings of the National Academy of Sciences*, *112*(28), 8567–8572. https://doi.org/10.1073/pnas.1510459112

Capaldi, C. A., Dopko, R. L., & Zelenski, J. M. (2014). The relationship between nature connectedness and happiness: A meta-analysis. *Frontiers in Psychology*, *5*, 1–15. https://doi.org/10.3389/fpsyg.2014.00976

Chawla, L. (2015). Benefits of nature contact for children. *Journal of Planning Literature*, *30*(4), 433–452. https://doi.org/10.1177/0885412215595441

Coscieme, L., Hyldmo, H. S., Fernández-Llamazares, Á., Palomo, I., Mwampamba, T. H., Selomane, O., Sitas, N., Jaureguiberry, P., Takahashi, Y., Lim, M., Barral, M. P., Farinaci, J. S., Diaz-José, J., Ghosh, S., Ojino, J., Alassaf, A., Baatuuwie, B. N., Balint, L., Basher, Z., ... Valle, M. (2019). Multiple conceptualizations of nature are key to inclusivity and legitimacy in global environmental governance. *Environmental Science & Policy, 104*, 36–42. https://doi.org/10.1016/j.envsci.2019.10.018

Dadvand, P., Nieuwenhuijsen, M. J., Esnaola, M., Forns, J., Basagaña, X., Alvarez-Pederol, M., Rivas, I., López-Vicente, M., De Castro Pascual, M., Su, J., Jerrett, M., Querol, X., & Sunyer, J. (2015). Green spaces and cognitive development in primary schoolchildren. *Environmental Sciences, 112*(26), 7937–7942. https://doi.org/10.1073/pnas.1503402112

Dhammika, S. (2015). *Nature and the environment in early Buddhism*. Buddha Dhamma Mandala Society.

Erikson, E. H. (1950). *Childhood and society.* W. W. Norton & Co. Inc.

Faruqi, Y. M. (2007). Islamic view of nature and values: Could these be the answer to building bridges between modern science and Islamic science. *International Education Journal, 8*(2), 461–469.

Fjørtoft, I. (2001). The natural environment as a playground for children: The impact of outdoor play activities in pre-primary school children. *Early Childhood Education Journal, 29*(2), 111–117. https://doi.org/10.1023/A:1012576913074

Fjørtoft, I. (2004). Landscape as playscape: The effects of natural environments on children's play and motor development. *Children, Youth and Environments, 14*(2), 21–44. https://www.jstor.org/stable/10.7721/chilyoutenvi.14.2.0021

Gidlöf-Gunnarsson, A., & Öhrström, E. (2007). Noise and well-being in urban residential environments: The potential role of perceived availability to nearby green space. *Landscape and Urban Planning, 83*, 115–126. https://doi.org/10.1016/j.landurbplan.2007.03.003

Gill, T. (2014). The benefits of children's engagement with nature: A systematic literature review. *Children, Youth and Environments, 24*(2), 10–34. https://doi.org/10.7721/chilyoutenvi.24.2.0010

Gould van Praag, C. D., Garfinkel, S. M., Sparasci, O., Mees, A., Philippides, A. O., Ware, M., Ottaviani, C., & Critchley, H. D. (2017). Mind-wandering and alterations to default mode network connectivity when listening to naturalistic versus artificial sounds. *Scientific Reports, 7*, 1–12. https://doi.org/10.1038/srep45273

Harte, J. L., & Eifert, G. H. (1995). The effects of running, environments, and attentional focus on athletes' catecholamine and cortisol levels and mood. *Psychophysiology, 32*, 49–54. https://doi.org/10.1016/0301-0511(95)05118-T

Hopkins, E. (1994). *Childhood transformed: Working-class children in nineteenth-century England*. Manchester University Press.

Hunter, M. R., Gillespie, B. W., & Chen, S. Y. (2019). Urban nature experiences reduce stress in the context of daily life based on salivary biomarkers. *Frontiers in Psychology, 10*, 722. https://doi.org/10.3389/fpsyg.2019.00722

Li, D., & Sullivan, W. (2015). Impact of views to school landscapes on recovery from stress and mental fatigue. *Landscape and Urban Planning, 148*, 149–158. https://doi.org/10.1016/j.landurbplan.2015.12.015

Matsuoka, R. H. (2010). Student performance and high school landscapes: Examining the links. *Landscape and Urban Planning, 97*(4), 273–282. https://doi.org/10.1016/j.landurbplan.2010.06.011

McCaig, B., & Pavcnik, N. (2013). *Moving out of agriculture: Structural change in Vietnam* (Working Paper No. 19616). National Bureau of Economic Research. https://www.nber.org/system/files/working_papers/w19616/w19616.pdf

McDonald, M., Wearing, S., & Ponting, J. (2009). The nature of peak experience in wilderness. *The Humanistic Psychologist, 37,* 370–385. https://doi.org/10.1080/08873260701828912

Morries, G. P. (2010). From revelation to resource: the natural world in the thought and experience of Quakers in Britain and Ireland, 1647–1830 (Doctoral dissertation, University of Birmingham). http://etheses.bham.ac.uk/id/eprint/631

Naor, L., & Mayseless, O. (2020). The therapeutic value of experiencing spirituality in nature. *Spirituality in Clinical Practice, 7*(2), 114–133. http://dx.doi.org/10.1037/scp0000204

Njuki, E. (2021, July 29). A look at agricultural productivity growth in the United States, 1948–2017. *Research and Science.* https://www.usda.gov/media/blog/2020/03/05/look-agricultural-productivity-growth-united-states-1948-2017

Plambech, T., & Konijnendijk van den Bosch, C. C. (2015). The impact of nature on creativity—A study among Danish creative professionals. *Urban Forestry & Urban Greening, 14,* 255–263. http://doi.org/10.1016/j.ufug.2015.02.006

Robbins, J. (2020, January 9). Ecopsychology: How immersion in nature benefits your health. *Yale Environment 360.* https://e360.yale.edu/features/ecopsychology-how-immersion-in-nature-benefits-your-health

Satterthwaite, D., McGranahan, G., & Tacoli, C. (2010). Urbanization and its implications for food and farming. *Philosophical Transactions of the Royal Society B, 365,* 2809–2820. https://doi.org/10.1098/rstb.2010.0136

Sen, B., Dorosh, P., & Ahmed, M. (2021). Moving out of agriculture in Bangladesh: The role of farm, non-farm and mixed households. *World Development, 144,* 1–10. https://doi.org/10.1016/j.worlddev.2021.105479

Spindelegger, C., Stein, P., Wadsak, W., Fink, M., Mitterhauser, M., Kletter, K., Kasper, S., & Lanzenberger, R. (2012). Light-dependent alteration of serotonin-1A receptor binding in cortical and subcortical limbic regions in the human brain. *The World Journal of Biological Psychiatry, 13*(6), 413–422. https://doi.org/10.3109/15622975.2011.630405

Taylor, A. F., Kuo, F. E., & Sullivan, W. C. (2002). Views of nature and self-discipline: Evidence from inner city children. *Journal of Environmental Psychology, 22,* 49–63. https://doi.org/10.1006/jevp.2001.0241

Tillman, S., Clark, A. F., & Gilliland, J. A. (2018). Children and nature: Linking accessibility of natural environments and children's health-related quality of life. *International Journal of Environmental Research and Public Health, 15*(6), 1072. https://doi.org/10.3390/ijerph15061072

Tillman, S., Tobin, D., Avison, W., & Gilliland, J. (2018). Mental health benefits of interactions with nature in children and teenagers: A systematic review. *Journal of Epidemiology and Community Health, 72,* 958–966. https://doi.org/10.1136/jech-2018-210436

Trust for Public Land. (2022, September 14). About us - our mission - 10-minute walk. 10. Retrieved October 27, 2022, from https://10minutewalk.org/about-us/

Tsai, H., Chen, K, C., Yang, Y. K., Chen, P. S., Yeh, T. L., Chiu, N. T., & Lee, I. H. (2011). Sunshine-exposure variation of human striatal dopamine D2/D3 receptor availability in healthy volunteers. *Progress in Neuro-Psychopharmacology & Biological Psychiatry, 35*(1), 107–110. https://doi.org/10.1016/j.pnpbp.2010.09.014

van den Berg, A. E., Maas, J., Verheij, R. A., & Groenewegen, P. P. (2010). Green space as a buffer between stressful life events and health. *Social Science & Medicine, 70*, 1203–1210. https://doi.org/10.1016/j.socscimed.2010.01.002

Vogel, D. (2001). How green is Judaism? Exploring Jewish environmental ethics. *Business Ethics Quarterly*, 349–363. https://doi.org/10.2307/3857753

Wells, N. M., & Evans, G. W. (2003). Nearby nature: A buffer of life stress among rural children. *Environment and Behavior, 35*(3), 311–330. https://doi.org/10.1177/0013916503035003001

Wells, N. M., & Lekies, K. S. (2006). Nature and the life course: Pathways from childhood nature experiences to adult environmentalism. *Children, Youth and Environments, 16*(1), 1–24. https://www.jstor.org/stable/10.7721/chilyoutenvi.16.1.0001

Williams, K. J. H., Lee, K. E., Hartig, T., Sargent, L. D., Williams, N. S. G., & Johnson, K. A. (2018). Conceptualising creativity benefits of nature experience: Attention restoration and mind wandering as complementary processes. *Journal of Environmental Psychology, 59*, 36–45. https://doi.org/10.1016/j.jenvp.2018.08.005

Wilson, E. O. (1984). *Biophilia*. Harvard University Press.

Wineman, A., Jayne, T. S., Modamba, E. I., & Kray, H. (2020). The changing face of agriculture in Tanzania: Indicators of transformation. *Development Policy Review, 38*(6), 685–709. https://doi.org/10.1111/dpr.12491

Wu, C., McNeely, E., Cedeño-Laurent, J. G., Pan, W., Adamkiewicz, G., Dominci, F., Lung, S. C., Su, H., & Spengler, J. D. (2014). Linking student performance in Massachusetts elementary schools with the "greenness" of school surroundings using remote sensing. *Plos ONE, 9*(10), 1–9. https://doi.org/10.1371/journal.pone.0108548

Yurich, G. (2022). *1000 hours outside: Activities to match screen time with green time*. DK.

Chapter 3

The history of children's play

As with the history of children's time spent in nature, the historical changes in regard to the importance of children's play across cultures are inconsistent. The time available for free play and the value placed on play itself have changed in noticeable ways across eras and geographical locations, including a range of countries with developed economies, those with developing economies, those with emerging economies, and indigenous populations. While the developmental stages of play across cultures do not vary, the importance and prominence of child-led free play does vary across culture and location. The impact of free play on learning and development, along with policy recommendations for inclusion of play in educational environments because of the proven positive impact on children's development, will be presented here. A definition of play to be utilized in this book will be outlined first, drawn from multiple historical perspectives. This definition is an important place to start so that the progression of understanding of play can be seen, and we have a common starting point for understanding and utilizing the prescriptive model of integrating nature and play therapy.

Definition of play

In general, pure, neurotypical play is a tricky thing to define. There is no one accepted definition of play. Historically, play (especially in the therapy realm) was defined loosely, depending upon the need of the researcher or practitioner (Smith & Vollstedt, 1985). No two definitions were the same, nor were they based fully in research. Researchers have outlined characteristics of play and presented a few similar yet different definitions. Even the differences in fields of practice changed the definitions—educators looking at child development had different definitions than biologists working with animals, and those were still different than psychological practitioners (Smith & Vollstedt, 1985). Krasnor and Pepler (1980) provided one of the first multimodal definitions of play, including external physical attributes and internal response-driven aspects, thus defining play

DOI: 10.4324/9781003332343-3

as consisting of four qualities: positive affect, flexibility, nonliteral, and intrinsic motivation. Flexibility refers to the ability for adaptive variability and changing the play moment so play does not become stereotypical and is ever-changing. It is the creative piece of play. Non-literality refers to the pretend "as if" and suspension of reality that is present in creative and pretend play. This is a piece we unfortunately seem to lose as we age—except when a toddler hands you a toy phone and you answer it, or you smile when a child skips down the sidewalk wearing a cape instead of walking sedately. The intrinsic motivation refers to playing for internal versus external reward to appease a desire for autonomy, competence, enjoyment, or interest.

Stuart Brown, in his book about play and its importance in life (Brown & Vaughan, 2009), spoke of this intrinsic motivation as true play invites a player to want to keep going. He writes that play has seven inherent properties. These include the inherent attraction (it's fun!), voluntary, apparently purposeless, freedom from time, improvisational potential, continuation desire, and diminished consciousness of self. The fact that play encourages creativity while easing typical societal norms, expectations, and concerns is key, as well as that true play invites a player to want to keep going. These properties lend themselves to the essence of freedom inherent in the play itself. Huizinga, a Dutch historian, discussed this concept of freedom in play in his work *Homo Ludens: A Study of the Play-Element in Culture* (2014; original printing 1944), calling the freedom of play one of its main characteristics. Huizinga spoke of play as being necessary for the development of a culture, and that play itself consists of multiple qualities ranging from biological or physical purposes to an internal meaning known only to the individual player. He wrote that the primary element of fun is the most important and most difficult to define—how does one define the concept of fun for another person, or even for oneself? Yet "it is precisely this fun-element that characterizes the essence of play" (Huizinga, 2014, p. 3). In defining play itself, Huizinga included the voluntary nature of the activity, the notion of pretending (or temporarily and knowingly stepping out of the bounds of reality), being limited by time and space, fixed beginnings and ends that lead to repeatable sequences, creation of order, and rules. He was clear that play is necessary for an individual and society as a whole, as play is an important part of what makes people human and helps societies thrive yet has no notable profit or material gain (Huizinga, 2014).

Smith and Vollstedt (1985) decided there was a need for an empirically supported definition of play and performed a study to see which criteria well-educated adults would use to judge a videotaped behavior episode as "play behavior." Smith and Vollstedt included the four criteria identified by Krasnor and Pepler (1980): positive affect, flexibility, non-literal, and intrinsic motivation. They included a fifth criterion of means/ends, which was seen in Rubin et al.'s (1983) work which suggests that children play for play's sake rather than to come to a determined result. This criterion also includes children figuring out how an object can be used in play, especially in ways other than original uses. Smith and Vollstedt (1985) determined non-literality, positive affect, and flexibility to be the three core aspects of play which adults observe and identify in preschoolers' play behaviors. These are the characteristics of play on which the adults had moderate to substantial agreement when rating video vignettes of preschoolers playing and then were able to rate as play moments.

Based on a literature review of these studies plus many more, Charles Schaefer defined pure play as having eight characteristics: positive affect, intrinsic motivation, non-literal, flexible, process oriented, voluntary, inner control, and active involvement (Schaefer & Peabody, 2016). Process oriented refers to the notion that the process of the play is more important than the outcome—that the means is more than the end. The play itself is more important than the perfect castle creation, a finished fort that needs no more alterations or tweaking, or a tower that never falls. Voluntary refers to how a player chooses to engage in play and that children freely choose to devote most of their time to play. Inner control refers to play being a time in which children are free from external constraints and get to be and do what they would like. It is the time when children are bigger and stronger than all other forces in their worlds. Active involvement refers to active engagement by the player to create and maintain the play, rather than passive involvement in which a person waits to be entertained. From this list and research compilations, Schaefer further narrowed down "play" to be an activity characterized by a suspension of reality, positive affect, and flexibility.

In my attempt to further explore these definitions and narrow down my own working definition of play, I asked my children and their friends the simple yet challenge question, "What is play?" Most children answered readily yet thoughtfully, while most adults tried to avoid the question! Without fail children identified play as "having fun" and "being happy," lending support to the idea of positive affect being a prime characteristic of play. There were also reports of play including "active games," "running around," and "spending time with friends," suggesting that active involvement is a key piece of play compared to passive involvement. This active involvement can be either physical or mental—true play does not need to include running, jumping, or skipping around. It could include active mental engagement such as seen in a board game or other engaging activity. What matters for pure play is that the players are fully engaged in the play instead of being solely an observer. In watching my children play, I see a non-literality or suspension of reality take hold almost instantly as they turn nearby materials into what they need and want for their activities. They also can change their play at a moment's notice to account for missing materials, a change of thought, or a new whim. That flexibility is another indicator of true play, as they use their creativity to expand their play worlds. My nine-year-old also identified the voluntary characteristic of play in his definition, saying "We play because we want to, not because someone tells us to!" My six-year-old phrases the voluntary aspect of play slightly differently, saying "Ughhh, now you told me I have to do something, and that makes it not fun anymore!" Thus, I define pure play as an activity consisting of fun (creating positive affect), suspension of reality, active involvement, flexibility or creativity, and voluntary intent.

Types of play

There are other types of play outside of pure play. Most often, children play to experience all the freedom, flexibility, and fun of the activity. This is considered child-led free play. Children are in charge. They choose who will play, what will be used, which rules (if any) will be followed, and so on. They direct their own play, and they make changes as they need to to keep the play going. This is considered within the pure play category.

Other times, adults encourage play of children and utilize these times for playful learning. Play makes learning fun, which in turn makes the learning stick more solidly. I can still remember definitions of terms from *Advanced Biology* back in high school because our teacher had us draw images to represent the words. He also acted out definitions whenever possible and brought a true element of fun and play to his education methods. Playful learning is not pure play, as the voluntary nature of it is missing, yet it is still fun and playful, and definitely educational!

Another type of play that is typically adult-led or encouraged is structured play. In this type of interaction, children receive guidance from adults in some way about what or how to play. Sports generally fall into this category, as do games with rules and any other type of adult-directed or coordinated activity. Once the kids get going in this play, it can retain many characteristics of pure play, but is definitely different than child-led free play.

Children also use play on their own to overcome challenges and traumas. Play is the first language we learn and can be fully nonverbal in its experience. As such, it is the way we can fully experience and understand the world. We can use play to figure things out, make sense of the world, and discover new ways to put the pieces back together without words. When a person experiences a traumatic experience, they understand it in a nonverbal way and therefore need to process it in the same nonverbal way (Perry, 2014). Post-traumatic play allows for a person to focus on their own psychological need and play through it repetitively. This play allows a person to approach the event and confusion to sort through it at a pace and intensity that is manageable. They can reexperience the event until the emotional experience becomes too much to support, stop until they can handle the combination of emotions and experience, and repeat the process until they are able to fully integrate all of it. This is one of the true hallmarks of play as therapy—that people can utilize the properties and therapeutic powers of play to meet their needs where they are and how they need to understand the world. While there are various theories of why we play that can hold different prominences in different cultures, the same aspects of what makes an activity play hold across people, places, and cultural groups.

The development of play

The development of play is also consistent across cultures as play development progresses through both cognitive and social stages. Piaget was one of the first to indicate stages of cognitive growth in play development, and his stage model was later expanded by Smilansky (1968) to include the four stages of cognitive development most cited today: functional, constructive, dramatic, and games with rules. The purely sensorimotor play that Piaget (1962) first highlighted is the primary type of play engaged in by the very young child, so should be considered the first of the stages. This would be followed by functional play, in which children engage in repetitive motor movements as they learn about their world and their impact therein. The third stage is constructive play, wherein children create, build, and develop while utilizing objects. The fourth stage is dramatic play, or symbolic play, wherein children engage in pretend play and further develop their thinking and cognitive skills through play. Rough-and-tumble play should be considered in this stage model, as engaging in rough-and-tumble play allows children to learn about their physical capabilities while understanding the limits of their bodies. This type of cognitive understanding is crucial for social cognitive development (Pellegrini, 1987). The final stage of cognitive development is games with rules, in which children can learn and follow fixed rules in a game. While children go through these stages in a sequential order, the amount of time they spend developing in each stage does differ (Rubin et al., 1976), which is typical of development.

Play also develops along a stage model in terms of social interaction. Parten (1932) identified a model consisting of six stages of social development in play that through later replication studies was understood to consist of four primary stages (Rubin et al., 1976). These stages include solitary play, in which children play alone and have little interest in the activities of others around them, and parallel play, in which children begin to play with similar toys or objects as others around them but do not interact in meaningful ways. The third stage is associative play, in which children start to share toys or objects and begin to interact verbally. There is still no interaction to reach an end goal. That type of interaction develops during the fourth stage of cooperative play, in which children share play objects as well as a common end goal (Parten, 1932).

Why we play and the role of play in societies

Early theories of why people play include the surplus energy theory posited by Spencer (1873), Lazarus's recreation or relaxation theory from 1883 as described by Patrick (1916), and the practice theory outlined by Groos (1901). In the surplus energy theory, it is said that children are not concerned with matters of self-preservation as are adults, so their extra energy comes out via play. The recreation theory suggests that play allows a person to restore energy expended through work. This helps us to overcome attentional fatigue and to continue giving our best effort in our work. Restoring our bodies and minds to be able to concentrate better is a hallmark of recess time, and the benefits of a play-based physical activity time during school are clear across cultures. In considering recess, more is better! In 2009, pediatrician Dr. Romnina Barros and colleagues found that latency-aged children who had more than 15 minutes of recess time per day performed better on school tasks and showed better behavior than those with less or no recess time. Stevenson and Stigler (1992) noted that children in Asian communities who received 15 minutes of physical play time after every class period showed improved concentration in class. Groos's (1901) practice theory takes this connection between play and learning in another direction and states that we learn and practice new skills through play. Indigenous populations in particular view early play as vital to learning skills needed later in life and encourage children to play games to learn about mathematical concepts and observational skills, among other topics. The importance of playing to learn cannot be overstated. I have seen it work time and time again and am a huge proponent of bringing free play back into mainstream education to help children explore concepts on their own. My children constantly play out what they just learned, and this really helps consolidate skills and identify gaps in learning.

On the other hand, Huizinga (2014) agreed that play for play's sake is a vital part of the development of a society. He believed that play is the basis of culture and must be seen in every aspect of society in some way to achieve complete personal development and a healthy society. This includes play in language, law, work, and so on. Play is seen in metaphors, learning and education, rituals, music, dance, and representations. Play allows a person or culture to fluctuate away from serious, moving from silly and fantastical, back to serious, to the high pieces of the spirit and sacredness (Huizinga, 2014). Erikson spoke to this point in terms of being able to access various aspects of the self when he stated that "to grow means to be divided into different parts which move at different rates" (Erikson, 1950, p. 204). The relationship between the importance and prominence of play in children's development must be considered within the development of the self as it helps a person synchronize the body and the self (Erikson, 1950), as well as cultural groups and societies throughout history.

The role and value of children and childhood by era and cultural or religious group are other considerations when looking at the historical development of children's play. For example, Puritans in the early 1600s tended to view children as sinful beings, and thus, play was not tolerated as it was considered to be based in devious and devilish behaviors. Yet the Puritans loved their children and wanted just to shield them from corruption rather than prohibiting growth and development. Games and activities were typically Bible-based to help introduce and reinforce moral lessons using structured play for learning. The Quakers had a more tolerant view of play and allowed purposeful play so long as it was not based in idleness. Children of these and later colonial times were significantly involved in the adult world, and often married young, starting their own families at young ages (Chudacoff, 2007, pp. 20–21). This also limited the importance placed on child-led free play as it reduced work time. However, throughout this era, children were valued and given some indulgences for youthful, fun behaviors, as the developmental benefit was understood for both the child and society (Chudacoff, 2007, p. 28). In England, there was no concept of a youthful, fun childhood before the seventeenth century, and the idea of a true childhood as we consider it now developed gradually over the eighteenth and nineteenth centuries as social changes took place including reforms laws, industrialization, and urbanization (Hopkins, 1994). The physical needs of children and their families took precedence in terms of the use of their time. Hopkins (1994), in his deep review of childhood in Victorian England, shared an example of a boy who spoke of preferring work over playtime because he would eat better in seasons of work. Hopkins (1994) also spoke about how all the "stuff" of growing up that we associate with childhood and the teen years that happens through time with friends, such as learning about oneself, the world, intimate relationships, and the like, would happen in the adult work world instead of childhood free play. Play did not have a significant role in this time of exploration and growth.

Not many first-person accounts of early play experiences exist across cultures and eras, and obviously the experiences children had differed by family and community. However, through autobiographies, biographical sketches of childhoods, and the like, the value and roles of children across eras can be seen on a societal level, as well as some documentation of the time they generally had available for or dedicated to play. For example, Laura Ingalls Wilder wrote extensively about her childhood during the late 1800s in the United States (i.e., Wilder, 1971), while Eric Sloane (2004) presented a history of Noah Blake's childhood based from diaries written by Blake himself. Laura's play was that of a younger child, keeping herself busy, entertained, and learning about the world alongside her siblings. Her story was written in a more whimsical fashion, even given the hardships she and her family continually faced, and thus, the play aspects were highlighted and respected in her stories. The children would run across the fields, create, imagine, and explore. Within the house they would create play scenes and sagas, and use whatever was available to them for play, such as paper dolls, a corncob wrapped in scrap fabric, and a thimble to make pictures in the frost on glass. Noah's play was that of a young man who appears to be part of a Quaker community. His story was told of an older child, on the cusp of manhood, and thus, he was wrapped in the chores and details of living life to survive and thrive. Play happened between these needs and included things like songs during house-raisings, blanket tents in his bed for fun and warmth, drawing designs into the dirt floors when visitors were due, and bumping a child into trees or water marking boundary lines. Some toys and activities happened for purely play's sake, including balancing figures called Hoe Boys or playing in a barn attic creating imaginary stories and pulling the ladders up to protect against their imaginary foes. Mazes were popular, drawn on either paper or wood, or large ones were even worked in the ground by turning turf or laying sheaves of wheat! For their birthdays, Laura was gifted a doll, while Noah was gifted panes of glass for his windows and a diary. These accounts show that play is a natural part of childhood and even adulthood and takes different priority depending on the needs of the family but has always had a place in a youngster's life.

Howard Chudacoff (2007) utilized journals, diaries, and other written records to derive the history of children's play in the United States from around the early 1600s on. One challenge of utilizing such resources is that typically only families who were literate are represented. The historian's accepted approach to handling this discrepancy is to look to the historical records of the day and observe reform laws and factory acts, changes in church patterns, welfare systems, and literature references (Hopkins, 1994). What has been clear across the centuries is that children have always been instinctively drawn to play and will most often choose to make an activity playful if the opportunity is present. Favorite toys also tend to be what they create themselves, and play happens in a large variety of ways, so absence of manufactured toys due to availability or finances has never been a deterrent to children's play.

As societies developed, so did the concept of playing for play's sake. As children participated in the family activities of farming and settling, there was little time for free play. That said, children have always been able to find ways to fit spontaneous play into their daily lives and activities! Children have an innate desire toward play and fun. The best toys have always been what children create for themselves and what allows for flexibility and creativity in their play. This is why sand, blankets, cardboard boxes, sticks, and paper airplanes are items in the National Toy Hall of Fame through The Strong Museum of Play (2022)!

Chudacoff (2007, p. 18) wrote that childhood has never been an unencumbered time for children. There has always been something, in every era, which has in some way restricted or challenged children's free play time. What is generally seen is that children have slowly lost the ability and time to engage in child-led free play over the centuries regardless of geographical location and socioeconomic status. As previously indicated, there is a difference noted between cultures in terms of what children are "allowed" and encouraged to do regarding free play. Chudacoff (2007, p. 18) noted that non-Western cultures tend to view children as capable of autonomy and unsupervised play noticeably earlier than Western (North American) populations, and that this is reflected in their free play time and structure. Indigenous populations would encourage children to play as a way to learn skills needed for adult life, such as math and observation skills. Boys were given more freedom to engage in playful behaviors that would strengthen their skills, such as spear throwing, running, and competing in tribal events (Chudacoff, 2007, p. 28). Children in the prairie days of the United States would be turned out of the house to roam free once the chores and lessons were complete and created their own toys and games to amuse themselves, often creating play sagas that would last for days. We still see this extended play saga occur today, especially when children are given ample free play time in green spaces. Children in affluent families in Victorian England were often relegated to nurseries where they would learn lessons under the supervision of governesses and tutors. Play was part of development but had its time and place.

The 1800s saw children engaging in more specific training for adulthood, as society strove to develop "virtuous citizens" (Chudacoff, 2007, p. 39). Play continued and over the course of this century was seen to be part of a more specific childhood period of life. The use of games and specific toys like Locke's blocks for learning and cognitive development began to be more commonplace (Chudacoff, 2007, p. 34). By the late 1800s, public schools were more widespread, and children were spending more of their daytime hours at their studies. At this time, manufactured toys were also becoming more prominent, yet parents struggled with the balance between occupying children's time for them and allowing freedom of imagination and expression (Chudacoff, 2007, pp. 83–84). This progression was true of other societies as well, and a similar process was seen in England at this time. The manufactured toys of this era were simplistic and easy to adapt to meet the child's imagination (Hopkins, 1994).

By the early 1900s, parents were more open to fantasy-based play and allowing children to spend more time developing their imaginations (Chudacoff, 2007, p. 120). Events and changes in society certainly impacted views of children and play, from the Great Depression to World Wars to Disney's animated films in the late 1930s. All these events eventually led to children becoming more immersed in consumerism and a larger focus on manufactured and scripted toys. While socioeconomic status influenced the level of immersion for children and families, differences here did not completely remove the impact (Chudacoff, 2007, pp. 124–125).

Interviews and records indicate that the first half of the twentieth century was when child-led free play—unstructured, adult-free play—really came into its own (Chudacoff, 2007, p. 126). While adults wanted children's play to have meaning and guidance, children chose to go off on their own more often and play in their own ways (Chudacoff, 2007, p 127). While not directly identified as the reason, it could easily be understood that the parents of the 1920s–1940s were balancing more roles and responsibilities while under different stressors and restrictions than in previous generations. History shows that as families engaged in agricultural pursuits and later in factory work, children also worked more (Gray, 2011), which fits within these timeframes. When children did play, they played outside of adult supervision and direction, leading to an increase in child-led free play (Gray, 2011), but typically only when required tasks and work hours were complete.

This is also the time when televisions were beginning to enter homes, from 1939 to the 1950s (encyclopedia.com, 2022), which changed how families were able to view leisure time. The commercialism directed at children through such shows as *The Mickey Mouse Club* in 1955 truly changed not only how children spent their free time but the toys (and advertisements) that were available (Chudacoff, 2007, pp. 154–155). The 1950s also saw changes in how toys and books were advertised in terms of marketing to specific genders and age groups rather than children as a whole, thus solidifying the peer socialization and age-groupings of schools that until then were not key determinants in play and development (Chudacoff, 2007, p. 161). Just after this timeframe, households were shifting as birth rates generally declined after the baby boom of the 1950s and 1960s, and mothers were more routinely entered the workforce. These changes in home dynamics often led to more adult-led activities as sibling groups (and thus built-in playmates) diminished and children's time home alone increased overall (Chudacoff, 2007, pp. 160–161).

Parenting guidebooks found their ways into homes in the late 1900s, giving parents many views of parenting styles, child development, and advice on socialization (Chudacoff, 2007, pp. 162–163). Parents began to put children and their needs at the forefront of their efforts and started worrying about "the endangered childhood" (Chudacoff, 2007, p. 162). Health concerns like polio were real and consuming, and the safety of children became a major focus for adults. Control of children's play began to spread, leading to more adult supervision and organization of children's play and play time, and things like playgrounds began to receive special attention and modifications (Chudacoff, 2007, pp. 164–165). These and other trends have led to a significant decline in child-led free play since around 1955 (Gray, 2011). While parents (especially mothers) view child-led free play as a thing of importance and value, it remains difficult for parents to truly allow and encourage such time, even when the health and developmental benefits are clear (Clements, 2004). In particular, risky adventurous play is vital to children's overall development yet has received a bad reputation over time. The importance of this type of rough-and-tumble play is being highlighted in more studies as of late and encouraged to help children develop more fully in all realms including physical, social, cognitive, and emotional. This will be discussed more fully in Chapter 4, but the impact of the historical shift is important to highlight here.

As caregivers take more notice of children's free play and supervise play more closely, the fear of injury tends to encourage caregivers to limit risky play. While limiting risky play does make sense on a visceral, protection-based level, allowing some risky play while making safety limits clear can have remarkable benefits for children. Researchers are seeing that children have the ability to physically regulate their bodies during risky play, and this carries over into nonplay settings. Problems with coordination and balance in the classroom are being seen in children who do not have such risky play experiences to build up physical strength (Hanscom, 2016). Historically, this shift away from risky play correlates with an increase in playground monitoring and development of "safe" playground spaces, which tend to include manufactured structures and ground covers, with less open green space available for children to explore. Longitudinal studies are showing that these spaces (specifically the rubber coating for the ground) correlate with more bone fractures for children than if the spaces had been left coated with natural materials, and the incidence of serious injuries has not decreased (Brussoni et al., 2015)!

Educators and policymakers are seeing the importance of free play in the educational world as the impact on learning is becoming more visible. Thus, particularly in the United Kingdom, recommendations are being made to include more play time throughout educational experiences. Whitebread and colleagues (2012) encourage policymakers to understand the importance of play and the role it holds in the development of people and societies, and to be sure that time, space, and opportunities for play are available to children. He further recommends funding opportunities and work to change the public's perception of child's play to bring the importance of this activity to light (Whitebread et al., 2012). After a systematic review of the literature, Gill (2014) drew similar conclusions in terms of policy planning and encouraged policymakers to include playful experiences in educational initiatives given the importance of playfulness to children's growth and development.

Concluding thoughts

In sum, the history of children's play and the importance both the activity and a sense of playfulness have taken in society have shifted over the centuries. As play therapists, we understand the importance of both and I for one am pleased to see calls for provision of more opportunities for child-led free play and the space and time in which to do so. Encouraging children to engage in play to develop their senses of self, resilience, creative problem-solving, emotional regulation, social competence, and more will only help our societies develop more strongly as we raise children capable of all of this and more. Development, growth, and application of these skills have been linked to time in both nature and play and will be discussed in greater depth over the next few chapters. The research continues to show that encouraging free play time in natural environments is also necessary, and discussions in Chapter 4 will demonstrate the value and importance of the intersection of nature and play, and the way in which nature-based play therapy can be utilized in a theoretically grounded way to meet the overall needs of the children.

References

Barros, R. M., Silver, E. J., & Stein, R. E. K. (2009). School recess and group classroom behavior. *Pediatrics*, *123*(2), 431–436. https://doi.org/10.1542/peds.2007-2825

Brown, S. L. & Vaughan, C. C. (2009). *Play: How it shapes the brain, opens the imagination, and invigorates the soul*. Avery.

Brussoni, M., Gibbons, R., Gray, C., Ishikawa, T., Sandseter, E. B. H., Bienenstock, A., Chabot, G., Fuselli, P., Herrington, S., Janssen, I., Pickett, W., Power, M., Stanger, N., Sampson, M., & Tremblay, M. S. (2015). What is the relationship between risky outdoor play and health in children? A systematic review. *International Journal of Environmental Research and Public Health*, *12*(6), 6423–6454. https://doi.org/10.3390/ijerph120606423

Chudacoff, H. P. (2007). *Children at play: An American history*. New York University Press.

Clements, R. (2004). An investigation of the status of outdoor play. *Contemporary Issues in Early Childhood*, *5*(1), 68–80. https://doi.org/10.2304/ciec.2004.5.1.10

Encyclopedia.com. (2022, September 8). *1950s: TV and radio*. https://www.encyclopedia.com/history/culture-magazines/1950s-tv-and-radio

Erikson, E. H. (1950). *Childhood and society*. W. W. Norton & Co. Inc.

Gill, T. (2014). The benefits of children's engagement with nature: A systematic literature review. *Children, Youth and Environments*, *24*(2), 10–34. https://doi.org/10.7721/chilyoutenvi.24.2.0010

Gray, P. (2011). The decline of play and the rise of psychopathology in children and adolescents. *American Journal of Play*, *3*(4), 443–463.

Groos, K. (1901). *The play of man*. D. Appleton and Company.

Hanscom, A. J. (2016). *Balanced and barefoot*. New Harbinger Publications, Inc.

Hopkins, E. (1994). *Childhood Transformed: Working-class children in nineteenth-century England*. Manchester University Press.

Huizinga, J. (2014). *Homo ludens: A study of the play-element in culture*. Martino Publishing.

Krasnor, L. R. & Pepler, D. J. (1980). The study of children's play: Some suggested future directions. In K. H. Rubin (Ed.), *New directions for child development: Children's play* (pp. 85–95). Jossey-Bass.

Parten, M. B. (1932). Social participation among pre-school children. *Journal of Abnormal and Social Psychology*, *27*, 243–269. https://doi.org/10.1037/h0074524

Patrick, G. T. W. (1916). *The psychology of relaxation*. Houghton Mifflin Company.

Pellegrini, A. D. (1987). Rough-and-tumble play: Developmental and educational significance. *Educational Psychologist*, *22*(1), 23–43. https://doi.org/10.1207/s15326985ep2201_2

Perry, B. D. (2014, October 10). *The power of early childhood* [Keynote conference session]. 31st Annual Association for Play Therapy International Conference, Westin Galleria, Houston, TX, United States.

Piaget, J. (1962). *Play, dreams, and imitation in childhood*. Norton.

Rubin, K. H., Fein, G. G., & Vandenberg, B. (1983). Play. In E. M. Hetherington (Ed.), P. H. Mussen (Series Ed.)., *Handbook of child psychology: Vol 4. Socialization, personality, and social development* (pp. 693–774). Wiley.

Rubin, K. H., Maioni, T. L., & Hornung, M. (1976). Free play behaviors in middle- and lower-class preschoolers: Parten and Piaget revisited. *Child Development*, *47*(2), 414–419. https://doi.org/10.2307/1128796

Schaefer, C. E., & Peabody, M. A. (2016). Glossary of play therapy terms. *Play Therapy*, *11*(2), 20–24.

Sloane, E. (2004). *Diary of an early American boy: Noah Blake 1805*. Dover Publications.

Smilansky, S. (1968). *The effects of sociodramatic play on disadvantaged children: Pre-school children*. Wiley.

Smith, P. K., & Vollstedt, R. (1985). On defining play: An empirical study of the relationship between play and various play criteria. *Child Development, 56*, 1042–1050. https://doi.org/10.2307/1130114

Spencer, H. (1873). *The principles of psychology* (Vol. 2). D. Appleton and Company.

Stevenson, H. W., & Stigler, J. W. (1992). *The learning gap*. Summit Books.

The Strong National Museum of Play. (2022, September 7). *Inducted toys*. https://www.museumofplay.org/exhibits/toy-hall-of-fame/inducted-toys/

Whitebread, D., Basilio, M., Kuvalja, M., & Verma, M. (2012). The importance of play. A report on the value of children's play with a series of policy recommendations. *Toy Industries of Europe*. https://www.waldorf-resources.org/fileadmin/files/pictures/Early_Childhood/dr_david_whitebread_-_the_importance_of_play.pdf

Wilder, L. I. (1971). *Little house in the big woods*. HarperCollins.

Chapter 4

The intersection of nature and play

Now that the history and importance of both nature and play have been explored, the intersections of the two and impact on children's development can be described here. The history of nature-based play across cultures, including current trends and concerns across cultures, will be examined. This includes the impact of reduced nature access and less child-led free play time, and the development of risk adverse societies in developed countries. The education trends of stating an understanding of the need for child-led free play, exploration, and time in nature, combined with the lack of time in which to do so, will be introduced, as the impact on children's development of increases in structured, adult-guided play is explored. This will naturally lead to a brief discussion of an increase in child mental health referrals, which often go to play therapists. Thus, the definition of nature-based play therapy will be described, and the need for a theoretically grounded model for understanding how to implement nature-based play therapy and techniques will be discussed.

When talking with my children and their friends about what defines play and why play is important, something beyond "a fun activity that is flexible, suspends reality, is voluntary, and includes active involvement" consistently came up that was exceptionally interesting and caught my attention. Many comments included "running around" in the definitions of play. Some specifically stated that "being outside" was a key piece of their play experiences. One child immediately described her outdoor play space before defining play (she has an old tent that became a clubhouse, in which she and her friends can play with mud and sticks and "just do whatever!"). The combination of these two attributes in the discussions spoke to the children's desires to run and act freely outdoors, and the fun that they experienced at these times. That fun encourages them to want to continue the activities and enjoy the results of the creativity they are allowed. The physical engagement of active involvement in play engrosses one of a child's senses. Being in nature engages the other senses, so the intersection of playing in nature truly helps a person experience through all senses most thoroughly. When all senses are more fully awakened, people can understand experiences and learn on deeper levels as they are taking in information along

DOI: 10.4324/9781003332343-4

various sensory pathways through multisensory learning, which is an optimal learning condition (Shams & Seitz, 2008).

Time to play freely in a nature-based setting is crucial for children's development, including physical, social, and emotional domains. Research from the occupational therapy realm indicates that when babies are allowed to crawl over grassy areas, their physical development is positively impacted as they learn to navigate inclines and changes in the ground elevation as they move. Their muscles automatically learn to move in new ways, strengthening not only muscles but improving neurological connections as they learn new ways to catch themselves, right themselves physically and develop balance, and explore new challenges. Feeling the grass and dirt on skin (direct skin-to-skin contact) also has multiple health benefits. Allowing our feet to contact the ground enhances our ability to move properly, take in sensory information, support our bodies in space, and the like (Viseux, 2020). Pounding the ground as children run and jump improves bone mass and density (Fuchs et al., 2002). These physical benefits encourage physical growth and strength, as well as a sense of accomplishment and potential, encouraging people to continue in these activities.

From a social development standpoint, encouraging children to play together outside strengthens their social skills and ability to interact well and appropriately with peers. Pellegrini's (1988) early research recognized that when children are allowed to engage in rough-and-tumble play (which most often occurs outside, unless you are the parent of boys and can attest to the fact that it happens wherever they happen to be at any point in time), those who are good at rough-and-tumble actions are rated by their peers as being better friends than those who are not good at such play. Children who have been given the chance to use their bodies to play tag, run around chasing peers in play, fall and help others up, and pound the ground as they run outside the confines of a building and walls learn to understand their own physical boundaries and respect the boundaries of others. They learn how to interpret when someone else is done playing or needs a break. When someone needs a break, they can wander away from the play space, take the time they need to regulate themselves, and then rejoin the group without an issue. The ability to practice social skills in this kind of a free-flowing setting while taking the time to self-regulate is key in terms of building and utilizing solid social skills.

Discussion of this opportunity to self-regulate leads into discussion of emotional development. In the natural play world, children are consistently exposed to things that are bigger and more powerful than themselves, while at the same time maintaining control over smaller objects directly in front of themselves. They are consistently experiencing large and small at the exact same time and learn to attend to what their brains and bodies need in the moment. This ability to shift directed attention as needed has been particularly important for children dealing with symptoms of attention-deficit hyperactivity disorder (ADHD), depression, and anxiety. Simply being allowed to play in open green spaces has been correlated with a decrease in severity of symptoms of ADHD, particularly the hyperactivity component when offered more open spaces rather than man-made structures (Taylor & Kuo, 2011). The amount of time and depth of activities do not need to be much to start seeing positive impacts. Taylor and Kuo (2009) found that 20-minute guided walks in a park were enough for children to show improvement in concentration and attention. Simply sending children outdoors to engage in their typical after-school and weekend activities led to significant decreases in children's symptoms of ADHD (Kuo & Taylor, 2004). In Kuo and Taylor's (2004) study, parents reported on the severity of their children's symptoms after activities were completed either indoors or outdoors, including low-intensity activities such as reading which are not typically viewed as activities to inhibit impulsivity! Encouraging time to explore and play freely in the natural world allows children to regulate their attention and responses depending on their bodies' needs. Sometimes they can focus on the large vista in front of them to help with a brain break, then refocus on the smaller, more detailed view in front of them. Such attentional shifts fill the need children's brains have for variety and help them learn to shift focus and attend to necessary individual stimuli while observing the whole in a gentle, accommodating experience. Studies have shown that simply living near green space is correlated with greater amounts of physical activity by children, and that being in nature helps children to learn self-regulation skills, show improvements in emotional regulation abilities, and make gains in overall mental health (Gill, 2014). This combination of availability of and exposure to nature and the increase in physical exercise and free play is quite powerful and can be encouraged and sought by all caregivers to promote well-rounded child development.

There has been a generational decline in nature-based play time seen in the United States and the United Kingdom (Dodd et al., 2022). As the statistics note a decrease in time playing outdoors, researchers suggest that children are choosing not to, yet that mothers see the need (Clements, 2004). They remember their own experiences of playing freely outdoors and want this for their children. However, as society has changed, so has entertainment and technology. In a study conducted in 2004, Clements found that 96% of children were regular television watchers. Children connect over video games where they can talk with people around the world as they play the same game. This increased use of technology is seen as a significant reason why children are not playing outside on a regular basis (Clements, 2004). Schedules have become more structured, and activities are more often adult-led. Many parents are concerned about their children's safety and want their outdoor play supervised, yet do not have the time nor inclination to go outside and play with them or watch them play (Clements, 2004), especially since caregivers are busy balancing many roles and activities themselves. Choosing to make outdoor time happen, let alone be a priority, is an active choice that often requires scheduling the down time into a calendar and making it happen at the expense of other activities. It is becoming clearer that indoor play tends toward more passive entertainment and children receiving the entertainment rather than creating play opportunities and becoming immersed in the entire play experience (Clements, 2004; Stephenson, 1998).

Outdoor play affords children the opportunity to move in ways they cannot do indoors. The active and physical play that occurs in natural environments is vastly important for success in a variety of developmental tasks including motor skills such as basic locomotion involving overall movement of the body, physical manipulation skills like throwing and bouncing, and stability skills. Development of these skills combines to help children learn more complex physical behaviors through play such as combinations of movements and being able to successfully complete a range of motions (Little & Wyver, 2008). Thinking of an activity like baseball, a child must be able to successfully complete many basic physical skills to be any good at the complete activity. Standing, bending, running, swinging, twisting, throwing, and catching are all crucial physical aspects of the game, which do not account for the attentional and cognitive abilities needed to be successful as well (directing attention, choosing to ignore stimuli, keeping track of the next play and where you should be standing and be going, etc.). Having the time and space to develop these individual skills through active play throughout childhood is important. Research also indicates that children seek this type of active movement play, and if they have not been able to engage in physical play for some time, they will seek to overcome the deficit the next time they are able to by showing more intense and sustained physical play (Pellegrini & Davis, 1993; Smith & Hagan, 1980). This certainly explains why tensions grow so quickly in homes and schools during times of extended rain, when children do not go outside as frequently. Adopting the maxim of there is no bad weather with the correct clothing and attitude helps with this dramatically! A glorious, enormous puddle develops in our driveway during heavy rain, thanks to a slow-moving town drain. The kids have named it, watch for it, and beg to go explore it when it has built up enough. This puddle is why we keep the ill-fitting rain boots and jackets instead of passing them along and keeping only those that actually fit so that the kids have the tools they need to explore, play, and have fun in all weather.

As noted in Chapter 3, we have seen a general trend of a decline in children's play (Gray, 2011), and mothers have reported a significant generational decrease in the amount of time children spend playing outside (Clements, 2004). This coincides with a decrease in adventurous, risky outdoor play which leads to negative effects on mental health, child development, and social abilities (Dodd & Lester, 2021). Risky play tends to be defined as play that allows opportunities for children to explore a challenge to their play that can include the risk of physical injury and determine their own course of action, which includes emotions of fear, thrill, and excitement as they play (Brussoni et al., 2015; Dodd & Lester, 2021). This type of play is also being called adventurous play, as the children approach these risk assessment tasks as adventures in which they experience the thrilling positive emotions through playfulness (Dodd & Lester, 2021). In addition to physical development, adventurous and risky play is important for mental health. Dodd and Lester (2021) propose that adventurous play encourages children to understand their physiological arousal and feelings of uncertainty and anxiety, which will help children learning coping skills for anxiety as well as improve their capacity for resilience. Research indicates that children who engaged in adventurous play showed a decrease in internalizing concerns and an increase in positive emotions (Dodd et al., 2022), both of which are protective factors in terms of mental health. Outdoor play has also been shown to help children develop prosocial cooperative behaviors, to manage conflicts in a less confrontational manner (Bento & Dias, 2017), and to improve focus and attention in the classroom (Barros et al., 2009).

Even very young children are able to navigate the physical challenges of risky play. Tangen and colleagues (2022) utilized chest-mounted cameras to explore toddlers' abilities in natural environments. They observed children between the ages of 17 and 25 months navigating a variety of terrains including rocky, wooded spaces with elevation changes, along with more open areas. The researchers found that the children could assess potential risk and developing strategies to manage the risk and physically explore the environments. Young children who engage in this type of play show improvements in balance and coordination (Fjørtoft, 2001), which is important for ongoing physical development.

Part of the challenge with encouraging child-led outdoor free play is safety. We have become a more risk-adverse society than we were even 10–20 years ago. We are more aware of crimes happening in our areas as the internet, social media, and cell phones have become avenues to share information freely and instantly. I suggest that we seek a happy medium between using these devices and letting our fears interfere with children's development. We should be aware of the dangers that lurk in the world (both online and outdoors), take appropriate steps to safeguard ourselves and children, and find a balance between safety and child-led free play. Part of this is teaching our children safety skills, letting them watch us use the skills, and observing them put the skills into action. Perhaps this means that a responsible adult is monitoring but not supervising (and thus leading or guiding) outdoor play, or free play happens in a defined area like a playground or a home's backyard. A lot of this will depend upon the location and availability of green space in the child's area. Whatever the decision and plan is, the important part is that children need to have time to explore the outdoors on their own terms, in their own ways, and using their bodies to the fullest.

Getting adults on board with allowing and even encouraging risky and adventurous play is necessary and a second key obstacle in encouraging the resurgence of nature-based child-led free play. Research suggests that adults' tolerance of the boundaries of a risky play situation does impact the child's ability to fully engage in the activity and utilize the natural features (Sandseter, 2009). Finding a balance between children's physical safety and allowing adventurous risky play activities is crucial for children's health and development and should be part of policy-planning and playspace development plans (Brussoni et al., 2015). This can also be an ongoing conversation held during parent sessions of play therapy, as helping parents to become more aware of their concerns about risky play and developmentally appropriate options can benefit the entire family.

There has been a societal shift for parents into hovering over children more often, not only watching but directly supervising their movements and offering (or just giving) help before the child has a chance to actively try something new for themselves. This is connected to a lack of risky or adventurous play due to caregivers stopping the play before the child can personally assess and moderate risk, which is related to negative impacts on physical, cognitive, and social development. Not long ago, my husband was leading a group of children (kindergarten through fifth grade boys) who were new to his scout group on a nature-based outing. The terrain was moderate—not too hard, not too easy, but a bit of a challenge hike for them. He commented on how many children struggled not with the distance or elevations but with the simple act of staying upright. The children struggled to maintain posture and balance control when the terrain was not perfectly smooth. It is not a stretch to view this as the impact of not having spent much time outdoors when very young to help develop their core strength, proprioceptive abilities, and understanding of what their bodies can and cannot handle. The children who had tagged along with their parents on outdoor activities on a regular basis or spent time routinely playing outside jumped off rocks and raced each other around obstacles while maintaining their conversations. There is also a lack of connection between children and their knowledge or understanding of the outside world. A friend of mine is a cafeteria worker at an elementary school and brought a small fruit tree to the cafeteria one day. She was amazed at how many children commented that they did not realize that fruit grew on plants. This lack of understanding of where something as basic as food comes from, or how it gets to the grocery stores, is concerning, and children do not have any connection with the earth as they once did.

We have begun to see the need to get children back outside and the importance of time in nature for their education. Early research indicates that parents do see the importance of outdoor play for their children, especially with their physical, social, cognitive, and communication skills (Clements, 2004). The challenge comes in making the outdoor play happen consistently. Even better would be child-led free play outdoors! One more recent positive improvement is that the popularity of nature-based school settings is growing. In the Netherlands, it is not uncommon to see preschool children stomping through the forest in rain clothes on their way to an outdoor classroom. The Forest School movement is growing around the world, having started in the United Kingdom, and encourages hands-on learning in natural environments (Worroll & Houghton, 2016). In the United States, nature-based preschools are growing in popularity especially in more heavily populated areas. Educators of older children are also seeing the benefit and are working to bring outdoor experiences to their students. Interest in and availability of outdoor schools for elementary aged children are growing, as are outdoor learning spaces on a smaller scale. Summer camps and experiences for teenagers are readily available and continue to thrive, with a focus on exploration, challenge, and self-discipline as one learns their abilities.

As we see a shift to more indoor activities and a significant decline of outdoor, child-led free play, we also see an increase in mental health referrals for children and teenagers. Research does not yet show a causal link between these events, but the relationship is there. As children in the United States saw decreases in physical activity levels of 18% between the years of 2016 and 2020, there was a corresponding increase in behavior and conduct problems (rising by 21% between 2019 and 2020). There has also been an increase in mental health needs of 32% that went untreated (Lebrun-Harris et al., 2022). Findings like these are not specific to the United States. An emergency room in Israel saw an increase beyond expected, ongoing yearly rises in 2021 for psychiatric visits for children and adolescents (Dror et al., 2022). Researchers in the United Kingdom reported an increase in mental health concerns (especially anxiety and depression) for children and adolescents since 2004 (Ford et al., 2021). Kauhanen and colleagues (2023) performed a systematic literature review of research across the United Kingdom, the United States, China, Australia, Italy, India, Canada, Iceland, Spain, and Germany. They found that in 2019–2020, children and adolescents reported general declines in their mental health. The specific changes ranged, with depression and anxiety increases being the most prevalent. What we see from these studies is that youngsters are experiencing and reporting more and more mental health struggles, and these struggles are manifesting behaviorally. These struggles are continuing to grow as children and teenagers spend more time indoors and less time outdoors, being physically active.

It is interesting that some of these studies noted that during 2020, the first year of shutdowns related to COVID-19, notable numbers of children and adolescents reported being happier (Ford et al., 2021), stressors were reduced related to the school setting, and social interactions and emergency room visits decreased (though this decrease in visits could have been due to perceived safety needs with staying home; Dror et al., 2022), and parents of young children reported reading to their children significantly more often (Lebrun-Harris et al., 2022). This suggests that as children engaged in activities that were meaningful to them in their own spaces, they felt better. In Shanghai, China, children tended to report a decrease in depressive symptoms and related this to positive lifestyle changes of being home more often and having time and space to engage in their own activities (Xiang et al., 2020). Taken together, these findings suggest that treating these mental health impacts through play and nature is an appropriate avenue of treatment as they give children the time and space necessary to slow their schedules and process the impact of their world on their lives, while at the same time growing their sense of self and ability to self-regulate while learning about themselves. Children are reporting the need to take the time and space to explore their worlds and engage in activities that are comfortable and stress-reducing, which describes both play and time in nature.

Many times, children and families are able to create this time and space on their own, while others benefit from support in the process or have larger issues that would benefit from professional help. Play therapy is a modality which helps people strive for growth and development while utilizing a theoretical model and the therapeutic powers of play, also known as the change agents of play therapy (Association for Play Therapy, 2022). Nature-based therapy is the integration of nature, natural materials, and nature spaces within traditional therapy models, or ecotherapy models which can take place in settings fully immersed in nature and the wilderness. Thus, adding the therapeutic powers of nature to play in this definition allows for the expansion to nature-based play therapy—using the therapeutic powers of both play and nature would encourage enhanced therapeutic benefit. Play and nature both provide immense benefits to children's holistic development. Harnessing the therapeutic powers of both while presenting children with the time and space to fully utilize play and nature has the potential to improve therapeutic outcomes and provide a solid foundation for continued growth and development. Play therapists who work from a nature-based perspective should be fully grounded in a theoretical model of play therapy, as well as understand the importance and impact of the therapeutic powers of play and how nature supports or furthers the therapeutic value therein. Thus, nature-based play therapy is a modality which utilizes a theoretical model and the therapeutic powers of play and nature to help people achieve their optimal growth and development across the age range.

Concluding thoughts

I hope the vital importance of integrating nature and play has been clear through these chapters. Children's overall development is impacted by both, and we can support healthier development of children and society by encouraging more time at play, especially in nature! This knowledge is important for both the layperson and the psychotherapist. To continue in our understanding of nature-based play therapy, understanding and utilizing a theoretically grounded model for play therapy is important because it helps play therapists develop and understand their worldviews in relation to child development (physical, social, emotional, cognitive), family systems, development and maintenance of psychopathology, and more. Having a solid understanding of how children typically develop allows for a stronger understanding of where challenges can and do occur, and how various symptom presentations come to be. This knowledge allows the play therapist to then address improvements to make, areas to further develop, and skills to learn so that a child can reach their full potential. Techniques should only be implemented after case conceptualization following a theoretical model is in process. The following chapters will contain explorations of how nature can and should be integrated into this thinking process. Understanding how nature can fit into both the theoretical understanding of child development and psychopathology and how it can be integrated into techniques are key aspects of nature-based play therapy.

References

Association for Play Therapy. (2022, September 7). *Why play therapy?* https://www.a4pt. org/page/WhyPlayTherapy

Barros, R. M., Silver, E. J., & Stein, R. E. K. (2009). School recess and group classroom behavior. *Pediatrics, 123*(2), 431–436. https://doi.org/10.1542/peds.2007-2825

Bento, G., & Dias, G. (2017). The importance of outdoor play for young children's healthy development. *Porto Biomedical Journal, 2*(5), 157–160. https://doi.org/10.1016/j. pbj.2017.03.003

Brussoni, M., Gibbons, R., Gray, C., Ishikawa, T., Sandseter, E. B. H., Bienenstock, A., Chabot, G., Fuselli, P., Herrington, S., Janssen, I., Pickett, W., Power, M., Stanger, N., Sampson, M., & Tremblay, M. S. (2015). What is the relationship between risky outdoor play and health in children? A systematic review. *International Journal of Environmental Research and Public Health, 12*(6), 6423–6454. https://doi.org/10.3390/ ijerph120606423

Clements, R. (2004). An investigation of the status of outdoor play. *Contemporary Issues in Early Childhood, 5*(1), 68–80. https://doi.org/10.2304/ciec.2004.5.1.10

Dodd, H. F., & Lester, K. J. (2021). Adventurous play as a mechanism for reducing risk for childhood anxiety: A conceptual model. *Clinical Child and Family Psychology Review, 24*, 164–181. https://doi.org/10.1007/s10567-020-00338-w

Dodd, H. F., Nesbit, R. J., & FitzGibbon, L. (2022). Child's play: Examining the association between time spend playing and child mental health. *Child Psychiatry & Human Development*, 1–9. https://doi.org/10.1007/s10578-022-01363-2

Dror, C., Hertz-Palmor, N., Yadan-Barzilai, Y., Saker, T., Kritchmann-Lupo, M., & Bloch, Y. (2022). Increase in referrals of children and adolescents to the psychiatric emergency room is evident only in the second year of the COVID-19 pandemic—evaluating 9156 visits from 2010 to 2021 in a single psychiatric emergency room. *International Journal of Environmental Research and Public Health, 19*(15), 8924. doi: 10.3390/ ijerph19158924

Fjørtoft, I. (2001). The natural environment as a playground for children: The impact of outdoor play activities in pre-primary school children. *Early Childhood Education Journal, 29*(2), 111–117. https://doi.org/10.1023/A:1012576913074

Ford, T., John, A., & Gunnell, D. (2021). Mental health of children and young people during pandemic. *BMJ, 372*(614), 1–2. https://doi.org/10.1136/bmj.n614

Fuchs, R. K., Cusimano, B., & Snow, C. M. (2002). Box jumping: A bone-building exercise for elementary school children. *Journal of Physical Education, Recreation & Dance, 73*(2), 22–25. https://doi.org/10.1080/07303084.2002.10607749

Gill, T. (2014). The benefits of children's engagement with nature: A systematic literature review. *Children, Youth and Environments, 24*(2), 10–34. https://doi.org/10.7721/ chilyoutenvi.24.2.0010

Gray, P. (2011). The decline of play and the rise of psychopathology in children and adolescents. *American Journal of Play, 3*(4), 443–463.

Kauhanen, L., Wan Mohd Yunus, W. M. A., Lempinen, L., Peltonen, K., Gyllenberg, D., Mishina, K., Gilbert, S., Bastola, K., Brown, J. S. L., & Sourander, A. (2023). A systematic review of the mental health changes of children and young people before and during the COVID-19 pandemic. *European Child & Adolescent Psychiatry, 32*(6), 995–1013. https://doi.org/10.1007/s00787-022-02060-0

Kuo, F. E., & Taylor, A. F. (2004). A potential natural treatment for Attention-Deficit/ Hyperactivity Disorder: Evidence from a national study. *American Journal of Public Health, 94*(9), 1580–1586. https://doi.org/10.1177/1087054708323000

Lebrun-Harris, L. A., Ghandour, R. M., & Kogan, M. D. (2022). Five-year trends in US children's health and well-being, 2016–2020. *JAMA Pediatrics, 176*(7), e220056. https://doi.org/10.1001/jamapediatrics.2022.0056

Little, H., & Wyver, S. (2008). Outdoor play: Does avoiding the risks reduce the benefits? *Australian Journal of Early Childhood, 33*(2), 33–40. https://doi.org/10.1177/183693910803300206

Pellegrini, A. D. (1988). Elementary-school children's rough-and-tumble play and social competence. *Developmental Psychology, 24*(6), 802–806. https://doi.org/10.1037/0012-1649.24.6.802

Pellegrini, A. D., & Davis, P. (1993). Relations between children's playground and classroom behavior. *British Journal of Educational Psychology, 63*, 86–95. https://doi.org/10.1111/j.2044-8279.1993.tb01043.x

Sandseter, E. B. H. (2009). Affordances for risky play in preschool—the importance of features in the play environment. *Early Childhood Education Journal, 36*, 439–446. https://doi.org/10.1007/s10643-009-0307-2

Shams, L., & Seitz, A. R. (2008). Benefits of multisensory learning. *Trends in Cognitive Science, 12*(11), 411–417. https://doi.org/10.1016/j.tics.2008.07.006

Smith, P. K., & Hagan, T. (1980). Effects of deprivation on exercise play in nursery school children. *Animal Behaviour, 28*, 922–928. https://doi.org/10.1016/S0003-3472(80)80154-0

Stephenson, A. M. (1998). Opening up the outdoors: A reappraisal of young children's outdoor experiences (Doctoral dissertation, Victoria University of Wellington).

Tangen, S., Olsen, A., & Sandseter, E. B. H. (2022). A GoPro look on how children aged 17–25 months assess and manage risk during free exploration in a varied natural environment. *Education Sciences, 12*, 361. https://doi.org/10.3390/educsci12050361

Taylor, A. F., & Kuo, F. E. (2009). Children with attention deficits concentrate better after walk in the park. *Journal of Attention Disorders, 12*(5), 402–409. https://doi.org/10.1177/1087054708323000

Taylor, A. F., & Kuo, F. E. (2011). Could exposure to everyday green spaces help treat ADHD? Evidence from children's play settings. *Applied Psychology: Health and Well-Being, 3*(3), 281–303. https://doi.org/10.1111/j.1758-0854.2011.01052.x

Viseux, F. (2020). The sensory role of the foot: Review and update on clinical perspectives. *Clinical Neurophysiology, 50*(1), 55–68. https://doi.org/10.1016/j.neucli.2019.12.003

Worroll, J., & Houghton, P. (2016). *Play the Forest School way*. Watkins.

Xiang, M., Yamamoto, S., & Mizoue, T. (2020). Depressive symptoms in students during school closure due to COVID-19 in Shanghai. *Psychiatry and Clinical Neurosciences, 74*, 664–666. https://doi.org/10.1111/pcn.13161

Chapter 5

The seminal and historically significant play therapy theories

Nature edition

Understanding and utilizing a play therapy theory is crucial to the application of play therapy. In order to fully understand and utilize a prescriptive model for play therapy, the core tenets of the seminal and historically significant theories of play therapy must be outlined and understood. Without a solid theoretical understanding, play therapists cannot provide true play therapy. The Association for Play Therapy recognizes ten seminal or historically significant play therapy theories: Adlerian, child-centered, cognitive-behavioral, developmental, eco-systemic, filial, Gestalt, Jungian, object relations, and Theraplay (Association for Play Therapy, 2022, July 1). In this chapter, we will review the core tenets of each of these theories and how the value of nature can be understood from the theoretical perspective. It will also include how nature and the integration of nature into play therapy can happen within each theoretical orientation and treatment model while staying true to the original core tenets of the play therapy theory. This chapter is not intended to give a substantial overview or in-depth training of any specific theory—this would be impossible in this amount of space! The objective is to provide an overview so the play therapist has a basic understanding of each theory, the core tenets or beliefs of each, and some ideas of how incorporating nature into play therapy fits into each of these worldviews. The hope is that this will encourage deeper thinking and your own exploration of the theory (or theories) that best fit your understanding of the world and child development.

Within each of these theories, nature should be considered and included from two perspectives: the physical aspects and the metaphysical. In terms of physical aspects, considerations of including nature range from the physical location of a session (such as in an outdoor play space, on a walking trail, or at the back of a parking lot), to the materials included or used in sessions, to discussion of the child's experiences in the larger natural world outside of session. The metaphysical aspects of nature in play therapy include considerations of the role of nature in the therapy relationship, the client's experience of nature itself and the impact these interactions have on the person's development and sense of self, and the personification of nature. The client's views on the importance of nature, cultural

DOI: 10.4324/9781003332343-5

and religious beliefs in regard to nature, and personal knowledge of nature (including previous experiences in a natural setting, both good and bad) all impact the metaphysical experiences of nature-based play therapy.

Within this model of understanding, the role of nature in the play therapy relationship can be brought into session, explored, developed, and utilized in the process of play therapy. Ecotherapists and other nature-based therapists have described nature as a co-therapist or adding a distinct therapeutic role, bringing a specific yet often undefinable shift or addition to the therapeutic relationship itself (i.e. Courtney, 2017; Naor & Mayseless, 2021). In a co-therapist role, nature itself can adjust perceptions of physical and mental or internally held boundaries and provide new or unique opportunities for metaphors, self-regulation, self-exploration, growth, and development. As a co-therapist, awareness of the relationships that develop between client and nature, therapist and nature, and the triangle of the three should be ever-present, encouraged, and utilized as possible. These relationships can help develop self-awareness, access the unconscious, and encourage growth and development of social, emotional, and even physical domains.

In terms of the personification of nature, this concept comes quite readily to most children. It is frequently presented in children's stories, with inanimate objects giving a moral lesson in a lead role (such as the tree that gives all to a young boy in *The Giving Tree* by Shel Silverstein) and animals used as the main character who can talk, dance, and teach in so many books. Children naturally give human characteristics to inanimate objects in nature, or project feelings states onto animals and plants. When actively utilizing the personification of nature, the client does not need to be in an outdoor space to engage and reap the benefits. Stories can be created with natural materials in the sandtray, books with animals as main characters can be shared, or photos of nature-based scenes or items can be used as story starters or metaphors. For the purposes of this chapter, the concepts of how the role of nature in the therapeutic relationship, the client's experiences of nature, and the personification of nature can be understood within each play therapy theory will be further explored within a brief description of each theoretical orientation.

Adlerian play therapy

In Adlerian play therapy, an active and directive approach, people are seen as socially embedded, goal-directed, and creative beings (Kottman, 2011). People's experiences are seen as subjective, which means that clinicians need to take the person's experience into account, not only the facts of what "actually happened" during an event, because what "actually happened" is what the client experienced. Adlerian play therapists also follow the concept of the Crucial Cs, developed by Lew and Bettner (2000, as cited in Kottman & Meany-Walen, 2016, p. 35). The Crucial Cs concept suggests that well-functioning children are connected with others with a sense of belonging, are capable of taking care of their own needs (leading to self-control, self-disciple, and competence), count in relationships and the world (knowing they matter, have significance, and are capable of making a difference), and have courage to face life's tasks and take the necessary risks to succeed (Kottman & Meany-Walen, 2016). Children who have incorporated each of these components into their belief systems about themselves and their place in the world tend toward happiness, fulfillment, resilience, and successful lives (Kottman & Meany-Walen, 2016).

Adlerian play therapists follow four phases of therapy: Build an egalitarian relationship, explore the child's lifestyle, help the child gain insight into lifestyle, and reorient or reeducate. Within the first two, the Crucial Cs are consistently being evaluated and assessed to determine how to plan interventions to support any areas that would benefit from improvement in the third and fourth phases of therapy, thus strengthening children's core belief system about themselves, the world, and their place therein (Kottman & Meany-Walen, 2016). Within these core tenets, people's views of themselves within the natural world and their relationship with nature should be explored and understood. As nature allows for creativity and exploration, understanding the role of nature (or lack thereof) in a client's life should be considered. Children's misbehaviors are often viewed within four categories of goals, and the reasons behind their misbehaviors should be assessed during Adlerian play therapy. These categories are attention (these children need attention to feel significant, and the attention can be positive or negative), power (these children need to feel in control to count or matter), revenge (these children need to get even with others or make up for wrongs committed against them to feel secure), and prove inadequacy (these children are discouraged and feel they are incapable so set out to prove their inadequacy; Kottman & Meany-Walen, 2016).

The first phase of Adlerian play therapy, building an egalitarian relationship, is an excellent place to begin assessing the child's view of nature and integrating nature into the therapy. Within the egalitarian relationship, no one person is better than or more than another. This holds true for nature experiences and knowledge as well. In the natural world, a child may know more or different information than the therapist, and in Adlerian play therapy, this is more than welcomed. Therapist and client can learn and explore together, and use the natural world as a joining ground for developing an egalitarian relationship. Exploration of a child's lifestyle should include understanding previous nature experiences. Adlerian play therapists can explore what role nature plays in the child's and family's life experiences, what relationships the family and child hold with the natural world, and how these experiences fit in with the child's community. As the client gains insight into his or her lifestyle, questions about how nature could be included going forward could be utilized, or even discussing whether there is a role for an increase in nature time. Through the assessment of the Crucial Cs in these two phases, looking at the child's understanding of the natural world is important. Is the child able to connect with the world around himself? Is he capable of being part of the natural world—can he safely explore his surroundings, understand what is around him, maintain the necessary body strength, and balance to explore outdoors? Does he count within the larger world—what is his place in the greater picture outside of the four walls of his home? Does he have the courage to attempt risky or adventurous outdoor play? In the reorientation and reeducation phase of therapy, Adlerian play therapists can work with parents and children to explore how they can work toward goals set in the gaining insight phase, and nature-based interventions could be considered part of this process. Both bringing nature into the play space to broaden a child's view (or to let them show their capabilities as many children would love to share their knowledge of natural materials with an adult!) and bringing a child into a nature-based play therapy setting to expand the opportunities for developing the Crucial Cs would be applicable to Adlerian play therapy.

In looking at the metaphysical aspect of inclusion of nature in Adlerian play therapy, the role of nature as a co-therapist includes allowing for and encouraging nature to join the egalitarian relationship between client and therapist. Nature can be an add-on or direct component of goal creation and enhances creative ability. Within the Crucial Cs, the development of a relationship with nature encourages improvements in all four domains: connect, count, capability, and courage. Clients can experience what it is like to connect with individual aspects of nature (little critters, streams, special spaces, and so on), count within something so much larger than oneself, develop physical capabilities as well as new knowledge of individual aspects of nature, and explore and grow their sense of courage to explore, try, challenge, and grow. The personification of nature encourages utilization of natural materials within these domains and can range from wondering how a tree would describe a client and their growth within therapy, to inviting an inanimate object to participate in an intervention or session.

Child-centered and filial play therapies

Child-centered play therapy and filial play therapy will be discussed together as filial is an offshoot of child-centered. Within this theory, children are seen as truly capable of self-healing, self-growth, and self-discovery given the right environment and responses from a caring adult with whom they have been able to develop a relationship (Sweeney & Landreth, 2011). Child-centered play therapists strive to be genuine and show empathic understanding and unconditional positive regard. The main endeavor through this theoretical orientation is the development of the relationship, with a focus on the child specifically rather than solely symptom presentation (Sweeney & Landreth, 2011). It is recognized that children use play as their primary method of communication, and children lead the therapy sessions. They have a need for both unconditional positive regard and acceptance and strive for actualization which is a main goal of the therapeutic process. Landreth (2002) outlines ten objectives of child-centered play therapy, primarily focused on helping children to develop stronger problem-solving abilities through the development of self-concept, responsibility, control, coping process, self-reliance, a decision-making process, and trust in themselves. Developing these core components of self gives children a strength-based understanding of themselves as whole and adequate people, thus enabling them to develop further as whole and functioning adults capable of forming solid and healthy relationships.

When it comes to understanding the role nature can play within this theoretical framework and model, simply having nature available to the child is a primary task of the therapist. This could be either having natural materials available in the play room or having an outdoor play space available for the child's use as Jaqueline Swank and her colleagues have been doing with success in outdoor play spaces with individual therapy clients (Swank & Shin, 2015b), gardening groups (Swank & Shin, 2015a), child-centered groups held in outdoor play spaces (Swank et al., 2017), and by bringing natural materials into indoor space for individual clients (Swank et al., 2020). As the sessions are child-led and directed, having the natural world available as an option allows children to utilize nature as they see fit at any given time. In terms of accepting the child for who they are, accepting the role nature plays in a person's life is also key. Nature is a huge part of human history and plays differing roles in children's lives today. Asking about this role during intake and being open to the child potentially wanting to explore, challenge themselves, and utilize nature in various ways is an important step in accepting the child for who they are. Along with this also comes accepting the literal dirt that can come with nature play! This goes along with genuineness: A play therapist must be okay with dirt in the play space and on the child, or the child will recognize the discomfort and react. A play therapist must also be genuine in understanding the role nature-based play plays in physical, emotional, and social development, and be ready to include this in the child's therapy world. In terms of a child's striving for actualization, it is important to recognize that being part of nature means we are part of something much bigger than ourselves as individuals. It is a part of our history, our growth, and our development. Children need to determine the role nature plays in their personal lives to actualize to their full potential.

As a major goal of child-centered play therapy is self-actualization and developing a stronger sense of self as a whole and adequate person, then the larger world of nature should be considered within this context. Nature-based therapists identify the experience of unconditional acceptance by the natural world as a therapeutic aspect of nature-based therapies as it leads to a sense of belonging and the presence of this fully accepting setting as important in the development of an authentic self (Naor & Mayseless, 2020). The child-centered play therapist is to provide an environment geared toward helping the child develop these inner structures. For many children, exposure to the natural world can help encourage them to explore themselves more fully and gives a safe and exploration-friendly environment to further develop their therapeutic relationships. In nature-based child-centered play therapy, the natural world can act as a co-therapist, thus providing new opportunities for relationship development and deepening connections that already exist between play therapist and child. Many of the objectives of child-centered play therapy can be explored from the context of nature-based play therapy with no extra effort. As Landreth (2002) encourages play therapists to guide a child in the development of problem-solving abilities, self-concept, responsibility, control, coping process, self-reliance, a decision-making process, and trust in themselves, nature provides a wonderful playscape for these attributes.

In filial play therapy, the play therapist teaches the parents how to play with their children in therapeutic ways during special playtimes. During these times, the parents are acting as the change agents and encouraging their children in the child-centered modality (VanFleet, 2011). They are trained and supervised by filial play therapists to strengthen relationships and attachments within the family unit and help expand and maintain changes from the therapy space to home life (VanFleet, 2011). In terms of integrating nature into this approach, the parents should be able to discuss the role nature plays in their family life and be open to exploring the child's hopes and expectations about nature in their own lives. Parents might need to explore their own feelings and reactions to nature and time in nature, including the tendency for children to get dirty, and figure out how to incorporate this into their special play times. As the child gets to choose activities from provided toys, including nature-based items in the selection would be an easy way to incorporate nature into nature-based play therapy from a filial play therapy perspective. Parents and filial play therapists could also identify appropriate outdoor spaces in which to provide special playtimes for children and their parents, bringing the usual assortment of toys and materials to this space.

In terms of the metaphysical side of nature within nature-based filial play therapy, the aspects of relationships should be explored. Bringing a family together in nature-based play therapy expands the number of relationships in the space exponentially. We no longer have only the client/therapist, client/nature, therapist/nature, and client/therapist/nature relationships of which to be aware and facilitating, but now include each parent (and sibling, if involved) within each of these dyads or triads. Familial relationships tend to change, often subtly, within a natural setting. As each person interacts with nature and is impacted by time and space, shifts are seen in how others are treated and understood, especially when family members are given the opportunity to explore the environment during these times. This phenomenon reminds me of how sometimes removing direct eye contact is the way to let people feel comfortable opening up about deep feelings. Sitting next to each other at bedtime or side by side in a car are great opportunities for unexpected connection! The same holds true for together time outside. In my family, our kids sometimes start hikes in a grumpy mood, but after walking for about ten minutes, they are chattering away about everything and anything. The attitudes are left back at the house, and we have the opportunity to get to know each other better as we are all on equal ground outside. The hierarchy of a family system is still present, but suddenly no topic is off limits, and we can connect in deeper ways than when surrounded by the "stuff" of the house and its implicit expectations. Facilitating and utilizing this shift can be quite helpful in filial play therapy and offers opportunities for deeper connections and strengthening of positive attachments.

Cognitive-behavioral play therapy

Cognitive-behavioral play therapy is founded on the principles of new learning. In this goal-directed and therapist-led modality, new learning is used to achieve cognitive and behavioral changes. Theoretically, cognitive-behavioral play therapists understand problems as occurring because of maladaptive behavioral patterns, reactions to traumas, and learned responses. People hold core beliefs, and when psychological symptoms (including behavioral changes) are present, this is likely because of dysfunctional assumptions or automatic negative thinking. Maladaptive cognitions or cognitive distortions can lead to children needing some help creating adaptive beliefs through talk or play therapy. Adaptive beliefs lead to positive coping skills and better ways of understanding situations and reactions. The new learning in cognitive-behavioral play therapy is psychoeducational and is brought into sessions to break the maladaptive cycle of thinking and responding to help the client create a new response pathway or pattern. A cognitive-behavioral play therapist sets goals for children and families and utilizes a directive, psychoeducational, and goal-driven approach to help children understand conflicts and maladaptive thought patterns and responses to create more appropriate ways of dealing with situations (Knell, 2011). In cognitive-behavioral play therapy, a goal is to establish or re-establish appropriate behaviors and responses, in terms of both cognitive and behavioral reactions.

Another aspect of cognitive-behavioral theory is related to the cognitive triad. In this model, Beck posited that individuals dealing with depressive symptoms are more likely to hold negative views of themselves, the world, and the future. Taken together, these three aspects contribute to feelings of unworthiness, inadequacy, a limited worldview especially in terms of opportunities for success, and ongoing challenges and difficulties that cannot be overcome (Marcetti & Pössel, 2022). When integrating concepts from the natural world in this therapy, a multitude of possibilities is present for metaphors and expanding a person's worldview outside of themselves, which brings in the metaphysical aspects of nature interactions. Cognitive-behavioral play therapists can help their clients look at themselves in relation to a bigger whole by thinking outside of the playroom and viewing the self in relation to the entire natural world. Oftentimes people dealing with depressive thinking watch their worldview become smaller and more focused on what is directly in front of them and their singular experiences. Expanding these horizons allows for a wider range of metaphors, stories, and examples to be utilized which can also help ground the person in a world that is larger and more encompassing than themselves. For example, watching a tiny ant hauling a piece of food back to the colony is a simple way to introduce the concept of inadequacy, and working against the concept by providing a metaphor of something so small achieving a great goal. Going back to the religious aspects to work with the concept of self-worth, biblical examples abound related to tiny aspects of nature being noticed and appreciated or counted, which are then related to people and their experiences to show how much people do and should matter.

Other physical examples from nature can be used as metaphysical metaphors to help change negative thinking patterns. For example, many times tree roots grow over rocks and other large impediments. As the soil erodes away, the impediments under the roots can wash away, but the root structure maintains the form with which it grew. This can be a powerful metaphor for overcoming trauma reactions and challenging negative thoughts. Clients can see that while the impact of the trauma may have shaped them and even carries on with them, the strength of the core system flourishes and grows while maintaining the beauty of its difference. Instead of seeing the root system as broken or challenged, the client can see the strength it took for the tree to overcome the obstacles in its path as it rooted in solid ground and grew around the obstacle. Another tree example is a burl, which is a growth the tree naturally produces to heal a wound. Many trees have none, some have one or two, and yet others are literally covered in these bulges. These burls can be viewed as problems that were overcome and represent self-healing, thus challenging negative thinking patterns.

In terms of specifically including physical activity in nature during cognitive-behavioral work, increasing exercise by encouraging clients to get outside more often or engaging in a specific exercise regimen can be helpful. Research indicates that people who exercise show improvements in mood states and also that exercising outdoors in nature leads to stronger benefits than exercising indoors (e.g., Harte & Eifert, 1995). Nature walks have been found to be associated with improved mood and memory functioning (Berman et al., 2012), while spending time in a natural environment has been linked with decreases of physical stress markers (Hunter et al., 2019). Thus, encouraging physical activity in the natural world can help reduce felt stress and improve mood and cognitive functioning, all of which would benefit cognitive-behavioral play therapy outcomes.

Of note is that cognitive-behavioral play therapy is often utilized to help clients deal with or overcome symptoms of attention-deficit hyperactivity disorder (ADHD). The goal-oriented, behaviorally based treatment plans of cognitive-behavioral work lend nicely to working with these impulsive and dysregulated behaviors. Research shows that utilizing green or outdoor spaces in psychological treatments for ADHD leads to greater improvements, even when the interventions were the same in both indoor and outdoor spaces (Taylor & Kuo, 2011). Simply walking outdoors helped children with symptoms of distractibility and impulsiveness to better concentrate on tasks (Taylor & Kuo, 2009). These are promising results that should encourage play therapists to support their clients in getting outside more often, bringing the benefits of both nature and play to their sessions.

Developmental play therapy

Viola Brody's developmental play therapy theory focuses on how vital touch is to human development. In this theoretical approach, play therapists understand that touch creates a connection between self and other, which supports a stronger understanding of the self. Expressive touch is seen as the first mode of communication between infant and parent, and psychopathology stems from disconnection from one's inner self, along with a deprivation of touch. If children do not have a strong awareness and appreciation for their own bodies and their relation to others and the world, they will likely struggle in their interactions with others and themselves. This is also true of a child who has experienced inappropriate touching and has a deep need for healthy, appropriate, loving touches to help heal their missing basic needs. Developmental play therapy as a model offers creative touch dialogues to give children what is needed to develop the core self through presymbolic play, singing, and the basic infant–caregiver interactions. Through this model, developmental play therapists can provide nurturing, loving, and healing healthy touches throughout their therapy sessions that will help them heal past traumas, get basic needs met, and progress on a path of developing maturity and organization of their sense of self and ability to relate to others. A big piece of being able to provide such touches as an adult is understanding what is needed of the adult in the process and how the adult needs to develop an understanding of what it means to be touched, how to guide a child's development through touch, and becoming open to being touched during sessions themselves (Brody, 1997). The Association for Play Therapy has developed guidelines regarding touch in sessions that are helpful when working from this theoretical perspective (Association for Play Therapy, 2022).

Occupational therapy research has shown how vital time spent in nature is for physical development, particularly for developing an understanding of how one's body works and what one is capable of doing. Babies who crawl on grassy slopes, for instance, experience sensory reactions to the multiple textures while developing physical responses to the changes in terrains. They get a stronger sense of what their bodies are capable of, how they need to adjust to maintain position, and how they fit in with the physical world. Nature is also full of a wide variety of textures and other sensory input, which allows for exploration and learning from all five senses plus the proprioceptive system (Hanscom, 2016).

The physical touches of the world are necessary for physical, emotional, and psychological development and healing. Being encouraged to touch the ground, explore spaces and textures, and feel connected with the greater physical world helps children to develop stronger connections with the world around themselves but also develop core physical strengths and a more strongly integrated sense of self. Clients can also engage in the repetitive, repeatable, routine-based physical interactions of developmental play therapy in a natural setting. Rocking, matching breathing patterns, and engaging in self-regulation can be enhanced with the addition of fresh air, breezes, and the feeling of the sun warming the client.

Integrating nature into developmental play therapy also allows a child to experience being part of a greater whole, thus bringing in the metaphysical aspect of nature. A client's relationship with nature is quite important here. How comfortable is a client in a natural setting? Will they allow the touches of nature to help them heal? Are there traumatic memories based in nature? Here nature can act as a co-therapist as a client explores the physical sensations of the natural world as they touch and interact with rocks, sand, grass, water, and so on. For the nature-based play therapist, it is important to understand if these interactions are seen as supportive and soothing, helping the client to connect, or if they are negative in any way.

Ecosystemic play therapy

The ecosystemic play therapy theory has a focus on the fact that children are part of and impacted by multiple systems in a hierarchical fashion, which are similar to those found in Bronfenbrenner's work and include (in top-down order) chronosystems, macrosystems, mesosystems, and microsystems which include people's mind–body connections as a unique system (O'Connor, 2011). The impact of these systems on individuals, both positive and negative, influences how the individual responds in different situations. Consequently, the impact of the systems influences how children develop, while understanding that children are dependent upon these systems yet do not have much influence over the systems themselves. Stressors and problems within these systems and their interactions can lead to negative reactions by the children (O'Connor, 2011). For example, if a child's parent is struggling at work, the tension from the workplace can be felt in the home, and the child might start seeking reassurance or acting out in response to this felt tension. Children can also be affected when there are challenges in the greater macrosystems, such as global conflicts or national economic changes. The impact of the macrosystem can be felt in the mesosystem and microsystems, and if they are not addressed properly on those levels, the child can experience the pull of tension from those sources as well.

In addition to microsystems, mesosystems, macrosystems, and chronosystems, ecosystemic play therapists utilize the concept of individuals being their own mind–body system, which is seen as a microsystem capable of being impacted by the other systems as well. Thus, challenges within the mind–body interaction can also lead to negative reactions that could use some support and redirection by a play therapist. A goal of ecosystemic play therapy is to break set or help children recognize and redefine problems to enable creative problem-solving. By helping a child to maximize development and functioning, normal developmental progress can be resumed, and needs can be met effectively and appropriately. Given the child's dependence upon and influence of these other systems, it is important to recognize the role others play in children's development of symptoms of psychopathology, and ecosystemic play therapists may need to become involved in changing these other systems to mitigate the impact on the child (O'Connor, 2011).

The importance and role of nature within each of the child's systems should be an important consideration in ecosystemic play therapy. What is the role of nature within the child's daily life, and thus the impact of nature in the microsystem? How the family views nature and time spent in nature should be explored at the mesosystem level? Is there time to get outside during school, or are instructors willing to integrate natural materials into lessons? What is available to the child for safe outdoor exploration spaces? Does the community value nature? Perhaps most importantly, what does the child believe about nature, the outdoor world, and their role therein? Are they able to use nature as a space to explore, grow, and reconnect with themselves? This is a part of strengthening the mind–body system as well as a way to connect multiple larger systems through exploration of the greater picture of the world as a whole. Research supports the idea that time spent in nature enhances creative problem-solving abilities and helps maximize personal functioning (Naor & Mayseless, 2021), both of which are important in the ecosystemic model for a child to be able to reach their full potential and improve their current levels of functioning. Encouraging a child (and family) to spend more time outdoors playing and exploring is one way to reap many benefits within this model.

Another consideration within ecosystemic play therapy is that the therapist chooses the toys or materials to be presented during any given session. This can be a wonderful opportunity to provide the physical aspect of nature-based play within a session by intentionally choosing at least one item that comes from the natural world. These items can range from wooden blocks to a basket of twigs, acorns, and leaves to create a world or for clients to make their own toys and games. Actively choosing the toys and activities for each session also allows for release play therapy activities to be highlighted. Release play therapy is a modality used to activate the therapeutic power of abreaction, which allows for a traumatic memory or experience to be relived while the appropriate affect is expressed. This encourages a person to achieve a mastery ending over the traumatic memory, while experiencing control during active repetition and miniaturization of the trauma. For clients who have experienced traumas outdoors or related to natural catastrophes, having release play therapy utilizing natural materials can be incredibly healing.

Gestalt play therapy

Through Gestalt play therapy theory, play therapists believe in the power of acceptance and the experience of acceptance. Violet Oaklander spoke of the need for a child to become aware of their own sense of self and place in the world (Oaklander, 1988, p. 53). The therapeutic relationship is truly vital, and the I/Thou relationship is prominent. Within this relationship, the therapist seeks to make and maintain contact with the client, pay attention, and meet the client where they are, accepting them for who they are and what they bring to the relationship with the therapist and client being equals. The Gestalt play therapist believes in being fully present and genuine with the client while respecting the personal boundaries of the therapist as well as the client. In the Gestalt theory, the client is responsible for personal change, and sessions remain content-focused rather than analytical. A second core tenet of Gestalt play therapy is organismic self-regulation, which refers to understanding that a body will work toward developing and maintaining homeostasis by whatever means possible (Oaklander, 1994). Strengthening or renewing a person's sensory experiences goes a long way toward rebuilding or strengthening contact with the environment and other significant relationships, and encouraging a healthy homeostasis (Oaklander, 1988, p. 57). The Gestalt therapist believes that the whole is greater than the sum of its parts, understanding that interactions with others and the cooperation that occurs often lead to greater outcomes than one person working alone (Upton et al., 2014).

The integration of nature into the Gestalt play therapy theory fits in multiple ways. Many of Violet Oaklander's techniques are rooted in imagined experiences of nature, such as imagining a walk through a wooded area as one develops a personal safe space or creatively associating themselves as a rosebush to prompt inner awareness and drawing activities (Oaklander, 1988, pp. 3 and 32–33), thus personifying nature and encouraging the metaphysical aspects of nature integration. Dr. Oaklander spoke of the development of imagination as a way to help increase a person's ability to cope with events and thoughts, as well to learn new things (Oaklander, 1988, p. 10). She often used nature experiences in her fantasy techniques intended to develop the imagination. This bridges the physical and metaphysical integrations of nature into play therapy. To experience nature in its purest form, one must be an observer while soaking in the surroundings, making it one's own. This connection, acceptance, and overall merging into the surrounding space while experiencing a transpersonal view of being part of something so much bigger than the self bring the meaning of the whole as being greater than the sum of its parts to a deeper level. Exploring the relationship a client has developed with nature is also important. Is it a nurturing relationship? Challenged? Scared? Supportive? Educational? Mutual? How clients determine and describe their relationships with nature is a key indicator of the role this element can take in Gestalt play therapy. Also, developing a client's senses and sensory experiences through exploration of nature can be quite beneficial in the work of improving contact functions and thus sense of self.

This is where utilizing the physical aspect of nature in Gestalt play therapy is important. As a client explores the textures of nature, perhaps through a nature-based sensory board, or a sensory scavenger hunt, the client is exposed to multiple opportunities to explore new or already-assimilated contacts with the larger world, thus growing their system of contact functions. Children need to use all their senses to fully grow and develop their sense of self through contacts with their environments. Allowing for and providing physical opportunities for a child to explore the environment utilizing all senses encourages minimization of impairment in contact functions or an opportunity to heal and improve where impairments have already been created (Oaklander, 1988). This helps to continue to grow and preserve the client's sense of self, which is a core tenet of Gestalt play therapy.

Jungian play therapy

Jungian play therapy is an analytically based theory in which Jungian play therapists believe that children are striving for wholeness. They seek growth as they become more aware of their unconscious material, which is experienced and explored through symbols, projection, and displacement. Throughout their development, children take on traits of parents and caregivers, and part of their developmental journey is separating or achieving individuation as they create their own sense of self. As children increase their self-awareness, they grow through self-healing. Archetypes are used in hypotheses and interpretations as archetypal themes are observed in children's play and behaviors to understand what is happening within the child's psyche and process of developing wholeness. These archetypes are not just symbols but ways of organizing experiences, thoughts, and feelings, and are often shown through images developed from the collective unconscious, which refers to generations' worth of knowledge that is passed down, often unknowingly. The connections people have with the past and their present relationships are paramount, and thus, connection with parents during Jungian play therapy is notable. Jungian play therapists work to help children achieve individuation through exploration of archetypal images and symbols, often encouraging children to ground themselves in reality through artwork before leaving sessions (Green, 2011). Sandplay, developed by Dora Kalff (1980), is used as another means to explore symbols and archetypes in Jungian play therapy.

Jung himself was a strong proponent of time spent in nature and the impact it has on human growth, development, and awareness. He often advocated for people to learn "to 'live in modest harmony with nature'" and to understand that nature is the "nourishing soil of the soul" as the psyche is truly nature from its earliest and most basic definitions (Sabini, 2008, p. 1). Symbols and archetypes abound in nature and are often experienced more strongly and in the most primitive forms in the natural environment, with nature encompassing all archetypes (Sabini, 2008, p. 18). In a letter written to a colleague, Jung implored the man to spend time in nature as the way to sort through a troubling dream and find himself saying, "Why not go into the forest for a time, literally? Sometimes a tree tells you more than can be read in books" (Sabini, 2008, p. 6). Here Jung suggests the role of nature as a co-therapist, providing the space and time for personal reflection, drawing on the connection between humans and nature to refresh and replenish the soul. Jung was deeply concerned about the growing lack of connection to and with nature that people were allowing to happen, both as individuals and as a society (Sabini, 2008).

The collective unconscious, a concept prominent in Jungian work, speaks to generations' worth of experiences, and the historical aspect of nature cannot be minimized here. Jung actually identified the collective unconscious as Nature, stating that Nature contains everything, including both the known and the unknown (Adler & Aniela, 1976). The meaning people place on experiences in nature is powerful. Do sunrises symbolize new beginnings or something else? Are rainstorms refreshing and cleansing, or devastating? What stories have their grandparents or other relatives told about natural disasters, working the land, exploring, surviving, flourishing, struggling, and so on? What has been both passed down and experienced? In seeing the disconnect Americans in particular have had from nature, Jung's worry was that separating from nature was causing many of the problems we as therapists see still today (Sabini, 2008). Reconnecting with nature would give people an opportunity to reestablish their sense of instinct (which is a particularly fascinating concept when considering the collective unconscious) and to let nature affect us in many healing ways (Sabini, 2008). Society has been developing its own collective unconscious through technology and human advances, often neglecting the natural world and its history, which Jung was already pointing out many years ago (Adler & Aniela, 1976).

Another way in which nature is incorporated into Jungian play therapy is through mandalas, which, at a very basic level, are circular creations that are often interpreted as divided into four domains with a center representing Jung's typology of the intuition, thinking, feeling, and sensation domains. This interpretation, however, keeps the mandala static and unchanging (Duran, 2012). In play therapy, mandalas can be created within circles to represent the self or can be pre-drawn images that a client is able to color or fill in (Green et al., 2013). From a historical and cultural perspective, mandalas are powerful, important, and deeply rooted in many cultures. For example, the Navajo tribe creates such images out of sand, cornmeal, or other natural items as part of healing and ceremonial rituals. These symbols connect the cosmos and energy powers of nature as part of the rituals. Tibetan Buddhists create intricate mandalas through painting with sand, also creating four domains representing four directions, as part of ceremonial proceedings. Some of the overall purposes of creating mandalas include symbolizing wholeness, harmony, connection, and balance. An overall purpose is to focus on the center, be it the inner center of the person creating or a larger focus of society or the cosmos (Krippner, 1997).

From a nature perspective, the use of mandalas in therapy has been expanded to include the use of labyrinths. This is a way to connect the physical to meta-physical aspects of nature incorporation, as both can be nature-based. With a labyrinth being a circular path along which clients can walk to a center point be-fore retracing their path to the outer edges, clients are encouraged to contemplate personal issues or concerns on the walk toward center and potential solutions on the path back out (Peel, 2004). The circular journey and movement, combined with the time in a natural setting, can be quite powerful and healing in itself. In a play therapy setting, small wooden labyrinths with raised cutout paths for clients to trace and follow with a finger can be used, or an outdoor space can be provided that encourages physical movement along a path.

Object relations play therapy

A relationally based theory, object relations play therapy theory is a psycho-dynamic approach that recognizes the importance of a secure attachment base for positive development and the impact that attachment trauma has on dys-functional development. Interactions that infants have with significant others develop into internalized concepts of self, other, and self in relation to others. These concepts form internal working models that impact perceptions, attitudes, and interactions across the lifespan. These early attachment patterns are instinc-tual and dependency-based, particularly with the mother, and are what tend to endure across the lifespan (Ainsworth, 1969). Thus, when there is attachment trauma that occurs in these early stages, the child develops negative internalized models which impact subsequent relationships as well as personal development (Patton & Benedict, 2015). The object relations play therapy approach integrates this psychodynamic understanding of relationship development with thematic play to address thoughts, feelings, and behaviors (Benedict, 2006) by utilizing attunement with the therapist, coregulation, and empathy through developing a strong therapeutic relationship and such sensory-based techniques as finger painting and sand work (Patton & Benedict, 2015).

When it comes to incorporating nature into the object relations theory, the idea of developing an attachment base and how that impacts future relationships and interactions with nature is clear. People develop different types of attach-ment to nature and aspects of nature, in similar ways as they do with caregivers. For example, someone who has lived through a tsunami and seen the devasta-tion caused could develop an avoidant relationship with water-based areas. They could experience refreshment and fulfillment being part of a wooded area, how-ever, and feel more secure and stable there. People who have hiked mountains and experienced spiritual awakenings watching the sun rise over a peak could claim a secure attachment to nature as they integrate their physical and spiritual experiences. These more secure attachments can then be used to help a person self-regulate and develop stronger coping skills for current or ongoing stressors. It would also be important from this theoretical perspective to incorporate nature histories into intake questions to determine what the child's primary caregiver has experienced in the natural world and the importance placed on time in nature. The caregiver's expectations, experiences, and perceptions of the outdoor world impact the child's expectations and perceptions as well, and thus need to be understood before attempting to integrate nature into play therapy sessions. For example, a different approach will be needed to introduce nature into sessions for a family who has developed and encouraged a positive relationship with the natural world compared to a family who has fearful expectations of the outdoors. With the development of relationships with nature comes the opportunity to develop and explore the concept of nature as co-therapist, which will differ depending upon each client or family's need.

Given the use of sensory-based play with object relations play therapy, integrating nature into the physical side of play therapy would be quite appropriate. Making finger paints from berries and mud, and utilizing sand for sand tray applications are great ways to physically bring nature into sessions while staying true to the theoretical basis of object relations play therapy. Sensory boards made with materials the therapist collects outside of session (or as part of a sensory walk or scavenger hunt with clients) and then attaches to a piece of cardboard or thin wood for a client to explore can be useful tools to physically connect a person to the textures of nature.

Theraplay

Theraplay is a historically significant approach to play therapy that is based on attachment, self-psychology, and object relations theories. The replication of early parent/child interactions helps a child make the first relationship a healthier one, with the intent of improving attachment. The first and primary goal of Theraplay is to increase attachment between the child and the caregiver (Munns, 2000). Other outcomes include building trust between the child and the caregiver and improving self-esteem. This method has been particularly successful with families who have experienced trauma and children who are rebuilding trust and attachment after neglect situations. Through the replication of the early parent/child interactions with many preverbal types of touches, games and experiences, the child feels nurturance, care, love, and value as a whole person. This allows a child to build a positive self-image with an inner sense of strength, competence, and worth.

During the development of this model, Ann Jernberg determined that the typical interactions between parent and child fit within four main dimensions, with playfulness being added later: structure, engagement, nurture, and challenge

(Munns, 2000). These dimensions often hold the needs of the child and family at the time of treatment. Structure refers to rhythms and schedules of a day for predictability including rules and boundaries for safety, which is why Theraplay is a highly structured modality in which the therapist takes and maintains the lead throughout the sessions. The challenge domain refers to risk-taking and mastery behaviors so children can grow through scaffolding and support as they try and accomplish increasingly challenging tasks appropriate to their age and abilities. Engagement refers to the attunement that caregivers develop for the child's needs and brings fun to the relationship. The nurture domain refers to care-taking activities that support a child's feeling of being loved, wanted, and protected within the relationship, knowing that an adult will be present for them whenever necessary. This is a key component of Theraplay, and many foundational activities are grounded in nurturance as all children (and adults!) need nurturance. In Theraplay, the play therapist chooses the interventions and schedule for each session based upon the child's needs in each domain to both model and support the need for structure within a child's life. Parents are encouraged to be involved in the sessions themselves, even receiving Theraplay interventions personally if they have histories of neglect or trauma (Munns, 2000). Theraplay is taught through a specific training program sequence that should be explored by anyone interested.

As Theraplay is a historically significant approach and not a theory of its own, the tenets of developmental, attachment, and object relations theories should be considered here when looking at the potential role of nature within the theoretical model. To integrate nature in Theraplay, the concept of strengthening the connection and attachment between the parent and the child must be the focus. The metaphysical pieces of this can be seen as outlined in the object relations and attachment section of this chapter, while the idea of nature as a co-therapist is seen in a more physical way in Theraplay. Integrating nature can also afford new opportunities for connection that are not typical or as expected within a typical office setting. For example, natural materials can be brought in and used during activities. Feathers or long pieces of grass can be used as part of touching and tickling or other connection-based activities. Small soft feathers or seed pods can be used instead of cotton balls during activities in the engagement domain. Holding sessions outdoors utilizing Theraplay methods would also be a great way to incorporate some movement activities that could help strengthen a child's physical development as occupational therapists are seeing a need for activities held on an uneven ground to develop core strengths and physical abilities (Hanscom, 2016), and the differing tactile experiences found in nature would bring more opportunities for exploring new avenues for nurturance and challenge. The challenge domain of Theraplay is particularly well suited to the incorporation of nature into play therapy sessions. As discussed in Chapter 4, children benefit from risky adventurous play outdoors (Dodd et al., 2022). Encouraging children to participate in outdoor risky play activities while a caregiver supports, encourages, and supervises their attempts toward mastery and achievement would support the tenets of the challenge domain in Theraplay. The rocking and singing activities of the nurture domain could also be held outside, rocking and swaying with the wind, or singing nursery songs while observing the larger natural world. These activities do not necessarily need to happen within the play therapy sessions but could be part of interactions encouraged on their own.

Concluding thoughts

Each of these theories and historically significant approaches provides an opportunity for deeper understanding of child development, strengths, and challenges. Once again, it is incredibly important for the play therapist to be grounded in at least one of these theories. Understanding how the whole child develops and where their supports are (and are not) allows for a deeper understanding of where symptoms originate, how and why they are maintained, and what type of intervention would be best suited for the presenting issue, child, and family. Each theory naturally tends toward activating or facilitating certain therapeutic powers of play in play therapy and understandings of what makes play therapeutic. Prescriptive play therapy encourages the matching of theoretical orientation and therapeutic powers with the presenting needs of the child and family so at least a working understanding of the therapeutic powers is necessary to fully utilize this model. Researchers are now highlighting the therapeutic factors that occur via nature exposure (Naor & Mayseless, 2021), and the major categories of the therapeutic factors of nature coordinate nicely with the therapeutic powers of play. In Chapter 6, we will discuss how the two align, how nature impacts the therapeutic powers of play, and the benefits of combining the change agents of nature and play in nature-based play therapy.

References

Adler, G., & Aniela, J. (Eds.) (1976). *Letters of C. G. Jung: Volume 2, 1951–1961.* Routledge.

Ainsworth, M. D. S. (1969). Object relations, dependency, and attachment: A theoretical review of the infant-mother relationship. *Child Development, 40,* 969–1025. https://doi.org/10.2307/1127008

Association for Play Therapy. (2022, July 1). *Credentialing standards for the Registered Play Therapist™.* https://cdn.ymaws.com/www.a4pt.org/resource/resmgr/credentials/RPT_Standards.pdf

Association for Play Therapy. (2022). *Paper on touch: Clinical, professional & ethical issues.* https://cdn.ymaws.com/www.a4pt.org/resource/resmgr/resource_center/Paper_on_Touch_2022__-_Final.pdf

Benedict, H. E. (2006). Object relations play therapy: Applications to attachment problems and relational trauma. In C. E. Schaefer & H. G. Kaduson (Eds.), *Contemporary play therapy: Theory, research, and practice* (pp. 3–27). Guilford Press.

Berman, M. G., Kross, E., Krpan, K. M, Askren, M. K., Burson, A., Deldin, P. J., Kaplan, S., Sherdell, L., Gotlib, I. H., & Jonides, J. (2012). Interacting with nature improves cognition and affect for individuals with depression. *Journal of Affective Disorders, 140*(3), 300–305. https://doi.org/10.1016/j.jad.2012.03.012

Brody, V. (1997). *Dialogue of touch: Developmental play therapy.* Jason Aronson.

Courtney, J. A. (2017). The art of utilizing the metaphorical elements of nature as "co-therapist" in ecopsychology play therapy. In A. Kopytin & M. Rugh (Eds.), *Environmental expressive therapies: Nature-assisted theory and practice* (pp. 100–122). Routledge.

Dodd, H. F., Nesbit, R. J., & FitzGibbon, L. (2022). Child's play: Examining the association between time spend playing and child mental health. *Child Psychiatry & Human Development,* 1–9. https://doi.org/10.1007/s10578-022-01363-2

Duran, E. (2012). Medicine wheel, mandala, and Jung. In N. Cater (Ed.), *Native American cultures and the Western psyche: A bridge between* (pp. 125–153). Spring Journal, Inc.

Green, E. J. (2011). Jungian analytical play therapy. In C. E. Schaefer (Ed.), *Foundations of play therapy* (2nd ed.). (pp. 61–85). Wiley.

Green, E. J., Drewes, A. A., & Kominski, J. M. (2013). Use of mandalas in Jungian play therapy with adolescents diagnosed with ADHD. *International Journal of Play Therapy, 22*(3), 159. https://doi.org/10.1037/a0033719

Hanscom, A. J. (2016). *Balanced and barefoot.* New Harbinger Publications, Inc.

Harte, J. L., & Eifert, G. H. (1995). The effects of running, environments, and attentional focus on athletes' catecholamine and cortisol levels and mood. *Psychophysiology, 32,* 49–54. https://doi.org/10.1016/0301-0511(95)05118-T

Hunter, M. R., Gillespie, B. W., & Chen, S. Y. (2019). Urban nature experiences reduce stress in the context of daily life based on salivary biomarkers. *Frontiers in Psychology, 10,* 722. https://doi.org/10.3389/fpsyg.2019.00722

Kalff, D. (1980). *Sandplay: A psychotherapeutic approach to the psyche.* Sigo Press.

Knell, S. (2011). Cognitive-behavioral play therapy. In C. E. Schaefer (Ed.), *Foundations of play therapy* (2nd ed.). (pp. 313–328). Wiley.

Kottman, T. (2011). Adlerian play therapy. In C. E. Schaefer (Ed.), *Foundations of play therapy* (2nd ed.) (pp. 87–104). Wiley.

Kottman, T., & Meany-Walen, K. (2016). *Partners in play: An Adlerian approach to play therapy* (3rd ed.). American Counseling Association.

Krippner, S. (1997). The role played by mandalas in Navajo and Tibetan rituals. *Anthropology of Consciousness, 8*(1), 22–31. https://doi.org/10.1525/ac.1997.8.1.22

Landreth, G. (2002). *Play therapy: The art of the relationship* (2nd ed.). Brunner-Routledge.

Marcetti, I., & Pössel, P. (2022). Cognitive triad and depression in adolescence: Specificity and overlap. *Child Psychiatry & Human Development.* https://doi.org/10.1007/s10578-022-01323-w

Munns, E. (2000). Traditional family and group theraplay. In E. Munns (Ed.), *Theraplay: Innovations in attachment-enhancing play therapy* (pp. 9–26). Jason Aronson.

Naor, L., & Mayseless, O. (2020). The therapeutic value of experiencing spirituality in nature. *Spirituality in Clinical Practice, 7*(2), 114–133. http://doi.org/10.1037/scp0000204

Naor, L., & Mayseless, O. (2021). Therapeutic factors in nature-based therapies: Unraveling the therapeutic benefits of integrating nature in psychotherapy. *Psychotherapy*, *58*(4), 576–590. https://doi.org/10.1037/pst0000396

Oaklander, V. (1988). *Windows to our children*. The Center for Gestalt Development.

Oaklander, V. (1994). Gestalt play therapy. In K. J. O'Connor and C. E. Schaefer (Eds.), *Handbook of play therapy: Volume Two. Advances and innovations* (pp. 143–156). Wiley.

O'Connor, K. (2011). Ecosystemic play therapy. In C. E. Schaefer (Ed.), *Foundations of play therapy* (2nd ed.) (pp. 253–272). Wiley.

Patton, S. C., & Benedict, H. E. (2015). Object relations and attachment-based play therapy. In D. A. Crenshaw & A. L. Stewart (Eds.), *Play therapy: A comprehensive guide to theory and practice* (pp. 17–31). The Guilford Press.

Peel, J. M. (2004). The labyrinth: An innovative therapeutic tool for problem solving or achieving mental focus. *The Family Journal*, *12*(3), 287–291. https://doi.org/10.1177/1066480704264349

Sabini, M. (Ed.) (2008). *The Earth has a soul: C. G. Jung on nature, technology, & modern life*. North Atlantic Books.

Swank, J. M., Cheung, C., Prikhidko, A., & Su, Y. (2017). Nature-based child-centered group play therapy and behavioral concerns: A single-case design. *International Journal of Play Therapy*, *26*(1), 47–57. http://doi.org/10.1037/pla0000031

Swank, J. M., & Shin, S. (2015a). Garden counseling groups and self-esteem: A mixed methods study with children with emotional and behavioral problems. *Journal for Specialists in Group Work*, *40*, 315–331. http://doi.org/10.1080/01933922.2015.1056570

Swank, J. M., & Shin, S. (2015b). Nature-based child-centered play therapy: An innovative counseling approach. *International Journal of Play Therapy*, *24*(3), 151–161. http://doi.org/10.1037/a0039127

Swank, J. M., Walker, K. L. A., & Shin, S. M. (2020). Indoor nature-based play therapy: Taking the natural world inside the playroom. *International Journal of Play Therapy*, *29*(3), 155–162. http://doi.org/10.1037/pla0000123

Sweeney, D. S., & Landreth, G. L. (2011). Child-centered play therapy. In C. E. Schaefer (Ed.), *Foundations of play therapy* (2nd ed.) (pp. 129–152). Wiley.

Taylor, A. F., & Kuo, F. E. (2009). Children with attention deficits concentrate better after walk in the park. *Journal of Attention Disorders*, *12*(5), 402–409. https://doi.org/10.1177/1087054708323000

Taylor, A. F., & Kuo, F. E. (2011). Could exposure to everyday green spaces help treat ADHD? Evidence from children's play settings. *Applied Psychology: Health and Well-Being*, *3*(3), 281–303. https://doi.org/10.1111/j.1758-0854.2011.01052.x

Upton, J., Janeka, I., & Ferraro, N. (2014). The whole is greater than the sum of its parts: Aristotle, metaphysical. *Journal of Craniofacial Surgery*, *25*(1), 59–63. https://doi.org/10.1097/SCS.0000000000000369

VanFleet, R. (2011). Filial therapy: Strengthening family relationships with the power of play. In C. E. Schaefer (Ed.), *Foundations of play therapy* (2nd ed.) (pp. 153–169). Wiley.

Chapter 6

The therapeutic powers of play and nature

The therapeutic powers of play are the change agents in play therapy. These are the facets of play that cause change to occur in clients. Researchers have begun identifying the therapeutic factors inherent in nature-based therapies (Naor & Mayseless, 2021b), and these factors coordinate nicely with the therapeutic powers of play. The focus of this chapter is on briefly defining the 20 established therapeutic powers of play, while discussing how they are each activated, facilitated, or initiated with the inclusion of nature. The question to answer here is, how does combining nature and play strengthen the therapeutic impact in nature-based play therapy? By exploring the therapeutic powers of both play and nature, and examining how nature enhances the previously established therapeutic powers of play, the benefits of integrating nature-based play therapy from a theoretical perspective will become more clear.

The therapeutic powers of play have been written about extensively in other sources, so full definitions and examples will not be given here. The focus instead will be on how nature improves the quality of the therapeutic impact and how nature can provide, encourage, or expand therapeutic opportunities outside of traditional play therapy. In short, the therapeutic powers are the change agents in therapy. They are the pieces of the therapeutic puzzle that cause or facilitate change to happen for a client. Therapeutic powers, or factors, are observable in talk therapy, play therapy, and nature-based therapy. They are not techniques or approaches. Rather, the therapeutic powers are parts of the therapy that can be spontaneous or guided and make play interactions therapeutic instead of "just play." The therapeutic powers of play connect the abstract notion of theoretical orientation with concrete use of techniques, merging the therapist's hypotheses of what is happening in a client's experiences or development (the "why") with what can be tangibly done in session to address an issue (the "how"). The therapeutic power in play therapy is the mechanism through which play connects the "why" from the theory and the "how" through techniques or interventions to lead to therapeutic change through play. The same change process is true of the therapeutic factors of nature-based therapies, and the two work together quite nicely. The process of how to connect all of these pieces during case conceptualization

DOI: 10.4324/9781003332343-6

will be fully described in Chapter 7. For now the focus will be on describing and understanding the therapeutic factors within nature-based play therapy.

Naor and Mayseless (2020, 2021b) have begun to identify and categorize therapeutic factors of nature-based therapies. This work can inform our current study of the specific therapeutic powers of nature-based play therapy and how nature further facilitates the play-based powers. Other therapeutic powers that initiate therapeutic change for clients in specific nature-based therapies have been identified (Naor & Mayseless, 2021b) and are in the early stages of research support and development. For example, in wilderness therapy, the powers of the wilderness, the physical self, and the social self have been identified. These factors relate to interactions between nature and the individual in various domains and also represent progression of wilderness therapy groups through multiple phases of personal development. Adventure therapy reports indicate other therapeutic powers including the natural world as restorative, risk, and challenge as leading to empowerment and uncertainty of outcome. These factors are strongly related to the individual's perception of self, including health, self-efficacy, and ability to expand comfort zones (Naor & Mayseless, 2021b). Ecotherapy reports indicate that environmental identity, in-the-moment awareness and mindful attention, embodiment as an ecological self, and the physical setting itself are the primary therapeutic factors (Naor & Mayseless, 2021b). In these and other developed nature-based approaches, the theoretical perspectives may differ in terms of goals, core tenets, and interventions, but the therapeutic factor of nature itself is consistent. The experience and interactions with nature in some way enhance, facilitate, or activate the therapeutic effect of the therapy itself. This is quite similar to the field of play therapy in which theoretical orientations differ, but the concept of play as being a therapeutic modality that facilitates or initiates therapeutic changes through these powers is consistent.

The four categories of nature-based therapeutic factors identified through Naor and Mayseless's (2021b) research comparing and compiling therapeutic factors from all published nature-based therapies, which encompass wilderness therapy, adventure therapy, ecotherapy, and other nature-based approaches, include the natural environment, challenge, the role of nature, and expansiveness and interconnectedness. In the context of a therapeutic setting, the first category, the natural environment, refers to three specific domains of nature: growth-oriented environment, nonjudgmental and accepting, and wholeness (Naor & Mayseless, 2021b). Here the concept of the therapeutic setting itself is key, as being present in a natural space contributes to therapeutic improvement. The second category is the challenge domain and refers to both physically challenging the body and overcoming physical obstacles, and engaging with mental or emotional challenges that encourage growth of mindsets, expansion of self-understanding, and creation of new or improved beliefs. Empowerment, perceptions of self and world, and changing behavioral patterns are part of this category of therapeutic factor (Naor & Mayseless, 2021b).

The third category of therapeutic factors in nature-based therapies is the role of nature. This is where nature is seen as truly influencing the process of therapeutic growth and change. Clients are faced with nature as a co-therapist, which is alive and constantly changing. New situations, stimuli, and understandings are constantly being provided by nature and thus impacts the therapy session as well as therapeutic process. This tends to be the domain most challenging to describe. The fourth therapeutic factor is that of expansiveness and interconnectedness. Here nature is seen as a space in which to expand one's sense of belonging. You are no longer solely an individual whose thoughts and actions impact no one but yourself. In nature you are part of a greater whole, and this sense of interconnectedness enhances the sense of self, belonging, and understanding of your personal relationship with the world as a whole (Naor & Mayseless, 2021b).

Charles Schaefer and Athena Drewes (2014) have listed 20 therapeutic powers of play within four categories for easier classification. The powers that facilitate communication are self-expression, access to the unconscious, direct teaching, and indirect teaching. Those that foster emotional wellness are catharsis, abreaction, positive emotions, counterconditioning of fears, stress inoculation, and stress management. The powers of the therapeutic relationship, attachment, social competence, and empathy enhance social relationships, while the category of increases personal strengths includes creative problem-solving, resiliency, moral development, accelerated psychological development, self-regulation, and self-esteem.

If we look at the four categories of therapeutic factors in nature-based therapies and the four categories of therapeutic powers of play therapy, we start to see how they can work together. It is not a perfect, one-to-one matchup, but generally, the therapeutic powers of play that are within the category of facilitates communication match well with the role of nature therapeutic factor in nature-based therapies. Here nature is playing an active role in encouraging participants to understand themselves and their personal connections more clearly, which relates to the accessing the unconscious and self-expression powers of play. The therapeutic powers of play within the category of fosters emotional wellness are often related to the challenge factor of nature-based therapies, as are some of those in the category of increases personal strengths. The natural setting therapeutic factor seen in nature-based therapies also tends to encompass other therapeutic powers of play from the category of increases personal strengths. Finally, the idea of nature increasing interconnectedness and expanding perspectives (expansiveness of thinking) are related to the factors in the category of enhances social relationships. This is a very general categorization of the powers, and many do overlap (for now!). As each therapeutic power of play is examined in a bit more depth in the following pages, the relationship it can hold to therapeutic factors of nature-based therapies will be explored. Some ways in which the therapeutic powers of nature support or facilitate the therapeutic powers of play are introduced in Table 6.1.

Table 6.1 How the therapeutic factors of nature support or facilitate the therapeutic powers of play

	Natural Environment	Challenge	Role of Nature	Expansiveness and Interconnectedness
Self-expression	Is nonjudgmental, is accepting, provides natural space	Challenges previously held beliefs about self and materials, expands self-understanding, changes perceptions of self and world	Is ever-changing, acts as co-therapist, offers new situations and stimuli	Expands sense of belonging, offers exploration of relationship with world, enhances sense of self
Access to unconscious	Is nonjudgmental, is accepting, offers wholeness	Challenges previously held beliefs, expands self-understanding, changes perceptions of self and world	Acts as co-therapist, offers new stimuli	Expands sense of belonging, offers exploration of relationship with world, enhances sense of self, becomes part of greater whole
Direct teaching	Provides natural space	Changes behavioral patterns, engages with mental or emotional challenges, fosters creation of new beliefs	Acts as co-therapist, offers new situations and stimuli	Offers exploration of relationship with world
Indirect teaching	Offers wholeness	Changes behavioral patterns, inspires empowerment, encourages growth of mindset, fosters creation of new beliefs	Acts as co-therapist, offers new situations and stimuli	Expands sense of belonging, offers exploration of relationship with world
Catharsis	Is nonjudgmental, is accepting, provides natural space	Physically challenges body and mind, encourages growth of mindset, inspires empowerment, changes behavioral patterns	Offers new situations and stimuli	Enhances sense of self

(Continued)

Table 6.1 (Continued)

	Natural Environment	Challenge	Role of Nature	Expansiveness and Interconnectedness
Abreaction	Is nonjudgmental, is accepting, offers wholeness, provides natural space	Physically challenges body and mind, encourages growth of mindset, inspires empowerment, changes behavioral patterns, changes perceptions of self and world	Acts as co-therapist	Enhances sense of self
Positive emotions	Is nonjudgmental, is accepting, provides natural space	Physically challenges body, creates new or improved beliefs, changes perceptions of self and world	Acts as co-therapist, offers new stimuli	Expands sense of belonging, enhances sense of self, becomes part of greater whole
Counter-conditioning of fears	Is nonjudgmental, is accepting	Encourages growth of mindset, inspires empowerment, changes behavioral patterns, changes perceptions of self and world	Acts as co-therapist, offers new situations and stimuli	Enhances sense of self, becomes part of greater whole
Stress inoculation	Is accepting, provides natural space	Expands self-understanding, fosters creation of new or improved beliefs	Acts as co-therapist, offers new stimuli	Becomes part of greater whole, enhances sense of self and belonging
Stress management	Is nonjudgmental, is accepting, provides natural space	Physically challenges body, expands self-understanding, fosters creation of new or improved beliefs	Acts as co-therapist, offers new situations and stimuli	Becomes part of greater whole, enhances sense of self and belonging, offers exploration of personal relationship with world
Therapeutic relationship	Is nonjudgmental, is accepting, offers wholeness	Inspires empowerment, encourages growth of mindsets	Acts as co-therapist	Becomes part of greater whole, enhances sense of self and belonging

(Continued)

Table 6.1 (Continued)

	Natural Environment	Challenge	Role of Nature	Expansiveness and Interconnectedness
Attachment	Is nonjudgmental, is accepting, offers wholeness	Inspires empowerment, encourages growth of mindsets	Acts as co-therapist	Becomes part of greater whole, enhances sense of self and belonging, offers exploration of personal relationship with world
Social competence	Is nonjudgmental, is accepting	Encourages growth of mindsets, expands self-understanding, fosters creation of new or improved beliefs, changes behavioral patterns	Offers new situations and stimuli, acts as co-therapist	Expands sense of belonging, becomes part of greater whole, enhances sense of self
Empathy	Is nonjudgmental, is accepting, offers wholeness, provides natural space	Surmounts physical obstacles, encourages growth of mindsets, expands self-understanding, changes perceptions of self and world	Acts as co-therapist, offers new situations	Expands sense of belonging, becomes part of greater whole, offers exploration of personal relationship with world as a whole
Creative problem-solving	Provides natural space	Surmounts physical obstacles and challenges, encourages growth of mindsets, fosters creation of new or improved beliefs, changes behavioral patterns	Offers new situations and stimuli	Enhances sense of self, becomes part of greater whole
Resiliency	Is nonjudgmental, is accepting, offers wholeness, provides natural space	Encourages growth of mindsets, expands self-understanding, fosters creation of new or improved beliefs, encourages empowerment, changes perceptions of self and world, changes behavioral patterns	Acts as co-therapist, offers new situations and stimuli	Expands sense of belonging, enhances sense of self and belonging

(Continued)

Table 6.1 (Continued)

	Natural Environment	Challenge	Role of Nature	Expansiveness and Interconnectedness
Moral development	Is nonjudgmental, is accepting, offers wholeness, provides natural space	Encourages growth of mindsets, creates new or improved beliefs, changes perceptions of self and world	Acts as co-therapist, offers new situations and stimuli	Expands sense of belonging, enhances sense of self and belonging, offers exploration of personal relationship with world as a whole
Accelerated psychological development	Is nonjudgmental, is accepting	Surmounts physical challenges and obstacles, encourages growth of mindsets, expands self-understanding, fosters creation of new beliefs, changes behavioral patterns	Acts as co-therapist, offers new situations and stimuli	Enhances sense of self and belonging, offers exploration of personal relationship with world as a whole
Self-regulation	Is nonjudgmental, is accepting, offers wholeness, provides natural space	Surmounts physical challenges, expands self-understanding, fosters creation of new or improved beliefs, changes perceptions of self or world	Acts as co-therapist, offers new situations and stimuli	Becomes part of greater whole, enhances sense of self and belonging
Self-esteem	Is nonjudgmental, is accepting, offers wholeness	Surmounts physical challenges, expands self-understanding, fosters creation of new or improved beliefs, changes perceptions of self or world, inspires empowerment	Acts as co-therapist, offers new situations and stimuli	Becomes part of greater whole, enhances sense of self and belonging

Self-expression

The power of self-expression facilitates communication in play therapy. The general principle is that children naturally express themselves through play. Self-expression through play allows a child to gain awareness of their affect and memories, which allows for self-healing. For example, the use of puppets encourages talking in third person, which gives distance from the challenging or scary topics while allowing the child to approach the topic. This is important as the process of communicating an experience helps a child to organize and give meaning to the experience (O'Connor, 2011). Doing so through play allows a child better mastery and understanding of the experience as well.

In a nature-based environment, the power of self-expression takes a variety of new or enhanced meanings. Expressive mediums abound in nature, from natural pigments to create artwork, to twigs and leaves and berries for collages, to symbolic representation for pretend play (sticks become swords, paddles, magic wands, and thousands of other things). These connections with the materials themselves are almost primal, as children rarely need to think about how to use them and instead move on to the crux of the play, and therefore expressive qualities, with ease. In a study of over 800 parents in the United States, 97% agreed that outdoor active play improves children's communication skills and encourages the development of self-expression (Clements, 2004). The power of self-expression in nature-based play is also seen when a child can showcase a new skill (Clements, 2004) and express the feelings that come with that learning process, from challenged to exuberant.

Access to the unconscious

Access to the unconscious is a therapeutic power of play that speaks to a child's ability to utilize play to transform wishes and desires into action (Schaefer, 1999). Play allows for projection, displacement, and symbolization to occur naturally for a child, which allow the unconscious impulses to be shown and dealt with in appropriate ways. The unconscious here includes preverbal trauma and implicit or repressed memories. Bessel van der Kolk (2006) writes that emotions do not occur by conscious choice, and thus, allowing the unconscious to be expressed through play encourages understanding of memories and responses. Fantasy-based techniques such as puppets, art, and sand are ways in which play supports access to the unconscious.

Specific to integrating nature with access to the unconscious, some natural materials are already consistently utilized in play therapy sessions for this purpose! Sand trays in particular are incredibly useful for encouraging access to the unconscious. Often simply touching the sand itself brings memories and experiences to the surface, as well as reduces anxiety and tension, allowing a greater depth to the play therapy work. Many people have experienced nature-based traumas, including earthquakes, tsunamis, hurricanes, and flooding. Clinical work outdoors can help a client work through these traumas on a larger scale by allowing and encouraging exposure on an unconscious level (Ohnogi, 2021). This will be discussed in more depth in the "Abreaction" section, but is important to note here as well.

Direct teaching

Direct teaching is a therapeutic power of play often seen in cognitive-behavioral play therapy and integrative forms of play therapy as it is directive and encourages playful learning to teach new skills. Direct teaching is particularly useful to help a child consolidate skills. This is why children often play out new experiences they have, in an effort to understand and learn in a way that makes the most sense to them. They can also try new skills in a safe environment where failure does not mean devastation. The fun of play encourages the learning process and makes it easier for new skills to be acquired for the child, while capturing their attention during the process.

As time in nature has been linked with improvements in multiple cognitive domains including awareness, reasoning, concentration, and imagination, children become more "primed" or ready for learning in outdoor environments (Dowdell et al., 2011). The role of nature within the direct teaching therapeutic power of play is not just to offer another environment in which to learn and grow, but to support the aspects of cognitive development necessary to engage in direct teaching and learning. Nature also allows for freedoms and autonomy that are not usually allowed or encouraged in other learning environments, which support ongoing learning (Schlembach et al., 2018) and thus directly impact the therapeutic power of direct teaching.

Indirect teaching

The therapeutic power of indirect teaching relates to metaphors and distancing oneself from painful or challenging emotions to be able to approach them as the person develops emotional readiness and coping skills to handle the experience. The different structures of the metaphor itself allow a child to understand a therapeutic story or experience related to their own, which can then be translated into their personal experiences. This process helps a child to manage the challenges while learning their own lessons. There are three structures to a metaphor: surface structure, associated deep structure of meaning, and recovered deep structure of meaning (Taylor de Faoite, 2014). The surface structure is the presence of the metaphor itself, in actual words. For example, the printed version of a story book represents the surface structure, with the actual words printed on a tangible page. The associated deep structure of meaning is activated because the metaphor is indirectly related to the person. This could be a role play or enactment of a story. The recovered deep structure of meaning is activated and directly related to the person. This would be when a listener is able to make links from the story to their own lives (Taylor de Faoite, 2014). Children are remarkably capable of understanding and utilizing metaphors.

The question then is, how is intentionally using nature going to change the metaphor? How does nature enhance the therapeutic benefit of the indirect teaching power of play? The selection of play items a child has access to, and interpretations made by the clinician are considerations here. The act of miniaturizing nature and making a way to encapsulate it adds to a much deeper experience of the image. We feel it through all our senses including proprioceptive ways, which triggers deeper nonverbal experiences as well. Combining this physical experience of sensory input with observation of behavioral patterns and development of deeper insight due to real experiences in real nature-based situations leads to deeper personal reflection, which is linked a greater impact and utilization of metaphors as nature serves as a mirror to personal experiences (Naor & Mayseless, 2021a). Fairy tales are often grounded in nature-based adventures, and including this setting allows for curiosity to expand a child's interpretation of the metaphors (Clements, 2004). Utilizing books and creating stories based in a nature-based setting can facilitate the therapeutic power of indirect teaching through nature-based play therapy. Playing in nature has also been linked to children learning scientific principles such as properties of objects without specifically teaching the concepts (Guddemi & Eriksen, 1992) as well as mathematics, language principles, and vocabulary (Bento & Dias, 2017). Exposure to a wider variety of experiences and objects to explore helps a child to conceptualize academic skills in fun ways that encourage ongoing participation.

A second aspect of indirect teaching is learning lessons or skills without a primary focus on the stepwise learning process. Play is particularly suited to encourage children to explore a variety of concepts and properties of objects as they begin to understand how things work, how they go together, and the flexibility of imagination and creativity. As children grow and develop, the ability to focus attention on specific tasks is a learned process. Play is a modality that encourages this indirect learning of such skills. Research indicates that exposure to nature helps children improve their abilities with directed attention (Kaplan, 1995), which is a key component of the self-discipline required to maintain focus, concentration, and attention (Taylor et al., 2002). In particular, the ability of natural spaces to softly capture attention while not overwhelming the senses (and, in fact, helping to regulate and moderate sensory input) allows for restoration of attention (Kaplan, 1995). Later research supports the idea that intentionally integrating nature time and open green spaces into children's play is related to a reduction in symptoms of attention-deficit/hyperactivity disorder (ADHD; Taylor & Kuo, 2011). Simple 20-minute walks have also been shown effective in improving concentration for children with symptoms of ADHD (Taylor & Kuo, 2009). Findings such as these support suggestions of daily doses of green time for children with symptoms of ADHD to help augment behavioral and psychopharmacological interventions (Kuo & Taylor, 2004) and help teach skills important for the development of self-discipline (Taylor et al., 2002). Thus, encouraging play in open green spaces relates to the ability to improve concentration, focus, and attention, which improves children's ability to learn.

Catharsis

The therapeutic power of catharsis is an important one to discuss. Catharsis is the physical release of pent-up emotions. In play therapy, this can take the form of throwing or hitting things as part of a physical release of internal feelings. When facilitating the therapeutic power of catharsis, it is important to consider the client's history and referral reason. Catharsis can be a powerfully healing aspect of play, except for clients who are referred for anger or aggression, or have a history of aggressive actions. For these clients, catharsis can exacerbate the symptoms, especially for those who have antisocial tendencies (Bemak & Young, 1988).

When nature is integrated into play therapy, the therapeutic power of catharsis can take on a deeper meaning and allow for further understanding and combining of therapeutic powers. Throwing rocks into a pond can release the physical expression of anger, which can then immediately be followed by recognizing the ripples on the water as aftereffects of the expression of anger. Using a hammer to drive nails into a piece of wood allows for physical release, and the physical connection with natural elements allows for a connection with the world while engaging in a release-based activity that connects children to experiences of their ancestors, bringing another level of connection and healing. Active and vigorous outdoor play can be part of a cathartic experience for clients, as pushing one's body in various ways and allowing for the release of other pent-up emotions can relieve stress (Clements, 2004) and is a reason many grown adults engage in sports, whether they consciously recognize these connections or not!

Abreaction

The therapeutic power of abreaction occurs when a person relives a traumatic memory or experience, with the appropriate emotional expression. There are four parts to an abreactive experience: miniaturization, active control, repetition, and mastery ending. When a person miniaturizes an experience, they become larger than the experience and people in it. Instead of being overwhelmed by the experience, they can contain it in smaller, manageable chunks, representations, or experiences. This is a step toward taking active control over the experience. When playing out a traumatic experience, the player can stop when the emotional experience gets to be too much. They can play up to the point that they can no longer handle emotionally, and then back away from that experience by changing the direction of the play or stop the play completely. This allows for the opportunity to learn how to deal with the emotional experience in a safe and controlled environment. When the player is able to handle that emotional piece, they can continue on to the next part of the playing through of the traumatic experience. The repetition and repeated simulated in vivo exposure to the pieces of the traumatic event in this controlled way also allow the player to work through their emotional reactions as many times as needed to overcome the stuck emotional experiences. Mastery ending is an important piece of abreactive work because it is how people can make some sense out of what happened to them and how they want to integrate the experience into their future lives. It is a chance to create closure and understand the experience and their reactions as much as possible.

Integrating nature into abreactive work can be particularly useful when considering the emotional regulation part of the play process. Interacting with natural elements allows for a sense of connection and calm that can help regulate a person's emotions and reactions more quickly and deeply than using manufactured objects. As mentioned previously, people have experienced nature-based traumas on both small and large scales throughout history. Encouraging in vivo therapeutic experiences directly in a nature-based setting can allow for the healing work to both be triggered and worked through more rapidly due to the abreactive experience. Voluntarily being and working in the same type of environment where the trauma happened allows for a person to take active control of the traumatic memories, engage in as much repetition and emotional regulation as needed, and make the surrounding environment more manageable as they become larger and more powerful than the event that happened to them. They can also then create their mastery ending in an environment similar to where the initial trauma occurred, leading to more in-depth healing as the sensory and emotional memories associated with the trauma will be impacted and new memories created (Ohnogi, 2021).

Positive emotions

The power of positive emotions refers to the fun and enjoyment experienced in play. The health and social benefits of positivity and happiness have been well documented. Overall, the fact that play leads to, encourages, and results in positive emotions makes play therapeutic in and of itself. Being able to utilize this power to facilitate or initiate therapeutic encounters is important. Fun and happy people are more fun to be around, and we are more likely to want to continue doing things that make us happy. The combination of these two facets helps make play therapeutic.

When one is in or around nature and natural objects, it is easier to feel free and unencumbered. Such feelings underlie happiness and contentment. Integrating nature into play therapy facilitates the therapeutic power of positive emotions as being in and connected to nature naturally encourages happiness

(Capaldi et al., 2014), lighter emotional loads, and fun. Time in nature has also been shown to reduce rumination in adults dealing with symptoms of depression (Bratman, Hamilton, et al., 2015), decreases anxiety (Bratman, Daily et al., 2015), and preserves positive affect rather than diminishing it as can happen in an urban setting (Bratman, Daily et al., 2015). Simply viewing pictures of nature-based environments compared to urban environments led participants to rate photos as more refreshing and enjoyable (Berman et al., 2008). Taken together, these impacts on positive emotions in turn help to facilitate the therapeutic power of the play itself. The amount of time one spends in a natural environment does not appear to alter the mood benefits, as studies suggest that even five minutes in nature leads to improvements in positive emotions (Neill et al., 2019). In particular, adventurous outdoor play has shown associations with increases in positive affect for children at school (Farmer et al., 2017) and in general (Dodd et al., 2022).

Counterconditioning of fears

Counterconditioning of fears, as a therapeutic power of play, is not a technique. Instead, it is the ability of play to initiate or facilitate the counterconditioning itself. Play provides a safe space and comfortable activity in which children can explore their fears and a chance to experience fun and enjoyment while so doing. This dual experience of fun and fear initiates or facilitates the opportunity for counterconditioning the fearful experience. Research has shown that utilizing play interventions with hospitalized children results in decreases in anxiety and fears (Li et al., 2016). Common childhood fears like fear of the dark can be well treated through play, and this fear has research support, indicating that playing in the dark is the best way to countercondition fears (Nash, 2018), as play creates the best environment to provide the therapeutic healing.

Integrating nature into the experiences of counterconditioning of fears offers a "new" way to explore both fears and ways to overcome them. Time in nature allows children to have experiences that push their limits in different ways. Building confidence by attempting new physical challenges like skipping rocks and climbing trees, learning about new plants as they discover them, and so on teach a child that they are capable of new and different things. This knowledge that a child develops about how they are able to learn new things, try new challenges, and be successful can be carried over to other fearful situations. Sandseter and Kennair (2011) suggest that adventurous outdoor play allows children to approach and challenge situations that cause fear, such as heights or getting lost, and utilize the fun and repetition of play to overcome the fears or phobias. For example, playing flashlight tag is a great way to bring fun into outdoor play to help overcome a fear of the dark by facilitating the therapeutic power of counterconditioning through nature-based play.

Stress inoculation

Stress inoculation occurs when a person can develop coping skills and prepare for upcoming, potentially stressful events. For example, this includes things like the start of school, medical appointments, or family changes. The therapeutic power of stress inoculation refers to how play is particularly suited to facilitating stress reduction. Here, play allows a child the safety and comfort of a familiar environment in which to practice and prepare for the new situation while having fun and often happily approaching the feared stimulus through play. The "as if" or pretend quality of play is important in the stress inoculation power of play as this allows children to learn about their "what if's" and challenge their own fears and assumptions in a safe manner while exploring.

Time in nature has been consistently shown to reduce stress, produce a sense of calm, and improve concentration. These outcomes are particularly important to the stress inoculation power of play, which is enhanced by the stress-reducing power of nature. When a child experiences a naturally occurring sense of calm, engagement in the play can be stronger and more therapeutic. Wells and Evans (2003) found that living near nature provided a buffering impact against life stress. Children who had higher levels of nearby nature reported less impact by life stressors (Wells & Evans, 2003). These findings were supported in research conducted with adults which found that high amounts of nearby nature (particularly green space) were related to participants being less affected by stressful life events (van den Berg et al., 2010). These studies suggest that simply being near nature has a buffering or stress inoculation impact that can be drawn upon for prevention of difficulties. Incorporating nature into play therapy can therefore positively compound the therapeutic powers within both nature and play therapies, thus improving the influence of the two.

Stress management

Stress management refers to handling, managing, or dealing with the stress of an event or experience that has already occurred. People have both positive and negative ways of managing stress, and the therapeutic power of play aspect indicates that play is particularly suited to helping children develop their positive stress management methods. Play facilitates children's abilities to regulate their own emotions and reactions to events. This is vital to recognize and utilize in the treatment of children's anxiety and general worries. Research suggests that engagement in unstructured play reduced cortisol (the stress hormone) levels in children who were hospitalized (Potasz et al., 2013). Many studies report the positive impact play has on children's emotional states, including reducing symptoms of anxiety and depression, and that children naturally engage in self-soothing, fantasy, and exploratory play as a means to understand and navigate their responses to stress (Bemis, 2014).

When spending time in nature, blood pressure rates are lowered, the nervous system becomes more regulated, and cortisol levels decrease. Hunter and colleagues (2019) noted a decrease in both salivary cortisol and alpha-amylase markers after time in nature, with the most benefits seen between 20 and 30 minutes of time outdoors. Alvarsson and colleagues (2010) found that listening to nature sounds instead of urban noise resulted in decreases in sympathetic nervous system activation after a stressor. These are all physical indications of stress reduction and management. When children play in natural environments, they then receive the positive benefits of both, and thus likely experience greater impacts on stress reduction potentials. Kaplan (1995) posits that the restorative effects of nature are particularly suited to stress management, especially when overcoming mental fatigue caused by too-constant directed attention. Specifically, the opportunity for reflection, richness of the natural setting, and expansiveness of the environment that leads to enough stimuli to take over mental space are healing (Kaplan, 1995). Ewert and colleagues (2014) noted that nature-based adventure therapy has been linked to stress reduction. Thus, it makes sense that combining the freedom, fun, and positive affect created through play with the reflective and grounding aspect of nature leads to enhanced therapeutic benefits.

Therapeutic relationship

The therapeutic relationship as a therapeutic power of play makes sense intuitively—of course, the relationship is important and impacts therapy outcomes! Research supports and deepens this concept, as clients who are able to create a solid relationship (or alliance) with their therapists are more likely to have positive therapy outcomes compared to clients who do not form solid relationships with their therapists (Stewart & Echterling, 2014). The question here becomes, what is it about the play relationship that facilitates this change? Playing with a child helps to meet them where they are. It is speaking the same language and allowing for nonverbal communication to happen. This is crucial, especially when children are processing previous traumatic experiences. Bruce Perry (2014) has spoken about how play therapy is the only way to process traumas effectively as it allows a client to remove the need for verbal communication, which was not accessible at the time of the traumatic event itself and therefore should not be relied upon for the treatment of the reactions. Encouraging children to create a strong therapeutic relationship with an adult through play is vital for children to feel heard and be able to express their inner selves.

When nature is added to the therapeutic relationship in play therapy, the ability to connect is altered in a positive way. Nature is a common-ground environment that is accessible by everyone. If play therapy sessions occur out of doors, the stigma and inherent biases about a therapy office (no matter how fun and playful it is) get removed. The therapist will still be seen as an expert, but altering the setting allows a child and family to be more comfortable from the initial interactions. When natural materials are brought into a playroom for free use by a child, there is now something available that has no expectations, guidelines, or "structured" use attached to it. There is no one correct way to play with a stick. There is no one correct way to move the sand in a sandtray. There is no one correct way to glue leaves to a piece of paper. A child can be an expert with natural materials. Children inherently understand this, and again, the playing field is leveled just a bit more and the therapist can be seen as someone who understands the importance of allowing a child freedom and their own expertise.

Naor and Mayseless (2020, 2021b) describe nature as being a therapeutic "other" or "partner" in the therapeutic relationship. Nature itself holds characteristics and elements that both build the relationship between a therapist and a client and create a separate relationship with the client (and with the therapist!). This wider perspective and feeling of belonging to something greater enhance the therapeutic value of the relationships between the client and the therapist as well as the client and nature (Naor & Mayseless, 2021b). Naor and Mayseless (2021a) describe the reflections of nature-based therapists who have observed clients developing and welcoming this therapeutic relationship with nature, and how this deeper connection with the environment facilitates therapeutic change within the client. These therapists further describe the healing powers of unconditional acceptance by the natural world, sense of interconnectedness with nature, and expanding perspectives of the greater world created by the relationship with the natural world (Naor & Mayseless, 2020). Taken together, discussions such as these indicate that the relationship developed with nature as a therapeutic "other" deepens the therapeutic power of the therapeutic relationship.

Attachment

The ability to form a healthy attachment is an important skill for children to develop and impacts relationships across their life spans. Being able to develop a healthy attachment with parental figures in childhood has been seen as indicative of being able to form healthy friendships and romantic relationships as adults, as attachment styles can play out over the life span (Hazan & Shaver, 1987). When a child is able to utilize play to form an attachment with an adult, or repair attachment wounds, the therapeutic power of attachment in play is realized. This skill is often practiced through play with inanimate objects as well. Dolls are made to explore various levels of relationships and types of attachments. Attachment patterns are revealed in the sand tray. Children practice attachment patterns with stuffed animals and show these when interacting with a play therapist through play!

In nature, we see many examples of different attachment styles. These examples can enhance a child's understanding of relationships as they are observable examples. Ant colonies can be explored, and the multitude of relationships and roles therein can be discussed. The relationships between birds and their young can be watched and detailed. The child can watch a mother robin feeding her baby bird, and the tough parts can be discussed as well. What happens if a mother bird does not feed her young consistently? What if a predator comes near a nest and a parent bird needs to protect it? Watching sparrows chase off a red-tailed hawk never gets old at my house! Using these examples to describe the strength of an innate early attachment is quite powerful. Nature is a historical piece of all of us, as outlined in Chapter 2. The biophilia hypothesis suggests that we are all innately drawn to nature, and this attachment is a core piece of understanding the therapeutic impact of nature-based play therapy. Giving children experiences in nature has been shown to encourage positive attitudes regarding nature as adults (Wells & Lekies, 2006), thus suggesting that developing an attachment to nature as a child has lifelong positive impacts. Many cultural and religious understandings of the world include nature as a historical piece of all humans, either from a creationist point of view or through the biophilia hypothesis.

Social competence

The therapeutic power of social competence is a two-part power: A child must both develop positive social skills (acquisition) and then learn when to use them appropriately (utilization). Many children are able to describe or show how to perform a social task, like enter a conversation appropriately, but then fail to do so consistently and instead interrupt or push themselves into a group in some other way. Play is particularly suited to encourage both aspects. As with direct and indirect teaching, both skills (acquisition and utilization) can be developed and practiced through game play, pretend play, and other interactive types of play. Children are often more willing to explore options and learn new skills when they are presented in a fun and playful way, especially as play provides the therapeutic environment most suited to this growth and development.

Nature allows for many cooperative activities to occur. These in turn provide opportunities to develop and practice new skills. Active fleeing games, as Clements (2004) titles them, such as tag and chasing each other around an open outdoor area, continue to be popular games in which children develop cooperation and other social skills. While organized sports have taken the place of outdoor games like hopscotch for many children, these child-led outdoor experiences continue to develop both the acquisition and the utilization of social skills. Parents agreed that outdoor active play improves children's social skills, with 75% of those surveyed agreeing with the statement (Clements, 2004). For examples of therapy interventions, children and therapists can take turns finding items in a nature-based scavenger hunt or share gathered materials to create art masterpieces. The relaxation benefits of nature contribute to success in developing these skills, as well as the ability to start fresh every session! It is also interesting that research suggests that fewer conflicts happen in nature-based group play than in indoor play, and cooperation is improved (Bento & Dias, 2017). Fewer conflicts and instances of bullying were reported by schools that encouraged playground play that supported risk-taking and challenge activities (Farmer et al., 2017). Children have also been seen to be less sensitive to conflicts when they do occur after engaging in risky outdoor play (Lavrysen, et al., 2017). It is of note that when children can play outdoors, they are more likely to engage in physical play together (Stephenson, 2002), and when popular children are able to engage in rough-and-tumble play, they are rated as higher on social competence by their peers (Pellegrini, 1988). These results suggest that allowing children some freedom within their challenge-seeking, rough-and-tumble outdoor play has multiple benefits to the individual as well as the social group.

Empathy

Empathy refers to the ability to understand another person's position and to recognize what it might be like to live in their shoes. This is an important skill to develop, and play is particularly well suited to help children explore different levels of empathic understanding. This goes along with good sportsmanship during cooperative games or board games, and being able to think about why others might act the way they do. The therapeutic power of empathy in play therapy describes actively utilizing and encouraging empathy in play-based situations to effect therapeutic changes.

Using nature in play sessions allows for unique examples of empathy to be explored in the moment. What happens if we intentionally step on this ant, or we let it go on its way? Why is it important to gather a small number of growing items instead of every one we can find? What is the impact we are having on the environment by interacting with it in this way? These questions naturally lead to a deeper understanding of not just how and why the natural world works in certain ways but the role a caring and empathic child can play in his or her small piece of that world. Like watching ripples grow in a pond after tossing a rock, this knowledge and understanding then extrapolates to other areas of life, thus encouraging the development of a stronger sense of empathy overall. Research has suggested that outdoor play helps children learn an appreciation for their environment (Clements, 2004) that can have a lasting, lifelong impact on environmental attitudes as adults (Wells & Lekies, 2006). Teaching skills like caring for resources and sustainably harvesting materials during sessions and at home go a long way in developing a sense of empathic understanding about how nature provides long-term for both people and the natural environment. Nature-based group play experiences also help children develop empathy skills as they have real-life opportunities to experience others' needs and feelings in a variety of environments (Bento & Dias, 2017).

Creative problem-solving

Play facilitates the therapeutic power of creative problem-solving by allowing the flexibility and freedom to try a multitude of solutions without needing to pick the "correct" solution right away, if ever. This ability to try new options and discover new possibilities is a hallmark of true play. In play, things (and people) can become whatever the player wants them to be, and nothing is impossible. This is true of interactions, uses of items, and combinations that can be created. Research supports the notion that play encourages the development of creative or divergent thinking (i.e., Garaigordobil & Berrueco, 2011; Yin et al., 2015), which is the first step in creative problem-solving. The development of the skill of creative problem-solving is important as it is the basis for creating and utilizing new coping skills, adjusting personal reactions to experiences, and even learning social skills. Facilitating the therapeutic power of creative problem-solving in play therapy encourages therapeutic growth as a client experiences multiple ways of solving a problem, creating alternative solutions, and engaging in flexible or divergent thinking about their own situations.

Encouraging play in nature enhances children's creative problem-solving abilities, especially since playing in outdoor spaces leads to more opportunities for open-ended play (Stephenson, 1998), which in turn leads to more opportunities to create, explore, and develop new methods for achieving play goals. Outdoor play as a means to improve creativity and use of imagination is a modality supported by parents, with 92% of a survey population stating that time in nature improves their children's ability to be more creative (Clements, 2004). A study by Atchley et al. (2012) found that immersing 56 adults in a nature setting for a few days led to an increase in creative problem-solving abilities of 50%. They hypothesized that exposure to nature stimuli while reducing technology-based stimuli helped participants to focus attention better while engaging restful introspection to enhance performance in divergent thinking ability (Atchley et al., 2012). Plambech and van den Bosch (2015) suggest that this creative ability is heightened through exposure to nature because nature encourages curiosity and the flexibility needed for divergent thinking. They also suggest that nature encourages exploration, as spaces are always changing and thus become intriguing. The loose parts theory is particularly well suited to play in nature, as children are exposed to and encouraged to utilize a variety of natural elements in many ways to encourage creative thinking (Bento & Dias, 2017; Nicholson, 1972). Nature also helps people see things from different perspectives (Atchley et al., 2012), which is key for coming up with creative solutions to problems.

Resiliency

Resiliency refers to the ability to bounce back from a situation, or at least come to an understanding of why something happened, how it changed you, and how you will act differently moving forward. The important part of resiliency is continuing to move forward, and play encourages this. When the tower falls, the child rebuilds it, often bigger and better than it was before. If a toy is missing, or a prop for pretend play is not available, children improvise. Play offers a multitude of opportunities for developing resiliency. Initiating the therapeutic power of resiliency in play therapy can encourage positive views of a situation or opportunities to develop and grow, bringing a sense of hopefulness to the client.

Integrating natural materials into play allows for even more flexibility and opportunities for the development of resilience. Very rarely is the stick you find the exact right size and shape for the purpose you had in mind, and then either the stick or your purpose must change. There are always more sticks available to try again if your attempt does not succeed. Yet that moment when you find the perfect stick … the one with just the right weight, and just the right bend, and it breaks down to just the right length … that is a moment when the effort it took to search and try again becomes worthwhile. The resiliency shown here, as the client tries and tries again until success is gained, becomes a basis for the development of resiliency in "real life." Resilience is also seen so clearly in nature when trees grow over the obstacles in their paths or start to "eat" objects placed on them, like trail markers, by growing a burl over the affected area. The tree identifies a wound and heals itself, constantly seeking the sun as it grows. These examples provide profound metaphors for human resilience and the effort and time it often takes to overcome our own moments of adversity. One of my favorite examples of resiliency in nature is when trees grow up and over rocks and solid dirt, and their roots grow up out of the ground as the young tree reaches for the sunlight. Once the tree is established, over time erosion or strong rains can wash the impediments away, leaving the fully formed root system visible in its twisted and imaginative shapes. Sharing how the tree worked to overcome literal obstacles and grew strong and solid in the meantime is quite powerful, especially as the "wound" the tree endured is still visible even though the obstacle is gone.

The development of resiliency is clearly seen in adventurous or risky play. This is the kind of outdoor play in which children take age-appropriate risks as they push their physical and psychological boundaries to see just how far they can go (Dodd & Lester, 2021). Through adventurous play, children face uncertainty, challenge, the possibilities of both success and failure, and coping skills. As children expose themselves to obstacles that challenge or even scare them, they build tolerance, skills, and coping mechanisms necessary for the development of resiliency (Dodd & Lester, 2021), and studies have shown qualitative reports of improvement in resilience following adventurous play (Bundy et al., 2009). Children as young as 17 months can manage risky play situations in outdoor environments and develop their own risk management skills and thus a sense of resilience (Tangen et al., 2022). As a society, we have become less risk-tolerant especially over the past 50 years in terms of what children "should" be allowed to do independently (Dodd et al., 2022). Links are now being seen between the decrease in adventurous risky play and the increase in children's mental health concerns (Dodd et al., 2022) and overall physical health concerns (Brussoni et al., 2015), suggesting that to help children build up resiliency and healthy overall development, we should be allowing and encouraging adventurous risky play outdoors.

Moral development

Moral development refers to a child's developing sense of what is right and fair, even if it goes against the printed rules of a game. Play facilitates the growth of moral development in multiple ways. For example, an older child might realize that the fun of the game is what is most important, not winning by a landslide, and therefore might alter his own turn so that a younger sibling can have a chance to make an excellent move and enjoy that moment. The joy and contentment the older child feels watching the younger child's reaction is reward enough and points to a developing sense of morality. Play also allows a child to take another person's perspective during pretend play or game play and explore what it might be like for that person if the rules are followed exactly (or not at all). This experience helps children decide how they want to act to include and encourage others through play. Activating the therapeutic power of moral development in play therapy allows for the growth and utilization of these skills to support therapeutic change.

Encouraging nature play during therapy sessions allows for another angle to be taken regarding moral development that is similar to that of empathy. Children can explore the concepts of right and wrong in ways that are not always acceptable outside of a therapy session. They can divert waterways, dig holes, break sticks, and see the impact these changes have on the environment (either in a stream or in a water tray in the office). Experiences like these can help get the child thinking about what could be done compared to what should be done and which avenue they would prefer to take and why. In an indoor session, these connections can also be made as the child interacts with real nature materials instead of manufactured items. There is a big difference between holding a nest made of fabric instead of twigs and moss or leaves made of felt, and a rock made from plastic instead of the real thing. The physical sensation of interacting with natural materials heightens the sensory understanding and connection with the natural world, thus improving the opportunity for moral development.

Accelerated psychological development

Accelerated psychological development refers to a child's ability to understand things presented at a higher level than the child's typical cognitive performance "in the real world." Play intrinsically encourages children to be more and do more than they think themselves capable of, and thus enhances the therapeutic power of accelerated psychological development. As children explore, experience, and try out activities that are above their developmental levels, play encourages trial and error (or means over ends, process-oriented aspects) without risk of major consequence if they do not initially succeed. Many times, with little encouragement, children are capable of significantly more than adults expect—or allow. Facilitating the therapeutic power of this type of play can lead to noticeable improvements in abilities, development, and self-respect.

In natural settings, children are constantly facing opportunities for accelerated psychological development during free play. Risky play is especially relevant here, as children have the option to climb a tree that may or may not hold their weight, and they must figure out how they feel about that and if they are ready to take on such a challenge from a physical as well as emotional or psychological standpoint. They must figure out ways to cross a waterway and plan out a route across rocks that might be slippery or unstable. They must figure out how to make a fort big enough to protect them from all the bad guys they create. Children may not be old enough or physically capable enough to accomplish all these activities, but in nature-based play, they are capable enough to try. That effort is what will help them eventually succeed and to learn valuable lessons about themselves and their abilities along the way.

Self-regulation

Self-regulation is something that many people struggle with these days. The therapeutic power of self-regulation suggests that play facilitates the development and strengthening of a person's ability to self-regulate. When engaged in pure play, a child experiences changes in their serotonin, dopamine, and cortisol levels as well as heart rate and symptoms of depression and anxiety that make it easier for them to manage their reactions to events. Play allows a person to increase or decrease their nervous system responses through energizing or calming play experiences, which leads to self-regulation. There are also many opportunities in social play situations to observe how personal reactions are accepted or not by others, and a child can then decide if they want to continue with their current behaviors or adjust their responses.

Natural materials offer immediate feedback crucial to the development of self-regulation. If you play too roughly with a leaf that has become the sail of your raft, it will rip and not serve the purpose you intended. If you run and grab at a pretty flower without noticing its surroundings, you might be pulling a thorn out of your hand before you can smell the rose. If you push through leaves to touch a tree without looking at the leaves first, you might be dealing with an itchy poison ivy rash for a few days. If you do not move quickly from a damp area, you might end up with wet shoes. While the free exploration of natural materials is desired, so is caution that comes only from regulating the nervous system enough to observe, recognize, and appropriately react to surrounding situations. Developing self-regulation in these in vivo experiences helps the lesson to be learned more completely. These in vivo experiences can be brought inside the office through the inclusion of water trays, sensory bins that include dirt and the ability to make mud, clay, and a selection of leaves, pinecones, rocks, and so forth. Nature is also full of images and sensations that help with relaxation, deeper exploration, and attunement that are necessary for developing self-regulation skills.

The ability to curb impulses is important in the development of self-regulation and self-discipline, and the lack of inhibition of impulses is a key feature of ADHD. Multiple studies have shown that exposure to nature can help children better regulate their impulsivity. For example, simply viewing nature around their homes has been found helpful for children to show improvements in their impulse inhibition (Taylor et al., 2002) or improved attentional functioning more generally (Wells, 2000). Utilizing green spaces for activities and encouraging children to play in open green spaces instead of playscapes or indoor areas has been linked to better attention and impulse control (Taylor et al., 2001). Taylor and colleagues (2002) suggest that regulating impulse control includes three aspects: inhibiting impulses, blocking stimuli, and considering alternative behaviors. All of these aspects have been shown to be supported by exposure to nature, thus suggesting that including nature in play therapy can improve facilitation of the therapeutic power of self-regulation.

Self-esteem

Self-esteem refers to a person's thoughts and reactions about their own self-concept and self-worth. Self-estimates can be made on yourself as a whole or individual aspects. These values can also change. For example, you could be having an off day and not feel good about yourself as a whole but could identify one area in which you performed well and choose to base your self-estimation on this combination so as not to judge yourself as all bad. In general, the therapeutic power of self-esteem is facilitated through play by the serotonin boosts that result from play and social support, and the realization that play is something that most children are inherently good at and do not need to learn. "Ability to play" is an area that can be self-evaluated and included in an estimate of global or specific self-esteem. Role-playing events that have happened or are upcoming allow for opportunities for children to figure out what they are good at and thus decrease anxiety, allowing the positive emotions to come through and self-esteem to blossom. Trying new activities in a play-based manner offers exposure to new things without fear of failure, thus opening new possibilities for areas of success. All these types of play can lead to facilitation of the therapeutic power of self-esteem in play therapy.

There is something in nature for every person to be good at and in which to feel confident. These feelings support a person's self-esteem with little extra effort. In my family, my children are very good at identifying tinder sources and building responsible cooking fires. My husband is very good at identifying trees and animals. A late bloomer in the field of nature studies, I felt the need to learn about an aspect of nature that I could feel confident in and chose herbalism. Every time I can identify a new-to-me plant or recognize a medicinal use for something we found, I get a little self-esteem boost and reminder that there is something in nature I too can understand and an area in which I can be knowledgeable. Parents agree that outdoor play encourages the development of children's self-worth, with 82% of a large sample identifying nature play as a way to do so (Clements, 2004). The positive feedback that adults offer to children during these activities also helps to build self-esteem (Clements, 2004). Being in nature leads to a sense of being part of something bigger than oneself. This inclusion can lead to increased self-esteem because when people feel they matter and are part of the larger whole, they can fit in, feel included, and naturally feel better about themselves. Incorporating nature into play therapy facilitates this feeling, thus enhancing the therapeutic power of self-esteem.

Concluding thoughts

Understanding the therapeutic powers of play and nature is crucial to being able to intentionally create or utilize interventions to best support clients' needs. Utilizing theory, research, and evidence-based knowledge to support clinical decisions and treatment planning leads to more effective and efficient play therapy. A play therapist should always understand why they are utilizing a particular treatment at a particular time and understanding the change agents within the therapeutic powers of play and nature—what makes play and nature therapeutic—is a solid starting point. Recognizing that both play and nature hold specific therapeutic benefits that can be facilitated or activated during nature-based play therapy encourages case conceptualization to guide specific treatment planning. A case conceptualization model will be presented in Chapter 7.

References

Alvarsson, J. J., Wiens, S., & Nilsson, M. E. (2010). Stress recovery during exposure to nature sound and environmental noise. *International Journal of Environmental Research and Public Health, 7*, 1036–1046. https://doi.org/10.3390/ijerph7031036

Atchley, R. A., Strayer, D. L., & Atchley, P. (2012). Creativity in the wild: Improving creative reasoning through immersion in natural settings. *PLoS one, 7*(12), e51474. https://doi.org/10.1371/journal.pone.0051474

Bemak, F., & Young, M. E. (1998). Role of catharsis in group psychotherapy. *International Journal of Action Methods, 50*(4), 166–184.

Bemis, K. S. (2014). Stress management. In C. E. Schaefer & A. A. Drewes (Eds.), *The therapeutic powers of play: 20 core agents of change* (2nd ed.) (pp. 143–153). Wiley.

Bento, G., & Dias, G. (2017). The importance of outdoor play for young children's healthy development. *Porto Biomedical Journal*, *2*(5), 157–160. https://doi.org/10.1016/j.pbj.2017.03.003

Berman, M. G., Jonides, J., & Kaplan, S. (2008). The cognitive benefits of interacting with nature. *Psychological Science*, *19*(12), 1207–1212. https://doi.org/10.1111/j.1467-9280.2008.02225.x

Bratman, G. N., Daily, G. C., Levy, B. J., & Gross, J. J. (2015). The benefits of nature experience: Improved affect and cognition. *Landscape and Urban Planning*, *138*, 41–50. https://doi.org/10.1016/j.landurbplan.2015.02.005

Bratman, G. N., Hamilton, J. P., Hahn, K. S., Daily, G. C., & Gross, J. J. (2015). Nature experience reduces rumination and subgenual prefrontal cortex activation. *Proceedings of the National Academy of Sciences*, *112*(28), 8567–8572. https://doi.org/10.1073/pnas.1510459112

Brussoni, M., Gibbons, R., Gray, C., Ishikawa, T., Sandseter, E. B. H., Bienenstock, A., Chabot, G., Fuselli, P., Herrington, S., Janssen, I., Pickett, W., Power, M., Stanger, N., Sampson, M., & Tremblay, M. S. (2015). What is the relationship between risky outdoor play and health in children? A systematic review. *International Journal of Environmental Research and Public Health*, *12*(6), 6423–6454. https://doi.org/10.3390/ijerph120606423

Bundy, A. C., Luckett, T., Tranter, P. J., Naughton, G. A., Wyver, S. R., Ragen, J., & Spies, G. (2009). The risk is that there is 'no risk': A simple, innovative intervention to increase children's activity levels. *International Journal of Early Years Education*, *17*(1), 33–45. https://doi.org/10.1080/09669760802699878

Capaldi, C. A., Dopko, R. L., & Zelenski, J. M. (2014). The relationship between nature connectedness and happiness: A meta-analysis. *Frontiers in Psychology*, *5*, 1–15. https://doi.org/10.3389/fpsyg.2014.00976

Clements, R. (2004). An investigation of the status of outdoor play. *Contemporary Issues in Early Childhood*, *5*(1), 68–80. https://doi.org/10.2304/ciec.2004.5.1.10

Dodd, H. F., & Lester, K. J. (2021). Adventurous play as a mechanism for reducing risk for childhood anxiety: A conceptual model. *Clinical Child and Family Psychology Review*, *24*, 164–181. https://doi.org/10.1007/s10567-020-00338-w

Dodd, H. F., Nesbit, R. J., & FitzGibbon, L. (2022). Child's play: Examining the association between time spend playing and child mental health. *Child Psychiatry & Human Development*, 1–9. https://doi.org/10.1007/s10578-022-01363-2

Dowdell, K., Gray, T., & Malone, K. (2011). Nature and its influence on children's outdoor play. *Australian Journal of Outdoor Education*, *15*(2), 24–35. https://doi.org/10.1007/BF03400925

Ewert, A. W., Mitten, D. S., & Overholt, J. R. (2014). *Natural environments and human health*. Cabi. https://doi.org/10.1079/9781845939199.0000

Farmer, V. L., Fitzgerald, R. P., Williams, S. M., Mann, J. I., Schofield, G., McPhee, J. C., & Taylor, R. W. (2017). What did schools experience from participating in a randomized controlled study (PLAY) that prioritized risk and challenge in active play for children while at school? *Journal of Adventure Education and Outdoor Learning*, *17*(3), 239–257. https://doi.org/10.1080/14729679.2017.1286993

Garaigordobil, M., & Berrueco, L. (2011). Effects of a play program on creative thinking of preschool children. *The Spanish Journal of Psychology*, *14*(2), 608–618. https://doi.org/10.5209/rev_SJOP.2011.v14.n2.9

Guddemi, M., & Eriksen, A. (1992). Designing outdoor learning environments for and with children. *Dimensions of Early Childhood, 20*(4), 15–24.

Hazan, C., & Shaver, P. (1987). Romantic love conceptualized as an attachment process. *Journal of Personality and Social Psychology, 52*(3), 511–524. https://doi.org/10.1037/0022-3514.52.3.511

Hunter, M. R., Gillespie, B. W., & Chen, S. Y. (2019). Urban nature experiences reduce stress in the context of daily life based on salivary biomarkers. *Frontiers in Psychology, 10*, 722. https://doi.org/10.3389/fpsyg.2019.00722

Kaplan, S. (1995). The restorative benefits of nature: Toward an integrative framework. *Journal of Environmental Psychology, 15*, 169–182. https://doi.org/10.1016/0272-4944(95)90001-2

Kuo, F. E., & Taylor, A. F. (2004). A potential natural treatment for Attention-Deficit/Hyperactivity Disorder: Evidence from a national study. *American Journal of Public Health, 94*(9), 1580–1586. https://doi.org/10.1177/1087054708323000

Lavrysen, A., Bertrands, E., Leyssen, L., Smets, L., Vanderspikken, A., & De Graef, P. (2017). Risky-play at school. Facilitating risk perception and competence in young children. *European Early Childhood Education Research Journal, 25*(1), 89–105. https://doi.org/10.1080/1350293X.2015.1102412

Li, W. H. C., Chung, J. O. K., Ho, K. Y., & Kwok, B. M. C. (2016). Play interventions to reduce anxiety and negative emotions in hospitalized children. *BMC Pediatrics, 16*, 1–9. https://doi.org/10.1186/s12887-016-0570-5

Naor, L., & Mayseless, O. (2020). The therapeutic value of experiencing spirituality in nature. *Spirituality in Clinical Practice, 7*(2), 114–133. http://doi.org/10.1037/scp0000204

Naor, L., & Mayseless, O. (2021a). The therapeutic process in nature-based therapies from the perspectives of facilitators: A qualitative inquiry. *Ecopsychology, 13*(4), 284–293. https://doi.org/10.1089/eco.2021.0004

Naor, L., & Mayseless, O. (2021b). Therapeutic factors in nature-based therapies: Unraveling the therapeutic benefits of integrating nature in psychotherapy. *Psychotherapy, 58*(4), 576–590. https://doi.org/10.1037/pst0000396

Nash, J. B. (2018). Play interventions for children's nighttime fears. In A. A. Drewes & C. E. Schaefer (Eds.), *Play-based interventions for childhood anxieties, fears, and phobias* (pp. 27–40). The Guilford Press.

Neill, C., Gerard, J., & Arbuthnott, K. D. (2019). Nature contact and mood benefits: Contact duration and mood type. *The Journal of Positive Psychology, 14*(6), 756–767. https://doi.org/10.1080/17439760.2018.1557242

Nicholson, S. (1972). The theory of loose parts, an important principle for design methodology. *Studies in Design Education Craft & Technology, 4*(2). Retrieved from https://ojs.lboro.ac.uk/SDEC/article/view/1204

O'Connor, K. (2011). Ecosystemic play therapy. In C. E. Schaefer (Ed.), *Foundations of play therapy* (2nd ed.) (pp. 253–272). Wiley.

Ohnogi, A. J. (2021). Nature as a part of play therapy. In R. J. Grant, J. Stone, & C. Mellenthin (Eds.), *Play therapy theories and perspectives: A collection of thoughts in the field* (p. 105). Routledge.

Pellegrini, A. D. (1988). Elementary-school children's rough-and-tumble play and social competence. *Developmental Psychology, 24*(6), 802–806. https://doi.org/10.1037/0012-1649.24.6.802

Perry, B. D. (2014, October 10). *The power of early childhood* [Keynote conference session]. 31st Annual Association for Play Therapy International Conference, Westin Galleria, Houston, TX, United States.

Plambech, T., & Konijnendijk van den Bosch, C. C. (2015). The impact of nature on creativity—A study among Danish creative professionals. *Urban Forestry & Urban Greening, 14*, 255–263 http://doi.org/10.1016/j.ufug.2015.02.006

Potasz, C., Varela, M. J. V. D., Carvalho, L. C. D., Prado, L. F. D., & Prado, G. F. D. (2013). Effect of play activities on hospitalized children's stress: A randomized clinical trial. *Scandinavian Journal of Occupational Therapy, 20*(1), 71–79. https://doi.org/10.3109/11038128.2012.729087

Sandseter, E., & Kennair, L. (2011). Children's risky play from an evolutionary perspective: The anti-phobic effects of thrilling experiences. *Evolutionary Psychology, 9*(2), 257–284. https://doi.org/10.1177/147470491100900212

Schaefer, C. E. (1999). Curative factors in play therapy. *The Journal for the Professional Counselor, 14*(1), 7–16.

Schaefer, C. E., & Drewes, A. A. (2014). *The therapeutic powers of play* (2nd ed.). Wiley.

Schlembach, S., Kochanowski, L., Brown, R. D., & Carr, V. (2018). Early childhood educators' perceptions of play and inquiry on a nature playscape. *Children, Youth and Environments, 28*(2), 82–101. https://doi.org/10.7721/chilyoutenvi.28.2.0082

Stephenson, A. M. (1998). Opening up the outdoors: A reappraisal of young children's outdoor experiences (Doctoral dissertation, Victoria University of Wellington).

Stephenson, A. (2002). Opening up the outdoors: Exploring the relationship between the indoor and outdoor environments of a centre. *European Early Childhood Education Research Journal, 10*(1), 29–38. https://doi.org/10.1080/13502930285208821

Stewart, A., L., & Echterling, L. G. (2014). Therapeutic relationship. In C. E. Schaefer & A. A. Drewes (Eds.), *The therapeutic powers of play: 20 core agents of change* (2nd ed.) (pp. 157–169). Wiley.

Tangen, S., Olsen, A., & Sandseter, E. B. H. (2022). A GoPro look on how children aged 17–25 months assess and manage risk during free exploration in a varied natural environment. *Education Sciences, 12*, 361. https://doi.org/10.3390/educsci12050361

Taylor, A. F., & Kuo, F. E. (2009). Children with attention deficits concentrate better after walk in the park. *Journal of Attention Disorders, 12*(5), 402–409. https://doi.org/10.1177/1087054708323000

Taylor, A. F., & Kuo, F. E. (2011). Could exposure to everyday green spaces help treat ADHD? Evidence from children's play settings. *Applied Psychology: Health and Well-Being, 3*(3), 281–303. https://doi.org/10.1111/j.1758-0854.2011.01052.x

Taylor, A. F., Kuo, F. E., & Sullivan, W. C. (2001). Coping with ADD: The surprising connection to green play settings. *Environment & Behavior, 33*, 54–77. https://doi.org/10.1177/00139160121972864

Taylor, A. F., Kuo, F. E., & Sullivan, W. C. (2002). Views of nature and self-discipline: Evidence from inner city children. *Journal of Environmental Psychology, 22*, 49–63. https://doi.org/10.1006/jevp.2001.0241

Taylor de Faoite, A. (2014). Indirect teaching. In C. E. Schaefer & A. A. Drewes (Eds.), *The therapeutic powers of play: 20 core agents of change* (2nd ed.) (pp. 51–68). Wiley.

van den Berg, A. E., Maas, J., Verheij, R. A., & Groenewegen, P. P. (2010). Green space as a buffer between stressful life events and health. *Social Science & Medicine, 70*, 1203–1210. https://doi.org/10.1016/j.socscimed.2010.01.002

van der Kolk, B. (2006). Clinical implications of neuroscience research in PTSD. *Annals of the New York Academy of Sciences*, *1071*, 277–293. https://doi.org/10.1196/annals.1364.022

Wells, N. (2000). At home with nature: Effects of "greenness" on children's cognitive functioning. *Environment & Behavior*, *32*, 775–795. https://doi.org/10.1177/00139160021972793

Wells, N. M., & Evans, G. W. (2003). Nearby nature: A buffer of life stress among rural children. *Environment and Behavior*, *35*(3), 311–330. https://doi.org/10.1177/0013916503035003001

Wells, N. M., & Lekies, K. S. (2006). Nature and the life course: Pathways from childhood nature experiences to adult environmentalism. *Children, Youth and Environments*, *16*(1), 1–24. https://www.jstor.org/stable/10.7721/chilyoutenvi.16.1.0001

Yin, L. C., Zakaria, A. R., Baharun, H., Hutagalung, F., Sulaiman, A. M. (2015). Messy play: Creativity and imagination amount preschool children. In F. L. Gaol (Ed.), *Interdisciplinary Behavior and Social Sciences* (pp. 299–306). Taylor & Francis Group.

Chapter 7

A prescriptive model for nature-based play therapy

Now that all the basics have been covered, it is time to put them all together. The purpose of this chapter is to explore how to best integrate theory with the therapeutic powers of play and nature to create nature-based play therapy treatment plans based in a solid framework. A model of conceptualizing the needs of clients as grounded in your theoretical understanding will be presented along with some basic examples of how to utilize this framework from different theoretical perspectives with various clients' presenting needs. Ways to incorporate nature into this model and develop nature-based play therapy treatment sessions based upon your understanding of play therapy theory and the therapeutic powers of both nature and play will also be presented.

Prescriptive play therapy

Prescriptive play therapy is a theoretical orientation through which clinicians view differential therapeutics, individualized treatment, and prescriptive matching as core tenets of case conceptualization and provision of treatment. While not considered a seminal theory by the Association for Play Therapy, prescriptive work has been explored in the literature for over 50 years and was first introduced as a play therapy theory-based model in *The Playing Cure: Individualized Play Therapy for Specific Childhood Problems* (Kaduson et al., 1997). This is not a spontaneous, "throw whichever new technique you just learned at your client" type of treatment. Rather, clinicians seek to answer, "*What* treatment, by *whom*, is most effective for *this* individual, with *that* specific problem, and under *which* set of circumstances?" (Paul, 1967, p. 111). Heidi Kaduson and colleagues (2020) added that needing to know how the treatment comes about is a key component of prescriptive play therapy. Knowing how the treatment comes about refers to understanding how and why you incorporate treatment modalities and interventions for each client and doing so in a planned and specific way. This is one of the main reasons to explore the inclusion of nature in play therapy from the theoretical perspectives. Utilizing the most effective form of

DOI: 10.4324/9781003332343-7

nature-based play therapy and resulting interventions is necessary for providing the most useful treatment! Research and empirically based interventions should be used to guide and support treatment planning for this reason. Understanding and working from your chosen theoretical orientation while actively utilizing the therapeutic factors of play and nature (instead of hoping they will be activated and work by themselves) are core components of the case conceptualization and treatment planning process in prescriptive play therapy.

Within prescriptive theory, individualized treatment is a core tenet. This is where case conceptualization begins. Individualized treatment means that the therapist takes into consideration the client's history, family, abilities and areas of challenge, etiology of the problem, and empirically supported interventions to determine the most efficacious and appropriate course of treatment for each client. A comprehensive assessment should be completed, along with ongoing monitoring of progress. Play histories and nature histories can (and should) be included in these assessments. Understanding what the family's values are in regard to play and time with nature is important, including the identified client, family system, and earlier generations.

The concept of differential therapeutics is another core tenet of prescriptive play therapy and suggests that some interventions work better for different presenting concerns. As the adage states, one size does not fit all, and various theoretical modalities and treatments are better suited to various presenting concerns. Play therapists should be well versed in a variety of interventions so that they are able to individualize the treatment to the client. Research supports the fact that specific conditions are best treated with specific treatments rather than a generalized treatment approach, and that clients may respond differently to different types of play therapy treatments (Kaduson et al., 2020).

In moving away from a purist approach to theory, a play therapist takes the time to prescriptively match the core needs of the client (and family) with the therapeutic powers of play that should be initiated or facilitated through the play therapy sessions. This prescriptive matching is another core tenet of prescriptive play therapy in which the most effective interventions to reduce or alleviate concerns are considered and applied based upon the matching of need and specific therapeutic change agents (Kaduson et al., 2020). As the therapeutic powers of play are the aspects of play that cause therapeutic change in clients, it is important to be familiar with how they can be specifically and prescriptively utilized in sessions and overall treatment goals to create an individualized treatment plan rooted in empirical data. As the therapeutic factors of the role of nature in nature-based therapies are being outlined and described, intentionally utilizing aspects of nature to activate the therapeutic factors of nature must also occur for encouraging effective therapeutic interventions. Combining the therapeutic factors of nature and play therapy in these ways leads to effective practice of nature-based play therapy.

Utilizing a case conceptualization model

When determining which intervention is right for each person, given their situation, strengths, and needs, it is important to incorporate theory and the therapeutic powers of play and nature in the decision-making model. I suggest that play therapists should seek to answer two questions:

1 "Given that this presenting concern is likely occurring because of (hypothesis based on theoretical tenets), the fact that play is (characteristic) leads to initiation or facilitation of (therapeutic powers), which will lead to (desired outcome).
2 Given that we want to achieve (desired outcome), how would we do that by utilizing (this specific therapeutic power) and (this/these play characteristics)?" (Nash, 2021).

This model is presented visually in Figure 7.1 and is used as a working model of how to actively engage all aspects of nature-based play therapy into a client conceptualization and treatment plan. Here the play therapist is encouraged to blend one's theoretical knowledge and beliefs with presenting problems, therapeutic powers of play and nature specific to the client's needs, and characteristics from the definition of play to create an effective treatment plan. Connecting the tenets of a theory with the therapeutic powers of play and nature is the key piece that will allow for efficiency in treatment planning. According to Nock (2007), therapeutic factors allow a clinician to bring order to the work, highlight effective

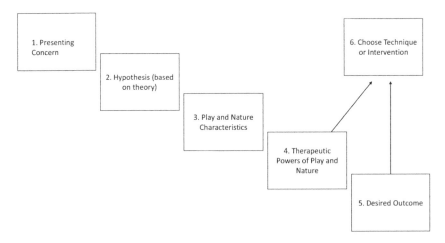

Figure 7.1 Model for treatment planning with therapeutic powers. Graphic adapted and reprinted with permission from Association for Play Therapy, Play Therapy™, 16(4) from the December 2021 issue. Graphic designed by Keith Cappelluti, Graphic Designer, Clovis, California.

parts of treatment, and eliminate the parts of therapy that are not effective or efficient. Prescriptively matching hypotheses rooted in theoretical tenets with therapeutic powers of play and nature that should be activated in nature-based play therapy encourage this order. As more detailed and specific case examples will be given in Chapter 8, the focus here will be on providing a basic overview to understand the model, what the pieces are, and how the pieces fit together.

There are a few main aspects to fully understand to help this model make sense. First is the theoretical understanding. Every trained play therapist should have a solid working understanding of at least one play therapy theory. The history, core tenets, and understanding of what causes change for a client through play must be understood from the perspective of what the theory outlines about human development and the etiology of psychopathology. Without this direct application of theory, nature-based play therapies become nothing more than techniques thrown at a client, which may or may not cause a therapeutic effect. This leads to frustration and the waste of resources and time! When a play therapist can understand WHY they are using a particular technique, because of their understanding of a person's development grounded in their theoretical understanding, nature-based play therapy becomes concrete and effective. Theory is the most abstract part of play therapy. It is the understanding that happens in a play therapist's head. The theories chosen for ongoing study should be based upon your understanding of the world, how strengths and problems develop for individuals and families, and what is needed for ongoing growth and development, as well as what is needed for intervention when challenges arise. In the prescriptive model, integration of two or more theoretical orientations is another core tenet and includes integration of both theoretical perspectives and treatment approaches (individual, family, and/or group work). Specifically following one particular therapeutic model is not the primary objective, but rather utilizing necessary interventions based upon a deep understanding (or theoretical conceptualization) of the client and their multidimensional, multidetermined presenting concerns.

To understand this concept more fully, it will help to explore some theories individually through general examples. A child-centered play therapist might say

> Because children are resilient and capable of self-healing, providing them with an opportunity for child-led free play in a playroom, supervised by a trained play therapist who can help them make sense of their unspoken words will lead to improvement in mood and behaviors.

A Jungian play therapist might determine that a child is struggling to understand and organize some previous experiences and thus is showing an incomplete understanding of themselves; thus, an exploration of their unconscious motivations and understandings through the viewing and interpretation of the archetypes they present in a play therapy session will allow the unconscious to become conscious and give the child the ability to work through their challenges. A Gestalt play therapist might understand a child's negative behavior as an outward expression of a fragile sense of self, and thus needs to improve awareness of themselves through play. A play therapist working from an ecosystemic perspective would look to the impact of the child's external systems on their current functioning and the importance of understanding the impact the systems have on behaviors (e.g., what role the caregivers, school officials, and peers play in a child's school refusal behaviors) as well as how the mind–body system impacts behaviors.

A prescriptive play therapist can integrate core pieces from each of these perspectives with current research, empirical support, and the therapeutic powers of play and nature to determine the most effective and efficient course of treatment. For example, a prescriptive play therapist might determine that a child's negative behaviors at school stem from inconsistent responses to behaviors in the home, which have led to the development of a fragile sense of self and inability to regulate their own reactions due to feeling like they have no control and do not count. Pulling aspects of ecosystemic, Gestalt, and Adlerian core tenets to understand the client and their needs more fully, the prescriptive play therapist can then consider empirically supported treatments to match with therapeutic powers of nature-based play therapy. Only once these WHYs are understood should a play therapist move into figuring out HOW to facilitate the therapeutic change the client needs. A key piece of this conceptualization model is that practitioners can work from any theoretical orientation, including prescriptive, and the model can be well utilized.

Connecting the characteristics of play with the therapeutic powers of play and nature that should be initiated or facilitated is the next step in the treatment planning model. The definition of play that I outlined in Chapter 3 describes pure play as an activity consisting of fun (creating positive affect), suspension of reality, active involvement, flexibility or creativity, and voluntary intent. These pieces are the characteristics of play included in this model and help describe why the therapeutic powers of play can be initiated or facilitated through play. This continues with the WHY portion of the question. What does the research say about treating this condition or presenting concern? Why is play the most appropriate modality for this client? What is it about play that makes it a therapeutic modality here? Given the therapeutic factors inherent in exposure to nature, why is integrating nature into therapy important for this particular client with this particular set of presenting circumstances? Why is nature-based play therapy the appropriate treatment modality? What about the integration of nature and play makes the modality therapeutic now? Here we look to the defining characteristics of play and nature, and match these with the presenting need of the client, our theoretical understanding of what is going on for this client, and which therapeutic factors of nature and powers of play should be activated or facilitated at this time. All of this explains why we are doing what we do and why we are planning the particular interventions we have in mind. It also helps us to weed out the interventions or aspects of therapy that are not particularly suited to this given client with this given need. Once we see why the client would benefit from specific help, we can figure out the best way or ways to meet that specific need. This is when the prescriptive play therapist also considers modalities of treatment and whether individual, parent, or family sessions are most conducive to effective treatment or if a combination is necessary.

To continue with the previous examples, a Gestalt play therapist who understands a child to need improvement in their awareness of self through play might decide that because play is fun and creative, it allows the appropriate platform for initiating the therapeutic powers of access to the unconscious and self-expression. Thus, a Gestalt play therapist can hypothesize that a child presenting for help with negative behaviors may need to improve their awareness of self, and because play is fun and creative, it encourages initiation of the therapeutic powers of access to the unconscious and self-expression, which would lead to a deeper and more thorough awareness and acceptance of self, which would result in fewer negative behaviors. A child-centered play therapist might hypothesize that a child presenting with acting-out behaviors in the classroom, potentially because of an impaired relationship with the teacher, is capable of self-healing through play, and thus, because play is a fun activity that encourages suspension of reality, play sessions can activate the therapeutic power of attachment and allow the child to work through feelings and reactions toward their teacher, resulting in the opportunity for a stronger relationship at school.

In nature-based play therapy, play therapists must also include their understanding of the characteristics of nature and subsequent impact on clients' development, and the consequences of lack of time in nature on development and psychopathology, especially considering research findings. This is the direct theoretical application of nature in play therapy. In the presented model, this aspect occurs in the understanding of theory and therapeutic powers, and the interventions chosen. How to integrate time in nature and natural materials into the play space logically follows this understanding. Here, I now encourage clinicians to not only look to the therapeutic powers of play and traditional play therapy theories but think through how adding nature will supplement, enhance, or facilitate the play therapy process. Where does nature fit into your theoretical understanding of play therapy? What is the importance of nature to this client's development? How does incorporating natural materials, or taking a client out into the natural world, improve the effectiveness and efficiency of play therapy? What does each client need currently, from both a theoretical play therapy and a nature-based perspective?

These questions encourage looking to nature as not just another place to gather materials or space to do a technique, even though natural spaces are useful for both, but to see WHY nature is important at a given point in play therapy. What will incorporating nature bring to the therapeutic relationship, treatment plan, and therapeutic powers of play that need to be activated or facilitated for this client? This may include the metaphysical aspects of nature, including nature as a co-therapist, sense of belonging, and access to the greater whole, as well as the biological benefits of physical exposure to nature. To continue with Gordon Paul's (1967) statement, "*What* treatment, by *whom*, is most effective for *this* individual, with *that* specific problem, and under *which* set of circumstances?" nature fits into both the "what treatment" and "which set of circumstances" parts. From a prescriptive nature-based play therapy standpoint, it is important to have a reason for incorporating nature into sessions and/or treatment plans that are grounded in theory and empirical support.

The neurosequential model of therapeutics and nature

In thinking about the most comprehensive ways in which to help clients overcome challenges and the biological benefits of exposure to nature, we should consider development from a neurological standpoint as well. The neurosequential model of therapeutics, developed by Bruce Perry, suggests that the brain and neurological processes develop in specific sequences. Maltreatment or neglect during these sequences disrupts typical development, specifically related to the monoamine neural systems which include norepinephrine, dopamine, and serotonin. While often known in psychopharmacology as monoamines that are important for mood regulation and emotional experiences, these are also the neurotransmitters that mediate and moderate signals between various systems in the brain. When the presence and impact of these monoamines are stable, consistent, regulated, and of normal intensity, the brain development (and overall functional development across the life span) is also consistent and regulated. When there is a dysfunction in the monoamine neural systems, including too much or too little of one or more of the neurotransmitters, dysregulation, or abnormal intensity, the person's development is also atypical (Perry, 2009).

Research indicates that time in nature supports regulation of these monoamines, particularly serotonin and dopamine. For example, the amount of time in the sun has been shown to be correlated with serotonin receptor binding, specifically in the limbic area of the brain (Spindelegger et al., 2012). Basically, people exposed to more time in the sun and more intense sunlight showed more serotonin binding in the brain (Spindelegger et al., 2012). Tsai and colleagues (2011) found similar results in a study looking at dopamine receptor availability—research participants who spent more time in the sunshine had a significantly greater amount of dopamine receptor availability than people who had less time in the sun. A logical assumption would be that integrating this brain-based understanding of development with play and with nature would truly utilize the importance of all three models (nature, play, and neurology) and encourage clinicians to match the need of the client with the benefits and opportunities provided by each, separately yet together.

When a person exhibits behaviors that indicate atypical development at these monoamine neural levels, treatment from a prescriptive perspective needs to meet that person where they are. Treatment should start at the lowest- or base-level need of the person, which could be at the brain stem or diencephalon level. This is where self-regulation, attention, and arousal are modulated, and thus, providing therapeutic activities that are patterned, repetitive, and focus on somatosensory experiences is key (Perry, 2009). From a nature-based play perspective, this would include nature walks on a consistent trail, use of labyrinths that have a true center and somatosensory experiences built in, and activities that target sensory experiences like multisensory scavenger hunts and seeking to identify things you can see, touch, smell, hear, and taste. Rhythm is particularly important for regulation when this system needs support (MacKinnon, 2012). Perry points out that there are many cultural rituals that include rhythm such as dancing and drumming (MacKinnon, 2012), which allows support of the mid-brain as well. The diencephalon and the cerebellum are found in the midbrain and are important with motor movement and coordination. Thus, incorporation of the rhythmic movement routines in the natural world (personal movement as well as incorporating the wind and waves, for example) can add to the therapeutic experience and activate therapeutic powers.

The next level of development in the neurosequential model is that of the limbic system. This is where emotional responses are understood. Dysfunction here would be evidenced by relationally based problems or trouble interacting with other people in the client's world (Perry, 2009). Perry (2009) recommends utilizing traditional forms of play therapy for challenges at this level of development. To integrate nature here, exploring one's relationship with the world as well as the symbiotic relationships found in nature would be helpful. The third level of development is the cortical level. Here is where verbal and more insight-oriented treatments are effective, as the dysfunction noted is more at the cognitive level (Perry, 2009). Negative thought patterns and misunderstandings are more common with this level of neurological difficulty. From a nature-based perspective, integrating verbal discussion of experienced place in the world, sense of self in relation to nature, and so on could be useful. Whichever level needs targeting for intervention, a key component of a neurosequentially focused treatment is repetition for maximum impact on that brain system (Perry, 2009).

The prescriptive model for integrating the therapeutic powers of nature-based play therapy

Incorporating all this together, the prescriptive model for nature-based play therapy becomes

> Given that this presenting concern is likely occurring because of (hypothesis based on theoretical tenets), the fact that play is (characteristics) and nature

is (nature characteristics), the therapeutic power/s of (therapeutic powers of play and nature), is/are facilitated or supported in play, which will likely lead to (desired outcome). Given that we want to achieve (desired outcome), how would we do that by utilizing (specific therapeutic powers of play and nature) and (this/these play and nature characteristics)?

These conceptualizations are visually represented in Figures 7.2 and 7.3. Let us look through a few basic examples of this before digging deeper into case conceptualization in Chapter 8.

Perhaps a child is presenting with dysregulated behaviors (acting out at home in particular) following his mother moving the children out of a long-term domestic violence situation. An ecosystemic play therapist well versed in the neurosequential model of therapeutics might discover that the mom and siblings are now living in a short-term shelter situation, while mom gets established in a new work situation. The children are in the same school and are not sure how long they will be in this shelter before needing to find their own accommodation. To include nature in the information-gathering and theoretical orientation aspects, this play therapist might learn during intake and assessment that the outdoor world has been the safest space for the child, and thus, including mom and child in an outdoor play therapy setting would strengthen that microsystem while building up more strengths and connections during the play therapy sessions. The therapist might then conceptualize the following: Given that these behaviors are likely occurring because of disrupted development of a felt sense of safety in his family system in the early years, the fact that play is flexible and nature is accepting, is nonjudgmental, and enhances a sense of belonging leads to the

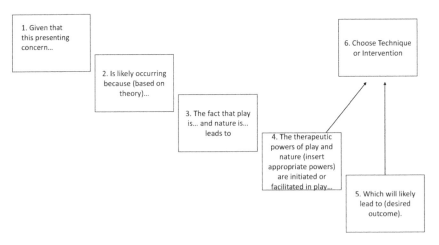

Figure 7.2 Prescriptive model for integrating the therapeutic powers of nature-based play therapy.

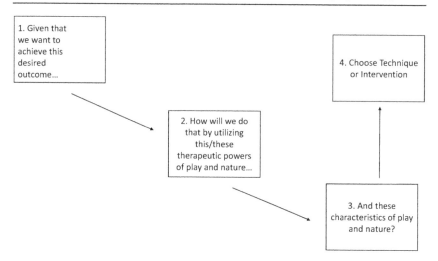

Figure 7.3 Prescriptive case conceptualization model for achieving desired outcome utilizing therapeutic powers of play and nature.

activation of the self-regulation power of play, which will lead to more regulated behaviors in the home. Given that we want to achieve more regulated behaviors in the home, the self-regulation power of play can be activated in a nature-based play therapy setting by engaging in outdoor drumming circles and nature walks along the same pathway (repetitive and rhythmic experiences). Mom can be included in these experiences to help improve the sense of felt safety between mom and son. The other siblings can be included in family sessions over time. In this scenario, nature is being incorporated as part of the therapy process or as an intervention (Figure 7.4).

This same family presenting to a nature-based play therapist who is trained in Theraplay would be assessed in terms of their attachment. Given that these behaviors are likely occurring because of disruptions in attachment between mother and children (likely related to the cycle of domestic violence and the children's exposures to this cycle), the fact that play is voluntary and fun, and that nature enhances a sense of self and of belonging, leads to the activation of the self-regulation and attachment powers of play. Facilitating these therapeutic powers will lead to a stronger attachment between mother and children, and thus, including the mother and all siblings in Theraplay sessions would lead to more regulated behaviors in the home. Given that we want to increase attachment and regulate behaviors at home, the therapeutic factors of self-regulation from nature and attachment through play therapy can be activated in nature-based play therapy by engaging in Theraplay sessions outdoors while also encouraging the family to engage in nature-based activities outside of session (Figure 7.5).

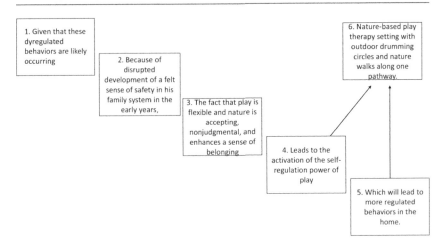

Figure 7.4 Example of case conceptualization from ecosystemic orientation.

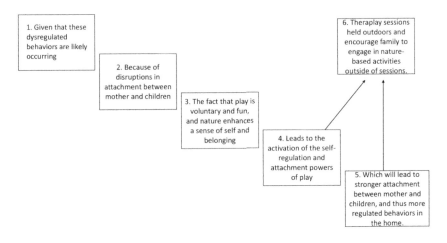

Figure 7.5 Example of case conceptualization from Theraplay orientation.

This type of conceptualization can and should happen for each client based upon your theoretical orientation. Doing so allows you to focus your treatment energies on the presented and actual needs of your clients. Determining treatment plans for the full scope of therapy flows naturally from this process as well, as does choosing specific interventions for individual sessions. Goals and objectives can be created based on play therapy theory and the therapeutic powers of nature and play, thus guiding your decisions on how to best incorporate both nature and play into therapy.

How to integrate nature into play therapy

Integrating nature into play therapy can happen in multiple ways. Some play therapists have a distinct, private outdoor space in which to bring clients. These spaces may or may not be directly linked to the office space. Sometimes there is a backyard area to the office, and sometimes the outdoor playroom is a completely distinct location where clients meet the therapist. Either way, the outdoor world becomes the playroom. Exploration, interventions, and everything play therapy related happen outdoors in a similar way as having an indoor playroom. There are outdoor play spaces that are open areas, while most that I have seen tend to incorporate the idea of centers within the outdoor world including specific areas designed for sensory play, big movement play, messy play, and so on. The children are encouraged to utilize these spaces in the same way that indoor play spaces are used, with the dirt and mess of play therapy sessions becoming more real in the outdoor world!

While I wish this opportunity for every play therapist, most of us must find ways to step into the outdoor world and bring nature into our indoor spaces. Sometimes play therapists can make a foray into the outdoor world with clients. Walks or playing in public spaces are possible with informed consent and assent. Utilizing trail systems or playgrounds has been done with success in nature-based play therapy sessions. These types of sessions often become parts of nature-based play therapy rather than the entire focus, with one or a few sessions being held outdoors when planned ahead of time. Bringing a client to a different space like this to incorporate nature into play therapy seems to be one of the more challenging methods of utilizing nature-based play therapy, or at least one of the more involved, simply because of the potential interaction with the public. Ensuring that the family is aware that you might run into other people and having a plan to deal with this is important.

Asking families to engage in activities outdoors between sessions is also a good option, as not only does the client get out and experience nature, but the family unit experiences the benefits! These do not have to be long and drawn-out adventures, as many families tend to think. Yes, some families enjoy hiking and biking and seeing how many miles they can add to their logbooks. Others are happier having a picnic lunch once a month or watching birds from the kitchen window. There are many options within this spectrum that help increase a family's time spent outdoors, and many resources dedicated to giving suggestions for these activities! Some suggestions are listed in Appendix 3. One of my favorite things to suggest is that children work on homework or read outside. They take a typically indoor activity and move it to the outdoor world. They do not need a huge space but having the open air and green space as part of their activities often helps them focus and concentrate and enjoy the experience. Working out math problems or practicing spelling words on a driveway or sidewalk with chalk is a distinctly different experience than using paper and pencils. Encouraging 10–20 minutes of child-led free play outdoors on a regular basis is quite important. If a safe outdoor space is not available at home, using school or town playgrounds, or setting kids loose in an open green park, is a good option. The playgrounds tend to help them burn off energy, while the green spaces let them explore and utilize their imaginations in deeper ways.

When spending extended time outdoors during sessions is not an option, a nature-based play therapist could also choose to have a client use natural materials collected outside the playroom. The therapist and client could collect these items together during a short time spent outdoors or have a client bring items collected at home between sessions. This gives the child some ownership over the materials and a deeper sense of connection to the items which attaches a different meaning to the work as well. This could include collecting any items that catch the child's interest to explore together or materials for a specific purpose such as collecting a quantity of leaves for making a collage, gathering sticks of assorted sizes for building miniatures during sessions, searching for materials to make boats during sessions, finding items of various textures to create a sensory board together, and choosing items to add to the sandtray or house furniture.

Having natural materials available for selection within the room is a great option. If you look around your current play space, you might be surprised by the number of natural materials already present. You likely have sand in the sandtray, wooden blocks for building or tower games, shells and stones for use as miniatures, woven baskets as miniatures or to hold your supplies, pictures of nature scenes on the walls, and books with pictures of the forest or other natural spaces. Intentionally looking for materials to supplement or enhance your current selection is an easy way to bring nature into your current play space without sacrificing your budget. Starting with miniatures and materials available for pretend play and crafts is an easy starting point. For example, can baskets of twigs, acorns or acorn tops, real seashells and stones, and leaves supplement the miniatures or craft supplies you currently have? Can a variety of mosses or lichens serve as sensory items for the client to hold, rub, or pull apart? When looking for new toys to add, look for those made of wood instead of plastic or metal. Obviously, this cannot apply to all toys, but once you begin intentionally seeking natural materials, you will be surprised by what is available! Remember, the toys children love the most are those they create themselves. Look to include natural materials that can be collected, used, broken, glued together, and replaced easily as needed to become permanent parts of your play therapy selections. Materials might change due to seasonal availability, which can make it exciting for children to see what you have to offer throughout the year.

Concluding thoughts

Integrating nature into play therapy sessions is an important way to increase the impact of the therapeutic factors at work during therapy. There are many ways in which to incorporate nature, with the key commonality being that interventions should be offered in a purposeful way, based upon your case conceptualization and understanding of the client's needs from your theoretical perspective. Prescriptively matching the client's needs from a theoretical lens with interventions allows you to offer what is needed both in the moment and across the course of treatment while eliminating the extraneous "stuff" that is not necessary for this particular client and consistently focusing on the end goals of the treatment from a nature-based play therapy perspective.

References

Kaduson, H. G., Cangelosi, D., & Schaefer, C. E. (1997). *The playing cure: Individualized play therapy for specific childhood problems*. Jason Aronson.

Kaduson, H. G., Schaefer, C. E. & Cangelosi, D. (2020). Basic principles and core practices of prescriptive play therapy. In H. G. Kaduson, D. Cangelosi, & C. E. Schaefer (Eds.), *Prescriptive play therapy: Tailoring interventions for specific childhood problems* (pp. 3–13). The Guilford Press.

MacKinnon, L. (2012). The neurosequential model of therapeutics: An interview with Bruce Perry. *The Australian and New Zealand Journal of Family Therapy, 33*(3), 210–218. https://doi.org/10.1017/aft.2012.26

Nash, J. B. (2021). Utilizing the therapeutic powers of play to create change. *Play Therapy, 16*(4), 26–29.

Nock, M. K. (2007). Conceptual and design essentials for evaluating mechanisms of change. *Alcoholism: Clinical and Experimental Research, 31*(S3), 4S–12S. https://doi.org/10.1111/j.1530-0277.2007.00488.x

Paul, G. L. (1967). Strategy of outcome research in psychotherapy. *Journal of Consulting Psychology, 31*(2), 109–118. https://doi.org/10.1037/h0024436

Perry, B. D. (2009). Examining child maltreatment through a neurodevelopmental lens: Clinical applications of the neurosequential model of therapeutics. *Journal of Loss and Trauma, 14*, 240–255. https://doi.org/10.1080/15325020903004350

Spindelegger, C., Stein, P., Wadsak, W., Fink, M., Mitterhauser, M., Kletter, K., Kasper, S., & Lanzenberger, R. (2012). Light-dependent alteration of serotonin-1A receptor binding in cortical and subcortical limbic regions in the human brain. *The World Journal of Biological Psychiatry, 13*(6), 413–422. https://doi.org/10.3109/15622975.2011.630405

Tsai, H., Chen, K, C., Yang, Y. K., Chen, P. S., Yeh, T. L., Chiu, N. T., & Lee, I. H. (2011). Sunshine-exposure variation of human striatal dopamine D2/D3 receptor availability in healthy volunteers. *Progress in Neuro-Psychopharmacology & Biological Psychiatry, 35*(1), 107–110. https://doi.org/10.1016/j.pnpbp.2010.09.014

Chapter 8

Case illustrations of nature-based play therapy

Now that a model for prescriptively integrating the therapeutic powers of play and nature with theoretical orientations to determine treatment goals and objectives has been introduced, case compilations will be used to more fully demonstrate this process. Along with these detailed examples, ways to include assessment of clients' histories with both nature and play, and comfort with nature in particular will be explored. This will allow for application of the prescriptive model to integrate the theory and therapeutic powers to determine potential interventions or techniques to incorporate nature and play into sessions. The following case examples are composites, and identifying information has been changed. However, the method of utilizing the prescriptive model with more common case presentations will help the model to make more sense as well as encourage clinicians to become more familiar and comfortable with ways to activate the therapeutic powers of nature and play therapy.

The first family we will meet here is the Summer family. Tommy Summer's parents and teacher noticed an increase in symptoms of attention-deficit hyperactivity disorder (ADHD), and his parents sought treatment to help him learn to better manage his behaviors at school and home. We will also meet Derek, a teenager who presented with depressive symptomatology and trouble with positive social interactions following the loss of a long-time friendship. Heather is our third client. She is a young girl who presented with perfectionist tendencies rooted in some anxiety that interfered with her school work, homework time, and overall family stress levels. Tucker is our next child to meet, and he had recently moved to a foster home following a long history of maternal neglect and truancy. The extent of his trauma history remained unknown, but the impact on his ability to appropriately attach to caregivers was clear. Finally, we will meet Jaylani, whose parents reported that she became more aggressive in her behaviors toward her siblings and that these behaviors became more difficult to physically manage as she became older and bigger. Some of these children were used to spending time outdoors with their friends and family, and for some it was a newer concept and more challenging to keep going on a regular basis due to their living situations. Together the stories of these children and their

DOI: 10.4324/9781003332343-8

journeys through nature-based play therapy will teach us the benefits of utilizing a prescriptive model to activate specific therapeutic powers of play and nature to integrate the most encompassing theoretical understanding and appropriate interventions for their current needs.

Taking play and nature histories

During intake assessments, it is useful to include questions about how much time children and families spend in play (both together and separately), how the child's school system views time for play, and the importance the family places on play. Questions can include how often the child and family play, what preferred activities are outside of school and work, what children are allowed and encouraged to play during recess or downtime at school, which activities the child prefers to do with their friends, what types of play the child likes when playing independently, and how often the child is encouraged to engage in child-led free play. Similar questions can be asked to assess the role of nature time in a family's life and the value they assign to time in nature. What types of outdoor activities the family enjoys, how comfortable the child and parents are in nature, how physically active they are and how often, and if they view the natural world as inviting or not are the important aspects to understand before suggesting and engaging in nature-based play therapy. It can also be interesting to know what the parents experienced in their own childhoods regarding the importance of both play and time in nature to understand how their experiences may be influencing their parenting approaches. If their answers do not suggest any comfort with nature, then you would be better served to slowly integrate natural materials into your sessions and work up to encouraging outdoor activities. If a family spends a lot of time outdoors and finds it to be a healing space to begin with, then it will be easier to integrate outdoor activities into both your sessions and suggestions for the family to try outside of sessions. Play and nature histories during intake will be shown separately for our first case study but incorporated into history and case formulation going forward.

The Summer family

Family history and symptom presentation

The Summer family sought treatment for their nine-year-old son, Tommy, who has been getting in trouble at school quite frequently over the past school year. School has always been a challenge for him as symptoms related to a diagnosis of ADHD that he had been managing for the past three years have started interfering with his school work now that the material and expectations of the teacher have increased as Tommy gets older. His teacher noted an increase in defiant behaviors as well as complaints of stomachaches and headaches multiple times in a week. His parents reported that Tommy has always been hyperactive and impulsive, often doing things without thinking even when he knew that he should not be doing something. He would then show regret over his actions but say that he was not able to slow himself enough to stop. As with his behaviors, his emotions would also be "all over the place," and he would express a wide range of big feelings. Tommy had always been an active child and started showing more destructive and "tornado-like" behaviors as he aged. Destructive behaviors did not typically happen in the classroom, but he would be loud and impulsive in his vocalizations. Tommy's mother noted that she thinks his anxiety helped to keep his physical behaviors in check at school as he worried about missing the presentation of new learning material, but he would still react strongly at home until around the age of seven.

Tommy's mother noted that he has shown a greater ability to manage his own behaviors as he ages, but this year has been hard. Tommy is quite smart and capable of managing a learning buting, but does not see the point of completing homework when he already knows the answers. The same is true of doing other busywork during the school day. Instead, he will fidget and move around, which distracts the other students and causes issues between him and the teacher. Tommy is typically a hard worker when he is interested in the material but can present as defiant when he does not want to complete his work. He has also been showing an increase in negative verbalizations when interacting with peers. He describes his thoughts as popping out of his mouth before he has a chance to figure out what he means to say. Tommy said he wants to have friends and is disappointed in himself when he says mean things or speaks too loudly with his peers. He likes to play team sports yet seems rather half-hearted in his efforts to truly join the team and work toward a common end goal. He seems to enjoy being on the field during baseball and enjoys being in the dugout and "messing around with people. It's fun to kick the dirt and pull the grass out in there."

Tommy's 12-year-old sister, Alex, also deals with symptoms of ADHD. Her symptom presentation is more physical in expression, as she will often fall out of her chair in the classroom as she is constantly moving and unaware of the full location of her body. She has been able to maintain herself more consistently in the classroom as she has gotten older but does still have days when it is hard for her to maintain her movements. Her mother described Alex as silly and giggly, often laughing for a long time over things that were not particularly funny but that caught her interest. She has more friends than Tommy but is able to more easily fit into a group of preteen girls who also liked to laugh. Mrs. Summer mentioned that Alex's symptom presentation was usually seen as "cute" or more acceptable for a young girl, so she did not get into trouble in her early elementary years as often as Tommy does now. Alex was also able to complete her schoolwork quickly, so her teachers did not recognize her behaviors as particularly problematic.

It is of note that Tommy's mother reported a history of ADHD symptoms herself. Mrs. Summer described a lifelong history of distractibility in her thought process often seen through daydreaming or doodling during her school days. She remembers also being frustrated with busywork in the classroom and much like Tommy, not understanding why she had to complete homework assignments on material already covered in class. Music or other background noise would help her focus enough to be able to complete assignments, but talking or voices as background noise were distracting. As an adult, she has found ways to keep her body moving frequently to help quiet her thoughts. She continues to experience times of having "a million ideas and things I want to do," but not having the ability to concentrate on one thing for long enough to see many projects to completion. Mrs. Summer realized early on that she performs better at jobs that challenge her mentally by providing a variety of tasks to complete throughout the day and those at which she can move around. She enjoys gardening and is successful in working at a garden center where she can work with customers as well as complete large planting projects over time. She finds herself able to understand Tommy's challenge with his symptoms and reports feeling annoyed by his need to constantly talk and ask questions, as the sound easily distracts her.

Mr. Summer reported no such symptoms of hyperactivity or distractibility himself. He has successfully managed his own business for the past ten years and enjoys working outdoors. As a couple, the Summers recognize that Tommy and Alex are smart children who want to do well in life but are currently struggling to fully manage their symptoms of distractibility and hyperactivity. Tommy's symptoms are currently causing more tension in the classroom and thus at home, so his parents continue to seek ways to help him slow his thinking as well as monitor his anxiety levels. He has used medications somewhat successfully in the past specifically during the school day to help him manage his behaviors, and he is willing to continue utilizing these but also does not like to take them outside of school and wants to learn "how to handle myself."

Play and nature histories

In looking at play and nature histories, both have always been considered important to the entire Summer family. They live on a quiet *cul-de-sac* so have space for the children to play outdoors without constant supervision, and both parents report this was key in managing behaviors at home until recently. When they noticed that Tommy was struggling with homework, he would be encouraged to run a few laps around the house or "just get his frustration out out there instead of in here!" Tommy reported enjoying when he can help his dad work on his truck and is usually "the runner" to get necessary tools for him. As Tommy has gotten older, his time outdoors lessened as homework demands increased, and his play became more structured as he started to join sports teams and play with his friends.

Case formulation

Tommy appears to be dealing with problems with impulse control and anxiety that has developed over time, potentially as a result of trying to unsuccessfully manage his impulsivity in the classroom as his academic load has increased. As he and his mother described his increase in symptoms and his typical day, it sounded as though his head becomes so full and busy that he must pick where to direct his attention—he can either manage his behaviors in the classroom or learn the new academic material. Doing both at the same time becomes overwhelming. Tommy agrees that the anxiety symptoms that bother him the most at the present time are related to the struggles he faces in school. He becomes nervous when he knows new information is coming, and it is hard for him to fully understand the topic in one sitting. He does not want to ask for help or further explanation because he does not "want to look stupid" and worries about making mistakes. So, he acts in ways that distract his teacher and classmates from recognizing that he needs more time to think and understand. He is a smart kid and fully capable of understanding the material, and he just needs a little extra time to put all the pieces together in his own way.

From an ecosystemic perspective, Tommy's feelings of being easily overwhelmed, distracted, and anxious make sense as the increased impact of the school system is weighing heavily on his ability to maintain his internal homeostasis. His family system remains secure and consistent, and this is a big benefit to maintaining his felt sense of safety and comfort at home, where he is allowed and encouraged to simply be himself at his own speed. His attentional concerns likely have a biological component leading to potential lifelong challenges, especially given the genetic picture presented in his family, but the focus here becomes the challenge interrupting his ability to meet his full developmental potential. The current problems impacting his ability to meet his full potential are needing a bit more time and space to figure out the new academic material at his own speed, and managing and regulating his behaviors until that happens. His parents are open to working with the school to help them understand his needs and create a plan that works for both parties.

Given the similarity in symptom presentation among three members of the family and the impact the identified client presentation is having on the family unit, the Summers agreed to integrate individual and family therapy sessions to learn ways to support and encourage each other in their progress. Their hope is that Tommy and Alex will each learn some new ways to cope with their symptoms and reduce the negative impact on their lives, while embracing their creativity and intellectual sides, and that Mr. and Mrs. Summer will learn ways to support them both. Tommy will continue to be the identified client in the case, and Alex will benefit from being part of the process. As they all like to move around and fully engage with their environments, family play therapy with an integrated nature-based portion was chosen as a primary treatment modality.

Goals of treatment

Tommy has two major goals that he would like to work toward:

1 Improve his self-regulation in the classroom so he can focus on the academic material and improve his interactions with his classmates.
2 Reduce his level of anxiety in the classroom.

Given that Tommy's increased negative behaviors and trouble with self-regulation at school are likely occurring because of increased attentional demands, the fact that play is flexible and creative while nature encourages physical challenges and growth of mindset leads to initiation or facilitation of the therapeutic powers of self-regulation and creative problem-solving in play therapy and challenge in nature-based therapy, which will lead to an increased ability to regulate his behaviors in the classroom.

Given that Tommy's increased anxiety is likely occurring because of his challenges with regulating his internal state and managing the increased academic workload to his own satisfaction, the fact that play is voluntary and active while nature encourages physical challenges and creation of new beliefs leads to the facilitation of the therapeutic powers of self-esteem, self-regulation, creative problem-solving, and challenge, which will lead to an increased ability to understand and manage his symptoms of anxiety.

Individual objectives

To achieve these overarching goals through the course of nature-based play therapy, individual objectives to guide the process will be determined. These are the smaller steps and include interventions that will help the client work toward the treatment goals.

Given that we want to achieve an increased ability to regulate Tommy's behaviors in the classroom, how would we do that by utilizing the self-regulation and creative problem-solving therapeutic powers of nature-based play therapy in a flexible and creative play session that encourages physical challenges? One activity to try will be building boats out of an assortment of natural materials and racing them during sessions, which will require creative thinking, focus, attempts with trial and error, and regulating breathing to make them move in specific directions. Other activities could include collaging and creating family art projects with natural materials like paints made from nuts and berries or playing board games using acorn tops and pinecones as the playing pieces.

Given that we want to achieve an increased ability to understand and manage Tommy's symptoms of anxiety, how would we do that by utilizing the therapeutic powers of self-esteem, self-regulation, and creative problem-solving by utilizing voluntary and active nature-based play therapy sessions that encourage physical challenges and creation of new beliefs? To achieve this, we could engage the family in timed outdoor obstacle courses with a variety of goals. For example, the family will have to work together to move a series of large blocks and small logs to cross a grassy space without touching the ground, attempting to beat their time records with each new trial. Other obstacles could include maintaining physical balance and completing cooperative tasks that involve more space than an indoor office would allow. The family could also engage in life-size board games by drawing game boards on the pavement with chalk and becoming the playing pieces themselves.

Model for treatment

Nature-based play therapy sessions took three forms for this family, including bringing nature into the sessions, taking the family outdoors, and encouraging nature-based activities at home. Bringing nature into the sessions involved having natural materials readily available for use with specific activities (in this case, building boats to encourage focus to details that would make them float and race the furthest while only working with materials provided). To take the family outdoors, we utilized a town park that was nearby. It was equal distance for the family to get there compared to the office and had a large enough space that afforded some privacy and space to engage in activities. Each family member agreed to meet there even with risks to confidentiality. They stated that everyone already knew the kids struggle in school, and they could use this as an opportunity to encourage others to better themselves as well, should anyone comment. The goal of these family activities was to encourage cooperation and self-regulation while utilizing the therapeutic impact of the natural environment on ADHD symptoms (as being in green spaces has been shown through research to have positive benefits on such symptoms). The family was also encouraged to spend time outdoors between sessions both together and separately. They discussed options such as completing homework at a picnic table and having dinner outside a couple of times a week as ways to increase outdoor time through daily routine activities.

Outcomes

One of Tommy's favorite activities that brought nature into the sessions was building boats out of nature materials and racing them. A selection of nut shells, twigs, and leaves was provided, and the family worked together to build small boats out of these supplies. They were able to glue them together using a hot glue gun and raced them in a dishpan of water using a small portable fan to create the wind at one end. They also ran races by using straws to blow their boats across the span of water. Tommy placed various rocks in the dishpan to serve as obstacles along the way and quickly changed the objective of the task from racing and winning against his family members to creating an ever-changing, ever more challenging obstacle course for everyone to maneuver through. He asked to change the direction of the "wind" at times and moved the obstacles at others. When he had finished, his face showed his excitement over the activity. He was asked to describe what he discovered through the trials, and he said:

> Sometimes I had to change the path to get through the obstacles, sometimes I had to change the direction of the wind, and sometimes I had to make the boat stronger. But the boat was always able to make it to the end when I helped it one of those ways.

After this conversation, the therapist spoke with Tommy's teacher about opportunities available for Tommy to remove himself from the classroom when he might need the opportunity. There was a sensory room in the school set up for children who needed the time to regulate themselves, and Tommy was able to make use of this space on occasion. In particular, his teacher suggested that he be encouraged to go to the room after she introduced new math topics so that he could physically work through and assimilate the new information. She offered to ask him if he would like to run an errand for her, so he had the option to accept or decline the time in the room without announcing to the class where he was going and why. In this way, she was offering to change the direction of the wind to help him through the obstacles and giving him some time and space to make his "boat" stronger in relative privacy.

The green space utilized for the family sessions appeared to serve as a great distraction for Tommy, Alex, and Mrs. Summer to help them stay better focused on activities and conversations. The activities utilized were basic board games that required attending to tasks and some group drawing activities. Mr. Summer was quite at home out of doors, so the green space was not a distraction for him but rather a calming influence. Tommy noted that the sounds, sights, textures, and wide variety of colors he could visually explore were not overwhelming or overstimulating but in fact gave his "brain a break," as he "didn't have to think so hard when [his] eyes could keep moving around." Mrs. Summer noted that being in nature helped her to feel more balanced, so she was not pushed to her limits as often as she usually experiences, and she was able to respond more calmly to Tommy's questions. Alex said that she did not feel as "confined" in the natural play space as she has in classrooms, buildings, or her house. She reported that it was easier to move around and move things in her physical environment to meet her fidgeting needs. Her movements did not have to be large as in the classroom to feel an effect because she was constantly receiving sensory input and stimulation from the grass that she almost constantly touched and ran through her fingers and other elements of nature. Mr. and Mrs. Summer reported that they often encouraged Tommy to take his homework outside to work at the picnic table so he could stand or move as needed, and that being positioned under or near trees seemed to help him quite a bit. They continued talking about ways they could spend more time outside both together and individually to help maintain their treatment gains.

Derek

Family history and symptom presentation

Derek is a 17-year-old male who presents as a quiet and withdrawn teenager. He is polite but answers questions briefly without making much eye contact. His school guidance counselor recommended that he seek therapy as he has become noticeably more withdrawn over the school year. Derek insists that "nothing is wrong," he's "just bored." When asked about social relationships, he revealed that a good friend moved last year, and he has not had any interest in making or pursuing other friendships mostly because it is hard for him to connect with others. Derek and his friend used to spend most afternoons together "just hanging out." When pressed to describe their afternoons a bit more, he mentioned biking and wandering around the neighborhood. They do not talk much anymore as his friend has become quite busy in his new school and district-wide activities. Derek's school performance has not changed dramatically, and he remains a consistent B-level student, yet admits that he does not put much effort into his schoolwork, which he believes is a new behavior over the past year. He is not involved in any extracurricular activities at this time though shrugged as he expressed interest in "maybe trying something" in the past. Derek said that he does not see the point in joining an activity as he does not see why he should bother making new friendships. When asked which activities he had been thinking about joining previously, he became even quieter as though he was embarrassed but said there was a men's singing group at school that he and his friend had discussed trying out for, but his friend moved before the auditions and Derek chose not to try out.

Derek is an only child whose parents work full-time. They are all home for dinner together multiple times a week and tend to pursue individual hobbies. They have enjoyed outdoor activities together in the past but not as frequently since Derek entered high school and his schoolwork responsibilities increased. On the weekends, they run errands and work around the house. Derek seems to enjoy doing yardwork with his father. Derek's mother reported a personal history of "minor depression" as a teenager and into her early 20s and attributes "growing out of it" and increased responsibilities at work for helping her to overcome her symptoms. His father presents as quiet and prefers individual activities to social events. His parents both expressed a desire to see Derek getting outside more often, and while they would like him to engage in some sort of group activity, they do not push him into groups because none of them are "particularly social creatures." While he does not play video games consistently, he does engage in some play for a couple of hours over the course of a week and says that he does not particularly enjoy the game itself but does like working with other people to achieve tasks.

Case formulation

While there does appear to be a genetic predisposition to some depressive symptoms, Derek is also dealing with the loss of a friendship and missing the good connection he had with his friend. From a Gestalt play therapy perspective, Derek is likely unaware of (or unwilling to be unaware of) the impact the loss of his friendship has had on his progress toward his ongoing development. This block in his ability to allow himself to understand and work through the loss of his friend and subsequent impact on his daily activities and sense of belonging has impacted the development of his sense of self. He seems to have a sense that he "should" be sad and "should" be withdrawn without his friend in his life and has trouble separating his inner beliefs and hopes for his ongoing development from this outside evaluation mentality. Derek also seems to have a fear of being left alone again and is finding a sense of safety in isolating himself from others.

Helping him to build his sense of self at the same time as improving contact with his senses and feelings while utilizing his intellect and ability to think about these aspects and strengthen his awareness of his inner self will lead to a better awareness of his needs and overall improvement in his functioning. Derek would benefit from the opportunity to safely express the emotions he has locked away regarding his friend leaving him and, in so doing, his sense of his friend taking away his opportunity with the singing group. Encouraging appropriate expression of this anger and disappointment should allow him to start moving beyond the hurt he felt at his friend leaving, but also the disappointment he felt in himself for not going forward with his own ambition. The Gestalt play therapy model will help Derek be able to give a voice to different aspects of his being and use this voice to talk with other parts, with the intention of more fully exploring and understanding his experience and felt sense of loss and current ambiguity. The goal here would be to help him get back to a healthy and normative path of development.

Derek would likely benefit from nature-based play therapy as exploration of the natural world will give him increased opportunities for exploring his senses and his sense of belonging. As he searches for equilibrium in his life and sense of self, and thus self-regulation and a more genuine acceptance of himself through self-awareness and mindfulness, encouraging time in nature and with natural materials will likely enhance this process. In Gestalt play therapy, there are techniques grounded in the natural world that would be helpful to introduce to Derek including the rosebush technique.

Goals of treatment

Given that Derek's depressive symptoms are likely occurring (or exacerbated) by the loss of a close friendship, and he is now struggling to understand and accept the emotions he has about the loss, the fact that play is voluntary and suspends reality leads to initiation or facilitation of the therapeutic factors of access to the unconscious in play therapy and challenge in nature-based therapy to enhance his ability in self-discovery, which will lead to a deeper understanding of his depressive symptoms as based in grief and allow him to explore and express these feelings with the intention of developing a healthier sense of self.

As Derek begins to understand his grief process, given that he is also likely dealing with depressive symptoms related to loneliness and disappointment with himself, the fact that play is voluntary and active leads to facilitation of the therapeutic power of social competence, while inclusion of nature leads to activation of the therapeutic factors of challenge and interconnectedness, both of which will lead to exploration of his need for friends during his development of balance in his life.

Individual objectives

Given that we want to achieve Derek's development of a healthier sense of self through understanding and expressing unconscious feelings of grief, loss, and disappointment, how would we do that by utilizing the therapeutic power of access to the unconscious in play therapy and the therapeutic factor of challenge in nature-based therapy? There are multiple techniques within the Gestalt framework that encourage this exploration that are or can be grounded in nature-based activities. Use of the rosebush technique encourages a person to describe a rosebush and then identify with parts of the image, connecting the description to their own thoughts, feelings, and experiences. Derek could use this as an opportunity to explore his connection or lack thereof to others around him and the unconscious experiences of being alone, left behind, and ambivalent about allowing others close to him for fear of being left again. Drawing techniques and using the sandtray to help him explore his inner parts could be useful.

Given that we want to explore Derek's desire and need for friends and connectedness, how would we do that by utilizing the therapeutic power of social competence in play therapy and the therapeutic factors of challenge and interconnectedness in nature-based therapy? This objective would be specifically approached only after some grief work was done. Derek's family used to be more active outdoors and are looking to find ways to include nature time in their routines again. Derek noticed that the local library would be hosting a geocaching class, and he was interested in learning more, so his father agreed to attend with him. Derek was hoping that he would find geocaching to be interesting enough to help him decide to get outside more often and explore new places around town, as he missed walking and riding his bike with his friend.

Model for treatment

Gestalt play therapy techniques will help Derek to explore his inner emotions and begin to understand the role these emotions have been playing in his psychological presentation. While Derek is open to spending time outside, he is hesitant to spend entire sessions outdoors as they would be in potential public view, and he did not want to draw any attention to himself. He agreed to revisit the idea of nature walks on quiet trails later in therapy and likes the idea of nature-based techniques being used inside the office. Expressive techniques like the rosebush technique and others will be used to bridge into nature-based play. To further bring nature-based play to the indoor setting, sandtray will be encouraged utilizing a combination of manmade and natural materials. Derek might be encouraged to build his own miniatures for the sandtray as needed. This will allow him to develop a stronger sense of ownership over the miniatures and investment in the process of exploration of his sense of self.

From a nature-based perspective, increasing physical activity and outdoor time will help to improve his mood at a biological level, which will likely allow him to access deeper emotional levels of understanding. Derek will be encouraged to engage in outdoor activities a few times a week especially since this is an activity he used to engage in with his friend and has let lapse. He can choose to engage in these activities alone or include his family.

Bringing Derek on a nature walk during sessions would allow him to explore the outdoor world at his pace and experience the impact on his various senses. He might be encouraged to try a sensory scavenger hunt in which he identifies different sights, sounds, smells, textures, and even tastes during an outdoor walk. Using a nature journal kit (blank paper, colored pencils, and watercolors) for a quiet walk down a town-owned trail system could encourage him to explore his surroundings and his reactions to the sensory stimuli more fully as he works to reexperience his awareness of his senses and his existence within the natural world. These activities will be explored later in therapy once Derek has a stronger understanding of himself and feels more comfortable moving more fully in the outdoor spaces.

Outcomes

Derek and his father were able to attend the geocaching class and reported being "instantly hooked." Derek said that he had not "felt that excited about something in a really long time," and his parents reported that they have been geocaching together at least once a week and have enjoyed finding new trail systems to explore through the activity. They were able to get out for at least 90 minutes of hiking each weekend and have all noticed improvements in their moods. Derek reported looking forward to the weekends with this time together and spends time during the week finding maps for new locations and planning the weekend trip. At the class, he saw a classmate and chose to sit near him. They made plans to search for some easier geocaches and were able to find a few by bike together.

Derek reported that he enjoyed the time with this new friend and only felt a little guilt about connecting with someone new.

Derek made good use of the techniques used in sessions to explore his unconscious self. When asked to describe a rosebush, he spoke of a rather neglected plant but pointed out that it had deep roots that were able to search for water for nourishment. He described a plant that was closed in on itself, but once it reached water, it was able to reach for some sunlight as well. When asked if he could relate to this plant, Derek paused for a long time before taking a deep breath. "Yes," he said. "I'm almost ready to reach out." He and his therapist spoke about needing to clear some of the overgrowth that was crowding the rosebush so that the sunlight could be seen, and Derek's shoulders visibly relaxed during this discussion.

The following week, Derek said he had thought about the overgrowth and wanted to figure out what was holding him back. He turned to the sandtray for this session and asked to create his rosebush so he could really see it. There was no miniature available that exactly described his vision, and he agreed to try to make one. Derek used a basket of twigs, lichen, and dry grasses to create a completely enclosed "plant" with a hot glue gun. He then glued twigs together to create a stacked fence and added rocks to the scene, burying some under the plant and adding others to the fence line. After he completed his creation, he sat back and observed it silently for a few minutes. The therapist asked him to describe the scene, and Derek spoke about a plant that was "weighing itself down" with all the overgrowth it was not yet pushing through. He spoke of the rocks and fences as obstacles obstructing its path, and the plant's desire to reach the water it knew was beneath the surface. The therapist encouraged him to identify with the plant and begin to describe it using "I" statements rather than "the plant." As he did so, Derek sat up a little straighter in his chair and began removing pieces of grass very methodically from the top of the rosebush. "I want to do this," he said. "I want to grow toward the sun. I just don't know how or what I actually need but know there's a lot of junk in the way." Derek decided that he enjoyed the sandtray and creating his own miniatures. He chose not to take nature walks during sessions but did agree to bring in some of his own materials that he found on the trails with his parents and enjoyed sharing and creating with these during sessions. He continued using the sandtray to explore his sense of self and began creating a scene at the beginning of sessions, leaving it, and returning before the end to adjust and open the scene up a bit more. The therapist gave him a small box in which to store his miniature creations and materials so that he could have a physical container to leave in the therapy room.

Heather

Family history and symptom presentation

Heather is an eight-year-old girl who "has been anxious forever" according to her mother's report. She met developmental milestones within normal limits but "seemed to do them only when she could do them perfectly. She took a couple of steps, then nothing for a few weeks, when she decided to walk across the room!" Heather's mother reported that Heather worries about "messing up, breaking things, and doing things wrong." She often takes extra time to complete chores, but now her need to be perfect is impacting her schoolwork as she struggles with completing assignments that are "not good enough." For example, she will erase spelling words multiple times, sometimes until there is a hole in the paper, because the letters are not "straight enough." She then becomes fixated on completing that assignment and will not be able to complete any other worksheets within the class time and is asked to complete them at home in addition to her regular homework sheets. Heather's mother reported that homework time is quite challenging and often ends in tears.

Heather is an only child and enjoys quiet activities. She has a large collection of stuffed animals and shared the name of each along with what the animal likes to play after school. Heather said that she likes making up stories with them and described many dramatic stories that she and her stuffed animals have acted out together. The themes of these stories seem to alternate between good and evil (she alternates playing each role herself, with the stuffed animals filling in for either an all-knowing, calming presence or a cowering and scared youngster afraid of being hurt, depending on the day's saga) and embarrassment. Heather said that the scene she plays out the most is when one of her animals (Sparky, a lightning bug) goes to school and must take a test but did not know it was scheduled for that day. Sparky thought the test was the next day and was not ready for it, and the test was given verbally rather than on paper. Heather laughed gleefully when she shared that Sparky became so nervous that he wet his pants and the other animals in class teased him about it for weeks, "especially because once he got wet, his light kept flickering! So, everybody always knew!"

Heather does have a few friends and enjoys spending time playing outdoors with them. Her mother stated that playing outside works best for them, because she notices that when they seem to be getting overstimulated or struggling with an interaction, they naturally drift apart for a bit. At those times they play or explore independently, and then regroup when they are ready. She does not see them specifically talking about these separations and joinings but said that they occur naturally and allow the play sessions to last longer. Heather will often separate from the group when she is spending an "excessive" amount of time focused on one task, as the other girls wander into another activity. Heather does not appear bothered by these times, and the one time her mother asked about what happened, Heather replied, "They wanted to do something, and I wasn't done organizing my leaves yet. So, they played, and I finished."

There is no history of abuse, neglect, or developmental traumas in Heather's life, nor any significant medical issues or delays. Her mother reported that Heather is the result of a healthy planned pregnancy and that she and her husband had wanted more children, but doctors advised against it due to her own medical history. Heather's father works full-time, and her mother works part-time during the school day, with the family being home together most nights. They report no other concerns outside of Heather's increasing anxiety and are worried about the impact this will have on her life, especially as she is getting older and "the hormones of puberty will be kicking in soon, and that's not going to help anything!"

Case formulation

From a child-centered play therapy perspective, Heather would benefit from therapeutic interactions that allow for unconditional positive regard, empathic understanding, and genuineness from a therapist seeking to develop a strong therapeutic relationship and the opportunity for her to share and learn her own story at her own pace. Pushing her to work through her challenges at any other pace will likely lead to an increase in her anxiety level and symptoms, while encouraging a safe space to explore her feelings will give her the strength she needs to build resilience and heal her own symptoms. Developing a strong therapeutic relationship will also give her the space and support to identify and work through her emotional needs. Providing her with opportunities to engage with natural materials in an indoor play space and to have the option to explore an outdoor place space will enhance this growth, as she will be presented with opportunities to utilize the therapeutic factors of the natural space as nonjudgmental and experiencing an expanded perspective to explore herself within the larger context of the world.

Heather's parents will be encouraged to engage in special play times with her at home, during which Heather is allowed to choose the family's activity and the focus is on simply spending time together. They would all benefit from some time away from expectations of what could or should be happening and an opportunity to enjoy each other's presence, reconnect, and strengthen their attachment and relationships.

Goals of treatment

Given that Heather's increase in anxiety and perfectionist moments are likely occurring because she needs the opportunity to develop her sense of resilience at her own pace and in her own way, the fact that play is voluntary and flexible while nature is accepting and expands one's sense of belonging leads to facilitation of the therapeutic powers of resilience in play therapy and the natural environment and expansiveness of nature-based therapy, which will lead to a decrease in perceived anxiety and perfectionist tendencies. Developing a solid therapeutic relationship with a child-centered nature-based play therapist will give Heather the space to explore her own needs and achieve self-healing.

Individual objectives

Given that we want to achieve a decrease in perceived anxiety and perfectionist characteristics, how would we do that by utilizing the therapeutic power of resilience in play therapy and the natural environment with expansiveness factors of nature-based therapies to create a therapeutic nature-based play therapy setting? From a child-centered perspective, it is anticipated that Heather will further develop her sense of resilience through child-led free play in a safe and supportive environment where she can explore her abilities and challenges at her own pace. The therapist will provide unconditional positive regard, acceptance, and empathic understanding, and nature will provide an accepting environment that encourages an expanded sense of belonging, while the child strives for self-actualization through play.

Model for treatment

For Heather, an indoor child-centered playroom was offered, as well as the option to explore an outdoor setting just outside the play therapy center. The outdoor space was accessed through a back door of the center and enclosed by fences. It had been arranged into "centers" including a garden area with various flowers and herbs, a sensory and movement area, a digging and constructive play area, and some open space. There were also a table and chairs set up in one corner. Heather was given the option of either staying in the indoor or outdoor space for the entire session or moving from one to the other as she chose. She often chose to spend part of her sessions indoors and then moved to the outdoor space, gradually adjusting the amount of time spent in each until she was spending most of the sessions in the outdoor play space. In the outdoor space, Heather was at first generally cautious and specific in her movements, verbalizing that she did not want to mess anything up. She explored and organized objects as she went, lining up the digging toys, organizing the tools on the potting shelf, and putting seed packets in alphabetical order "so you [the therapist] can find them when you want them." Over the course of treatment, Heather gradually explored the more open areas of the space and was asked to explore the tree line. As the therapist reflected Heather's desire to explore the areas that were a bit further away, Heather darted off to touch and examine the trees more closely.

Heather's parents were asked to encourage 20–30 minutes of outdoor free play each day before attempting homework to give Heather a chance to decompress from the school day and engage in physical activity before trying to sit and work. While she often played outdoors with her friends, the thought here was that encouraging her to have some individual time to explore would help Heather further her in-session treatment progress. It was also suggested that Heather be allowed to spread a blanket on the back steps to sit outside with a couple of her stuffed animals while working on homework. Given that spelling and math lessons were typically triggers for her anxiety, it was suggested that Heather be allowed to practice writing her words in the dirt using her finger or a stick and to work math problems in the same way. By replacing the paper and pencil with natural materials that would not allow for perfection, the goal was to allow Heather to focus on the lesson practice rather than its presentation. Heather's parents were offered some sessions to explore filial therapy components and ways to integrate these concepts into their interactions with Heather, but they chose to not utilize those sessions at this time.

Outcomes

Heather and her play therapist spent multiple sessions outdoors by Heather's request. She spent a lot of time simply exploring the space and observing the garden, eventually moving outward to explore the trees along one fence line. She would occasionally ask to bring drawing materials out to the table and would attempt to capture a leaf. Sometimes she would try to draw it freehand, and other times she would trace or take a rubbing of the leaf. During one session, Heather noticed tree roots that were quite prominent, raised up from the ground with many open spaces present in the root system. Heather stopped walking and stared at this tree for some time. After about five minutes of staring, walking around the tree, touching the roots, and looking at the roots from all angles, Heather said it was beautiful and asked if the therapist knew why the tree grew like that. The therapist responded that sometimes when trees are growing, they meet obstacles. In their efforts to reach the sun, some trees push around whatever the obstacle is. She suggested it was likely that this tree met a rock or large, hard area of dirt and began to grow around it. When the tree was bigger, the dirt or rock probably loosened and washed out of the roots over multiple rainstorms. Heather nodded slowly, continuing to gaze at the root system. "But it's still really strong," she said. "So it held on, grew stronger and taller, and was still sturdy when the problem washed away?" Her therapist nodded in agreement. "Wow," Heather said.

> Even though the problem washed away, the roots were still there. They still held the tree up even though it was hard, and they were bent. And look! The tree is happy and healthy! Look at those leaves it has!

Heather then skipped further down the path and looked under some rocks for a few minutes before turning and heading back to the indoor playroom. Heather's mother reported that Heather drew a picture of the tree during the week and kept it next to her bed. She said that sometimes Heather would get up during homework time to go look at the tree and then come back to the table and noticed that Heather was not erasing her spelling words as frequently. This gradual growth in her observations and ability to see herself and the world as part of a bigger picture was seen through progression from her repetitive initial observations of small objects (exploring short plants in the garden, drawing a leaf multiple times, and so on), to looking at the trees as they grew over the fence line, to observing the core strengths of the trees themselves. The progression of depth of observations seen here translated to her ability to see herself as growing and seeing her whole self instead of only one aspect of her abilities (such as how perfectly she performed on individual homework assignments).

Heather's parents were asked to speak with teacher about setting amounts of time to work on homework rather than focusing on full completion of the assignment. For example, Heather would be expected to spend ten minutes a night working on her spelling lists verbally (reading, spelling, reciting the words) instead of turning in a completed spelling list. For math, she could spend a certain amount of time working through the problems for practice and show proficiency in the concept rather than completing ten practice problems correctly. Her teacher agreed to alter assignments for a month or two to see how the changes might impact Heather's anxiety. Initially, Heather was the one to balk at the changes and reported worry that her classmates would notice that she was being treated differently. Her parents talked this through with her and helped Heather to see that no one in the class knows what is inside each homework folder, as the teacher simply announces that homework is either completion of the lesson practice not completed during class or is the worksheet in their folders. Heather's teacher also accepted emailed photographs of Heather's work written in the dirt as proof of lesson practice and enjoyed the concept so much herself that she offered small trays filled with salt for the other students to write their spelling words with their fingers, too! Heather was eventually able to show some decreases in the number of times she erased and changed her answers. Her parents were pleased with the decrease, and it was unclear if they would choose to continue with play therapy to allow Heather time and space to continue her growth or if they would be taking a break from treatment.

In this case, it was hard to get Heather's parents completely on board with the treatment. They saw the need for the work and were grateful for the improvements noted. However, they expressed concerns about the amount of time therapy would take and were reluctant to change their routines at home to continue Heather's progress. They were willing to encourage Heather to spend time outside and change her homework routine but would not fully engage in changing their own routines. A parent-only session was planned to discuss their reluctance and encourage them to see how Heather's symptoms were impacting the family unit and being impacted by the family unit. This had been explored at the beginning of treatment, but their continued reluctance to engage suggested that further work needed to be done in this domain.

Tucker

Family history and symptom presentation

Tucker is a seven-year-old boy who is currently living in a long-term foster placement, where he has been for four months. He was removed from his biological mother's care after neglect charges were substantiated. Tucker was left alone overnight many times since around the age of five. Prior to age five, he and his biological mother often lived with his maternal grandmother until she gave Tucker's mother an ultimatum which was not met. Tucker and his mother then lived in their own apartment with very limited contact with his grandmother. It is not clear if Tucker's mother had a drug history or not, but as far as his foster family is aware, he met all developmental milestones on time and there was no concern about the presence of drugs in his system at birth. His foster family does not have details about why his biological mother would leave Tucker home alone, but Tucker's understanding is that she was working. Thus, his school attendance was sporadic, and he was often left to find his own breakfast out of whatever food happened to be in the apartment. He came to the attention of child protective services after his school reported truancy. Tucker's school counselor reported that he often wore the same clothes throughout the week and had trouble concentrating in school, staring out the window. He would perk up at lunchtime but would sit alone at the end of a table, eating the school meal quickly. Anything he did not finish would be carefully wrapped in a napkin to go into his backpack to be later stored under his bed. As his academic record is spotty, Tucker is now receiving extra support during the school day to help him catch up in his core academic subjects. His foster mother reports that he is making good progress in many areas and is smart and a quick learner. She mentioned that he tends to notice patterns quickly and is often alert to changes in these patterns, which is also seen in his ability to notice changes to daily routines. When there are even small changes to routines, such as being a few minutes late to school or a parent running a few minutes behind at pickup time, Tucker appears to "freeze up" and turns away from the people around him to engage in his own ritual-like behaviors of tracing patterns on a wall with his finger or tapping a rhythm on his leg.

He presents as a quiet child, interested in the toys around the room and easily able to entertain himself without choosing to interact with the therapist. His foster parents report that he does not engage much in family activities, and they often find food hidden under his bed. Tucker enjoys being in the same room as his foster family members including two foster siblings aged six and nine but does not actively engage in activities with them. His play tends to move between the parallel and associative stages of social play development, which would be expected developmentally between the ages of two to five years old. The foster family lives in an apartment building that has a shared backyard that three other families often use as well. It is a small space, but the family enjoys cooking dinners outside at least once a week during the warmer months when there are multiple children playing in a small kids' pool or running around the outdoor space.

Case formulation

From an attachment-based perspective, Tucker is dealing with the effects of irregular and neglectful attachments. He did not receive consistent attention or experiences of unconditional love from his biological mother, and that has translated into Tucker not being able to consistently develop strong attachments with others. His sense of self is quite limited, as he cannot view himself as worthy of love and attention given his early history. His early understanding of his basic needs being met is wrapped up with his mother needing to go to work and leave him alone, so he is likely struggling with the idea that his needs are so big that they impact an entire family system and therefore he is burdensome. Tucker has not experienced a consistent loving relationship with a caregiver until this foster placement. He has also experienced being left by two caregivers (his grandmother and mother) when money and food ran out. Thus, it makes sense that he keeps extra food safe so that he knows he will always have a little in case he needs it. He does not trust adults to meet his basic needs, nor does he see himself of worth their love and attachment. When Tucker sees adults as failing him, such as being late or not adhering to the schedule they said they would keep, he reverts to meeting his very basic needs by tapping out rhythms or tracing patterns with his fingers on his leg. These actions likely help him to regulate his central nervous system and focus his attention on meeting more basic, primal needs. Thus, Tucker would likely benefit from regulating physical activities mimicking early parent–infant interactions and thus helping him to grow through this developmental stuck point. Given these needs and Tucker's history of attachment-related traumas, Theraplay interventions will be used to build some attachment with his foster family and help him deal with trust issues. Part of this work will be educating his foster parents on the potential impact of his early traumas and ways in which they can support his growth at home and school.

Goals of treatment

There are multiple goals to address for Tucker, and the two that will be highlighted here are his attachment challenges and storing of food in inappropriate places, as these have the most day-to-day impact on his home life.

Given that Tucker's lack of engagement with his foster family is likely occurring because of a traumatic pattern of inconsistent attachment and neglect during periods of critical development, the fact that play is voluntary and fun while nature is nonjudgmental and expands one's sense of belonging leads to initiation of the therapeutic power of attachment in play therapy and natural environment and interconnectedness in nature-based therapy, which will lead to improvements in his ability to actively engage in activities and connection with his foster family.

Given that Tucker's propensity to store food under his bed is likely occurring because of a history of not having enough food readily available and fear of going without food, the fact that play encourages creativity and positive emotions while nature helps create new beliefs leads to initiation of the therapeutic powers of direct teaching and creative problem-solving in play therapy and challenge in nature-based therapy, which will lead to Tucker making more appropriate decisions about where to store extra food.

Individual objectives

Given that we want to help Tucker actively engage in activities with his foster family, how would we do that by utilizing the therapeutic powers of attachment, natural environment, and interconnectedness in a voluntary and fun nature-based play therapy setting? Using a Theraplay modality to improve the attachment between Tucker and his foster parents while helping to repair early developmental traumas grounded in neglect, the domains of structure and nurture will be the initial areas of focus. Routines and structure to the session will be announced and written out on a whiteboard in the room so Tucker and the adults in sessions can easily refer to it and be aware of upcoming changes. As Tucker shows evidence of central nervous system dysregulation when he senses potential disruptions in primary relationships, incorporating nature-based play to meet his regulation needs through repetitive and rhythmic activities will be incorporated into sessions.

Given that we want to help Tucker make more appropriate decisions about where to store extra food, how would we do that by utilizing the therapeutic powers of direct teaching, creative problem-solving, and challenge in a nature-based play therapy session that encourages creativity and positive emotions? From the Theraplay perspective, this issue will be addressed through the challenge domain of activities, as well as during nurturing activities involving food and feeding by his foster parents. Tucker will be encouraged to engage in activities that support him taking age-appropriate risks and needing to make decisions about how to best approach the task with the support of his foster parents.

Model for treatment

Theraplay sessions will first be held indoors. As Tucker also appears to be overwhelmed by competing stimuli, bringing nature-based materials into the play therapy sessions will be the initial way to incorporate nature. For example, during touch and tickling activities, feathers will be used for light touch and soft moss for a slightly deeper yet soothingly soft touch. As he grows in his ability to incorporate competing stimuli, he and his family will be offered the option of trying Theraplay activities on a blanket outdoors. They will also be encouraged to find a quiet and private space outdoors themselves to be able to engage in some of the nurturing activities and spend time sitting together exploring the natural world. This might be choosing a big rock, base of a tree, or a grassy open space at a local park or on a trail where they could sit together and sway or rock back and forth while watching the world around them, claiming the spot as their own. This would be a great time to engage in sit-spotting, during which they quietly observe changes in the environment as the seasons change. The family will also be asked to encourage Tucker in some risky play activities on playgrounds and during their own time spent in nature. This kind of play will complement the Theraplay domain of challenge and encourage Tucker to continue to develop his creative problem-solving abilities and take developmentally appropriate chances and trust himself.

Outcomes

Tucker presented quietly to each session, waiting patiently to hear what the schedule for the session would be. He did not talk much but willingly offered his hands and feet to have lotion applied during the introduction to Theraplay. He smiled briefly during the early engagement activities and appeared willing but slightly hesitant to relax into his foster mother during the nurturing activities. This slowly changed over time, and Tucker's willingness to engage with his foster mother was seen as his eye contact shifted. At first, he looked at the therapist or out the window when he and his mother were engaging in activities, and he gradually began to glance at his foster mother as sessions progressed. One day a few weeks into treatment, Tucker's foster mother was offering him bites of a snack as she verbally gave him a compliment or noticed one of his abilities. Initially, Tucker reached out for the food with his hand, but was able to quickly relax and wait for her to finish her statement before accepting the bite. Over the course of a few minutes, Tucker was observed to wait patiently, eyes bright and focused on hers, listening with his mouth closed to hear her comment before smiling and opening his mouth for the treat. Her eyes lit up as well, and the burgeoning connection between the two was palpable.

Tucker's foster family reported that they were able to choose an outdoor spot to claim as their own, and Tucker participated in finding the location. He chose a large oak tree whose roots formed little "seats" around it so that his foster siblings could also comfortably participate. While he was reluctant to talk about the tree and the experience of choosing it, his foster mother reported that he seemed happy to search as a family and that Tucker was incredibly content to snuggle first against the tree, and then into her lap as they settled in to observe their surroundings. After they had visited their tree three times, Tucker told his therapist about some changes he had noticed in the surroundings, mostly about the number of leaves that were on low-hanging branches. He said he was waiting to see an animal nearby as he had seen a hole dug at the base of a nearby tree and had some thoughts about who could be living in there. He wondered about how the animal would find and store food for the coming winter, which allowed for opening a discussion about appropriately storing food and how much was reasonable for one creature to have available.

Tucker's foster mother continued to engage in feeding activities during Theraplay sessions. He slowly began to see her as capable of providing his food. She also began to specifically tell him how much food she was preparing for meals and involved him in cleaning up afterward so he could package the leftover food to store in the refrigerator. Tucker was told that he was welcome to eat any of this food if he was hungry later in the day, and they made sure he had access to a plate that was stored on a lower shelf so he could easily reach it. Tucker was asked to choose a snack to take to school to supplement his lunch or to have available in his backpack should he feel he needed one during the day. Gradually, he stopped taking leftover food home from his lunch and began finishing his meal in the cafeteria. At one point, he asked if he could keep a snack on his night table overnight. His foster mother agreed, and they chose some snacks that were prepackaged so he could choose one to keep nearby. In this way, she was both showing that food would always be provided for him in this household and giving him some of the control over how and when such food was accessed. As his basic needs were consistently met in all of these ways, the nurture activities helped to solidify his basic need of being cared for and protected.

Jaylani

Family history and symptom presentation

Jaylani is a 12-year-old girl who lives with her parents and two older brothers (aged 16 and 14). Her mother brought her to play therapy at the suggestion of her guidance counselor, as Jaylani has been getting into fights at school. Recently fights have escalated from verbal arguments to hitting, pushing, and punching on the arms. Her mother reports that Jaylani has been arguing with her brothers more frequently at home and "always has a mean word to say." The siblings have always been physical with each other in terms of roughhousing and appropriate physical play, but Jaylani's mother has noticed an increase in Jaylani initiating arguments and said she has begun hitting her brothers with little provocation. They do not typically hit back, at least not with full strength, but her mother is having a harder time stopping Jaylani physically and is worrying for everyone's safety. Jaylani has no solid answer for why she has begun engaging in physical fights but says "no one listens anyway" and "everyone is always yelling at and with me so why am I the one getting in trouble?" Her mother reports that tempers do flare quickly at home, but it also feels like there is a standing tension throughout the week from everyone, as though they are just walking in the door expecting a verbal fight, so everyone is always on edge. Jaylani is the only sibling to start physical altercations, and typically her father would pick her up and bring her to her bedroom when she started getting "too handsy" when slapping at her siblings to remove her from the situation. Now that he is working a second shift job, he is not typically present after dinner when these fights are occurring. Jaylani's mother tries to physically remove her from the situation or at least restrain her movements by wrapping her arms around Jaylani's arms, but now that Jaylani is around the same height as her mother, this does not work well.

Jaylani and her family live in a three-bedroom inner-city apartment in which she has her own room. Jaylani reports that her parents both work two jobs, with her mother cleaning houses and her father doing landscaping jobs during the day and working in a local grocery store in the evenings. Her oldest brother works after school at the grocery store as well. Her 14-year-old brother would like to get a job when he turns 15, but for now he helps older neighbors with their household chores and errands on Saturdays. Jaylani says she is not able to even help her neighbors right now because her parents do not trust her to be in other people's apartments without one of her siblings present. So, she tends to come home after school where she watches television and does part of her homework. The entire family keeps Sunday as a day to be together as often as possible. They tend to stay around the apartment, catching up on chores, enjoying a special dinner, and attending a Baptist church at least a few times a month. Their church has some programming for teens and preteens, but the family does not attend many of these events. Jaylani says this is because there is no one to take her to church on Friday nights, and her parents will not let her walk alone.

Outside of the arguments and fighting at school, Jaylani's school reports are fine. There are no academic concerns for her, her homework is mostly turned in on time and complete, and her teachers have no concerns about attention per her guidance counselor's report. There are no symptoms of depression or anxiety reported from any sources. She has a core group of two female friends with whom she spends much of her downtime at school and likes to get to school a bit early to hang out with them when she can. There is no family history of mental health concerns for any of her siblings, parents, or grandparents. There are no grandparents or extended family members in the area, but the family all gets together twice a year (Thanksgiving and the Fourth of July) at Jaylani's maternal grandparents' home. Jaylani reports enjoying these times and is looking forward to the upcoming Thanksgiving holiday so they can all be together. She misses her cousins.

Jaylani's mother brings her to therapy sessions as her father's work hours interfere with the schedule. The two sit next to each other on a couch in the waiting area, and Jaylani touches her mother's arm or hugs her before entering sessions. Her mother routinely appears tired, but her eyes brighten noticeably when Jaylani returns to the waiting area. Her mother's description of the family is of a solid lower working-class unit who enjoys their downtime together and "earns" this time by working quite hard during the week. She enjoys the quiet Sundays and how the family can stay around the apartment together. They do not typically spend much time outdoors as it is not a priority for them given the amount of time they are away from home and are busy just maintaining their daily lives.

Case formulation

Jaylani was introduced to nature-based play therapy from an Adlerian perspective. Her therapist spoke with Jaylani and her mother separately, and it quickly became clear that Jaylani was struggling with a sense of not counting in her family unit. Everyone else was contributing financially to the family's daily life, and she was unable to do so. She did not feel capable of making a difference at all and was responding by both seeking negative attention and asserting power over her peers in a negative way. Getting into fights at school had the joint benefit of bringing her to her parents' attention and giving her an area in which to feel strong and capable. Obviously, this was not the healthiest way to gain the attention and sense of making a difference, but it was certainly tangible and provided immediate results. It was determined that helping Jaylani to discover her own strengths and contributions to the family would help her to feel more capable in her growing abilities as a preteen and show her various ways in which she could count in her family's daily lives.

Goals of treatment

Given that Jaylani's power struggles and fights at school and home are likely occurring because she does not feel that she counts within her family system and she is trying to seek attention in a negative way and feel powerful, the fact that play is flexible, voluntary, and fun while nature enhances one's sense of self and expands one's sense of belonging leads to initiation of the therapeutic powers of resiliency, self-esteem, and self-regulation, with the nature-based therapeutic factor of interconnectedness, which will lead to improvements in her ability to appropriately engage with her brothers and peers, and help her develop a sense of counting and making a difference in her world.

Given these needs and Jaylani's potential feelings of inferiority and not counting in her family unit, the overall goals here became to increase Jaylani's sense of positive power in her own life and help her see how capable she was of making a meaningful difference in the lives of herself and her family. Finding an appropriate role within her household, especially since she wanted to contribute in a meaningful way to the family's daily life and overall connection, was important for Jaylani. As every other family member held a meaningful role not only within the family but also by contributing to society, it was important to help Jaylani see how she could make an impact in the larger scheme as well.

Individual objectives

Given that we want to help Jaylani reduce how often she is engaging in fights with her brothers and peers, how would we do that by utilizing the therapeutic powers of self-esteem, self-regulation, resilience, and interconnectedness in a nature-based play therapy session that encourages her to develop a sense of belonging and counting within her family and the greater whole? As Jaylani often feels pushed aside at home, she has learned to react very quickly and strongly to any perceived insult to her capabilities. Integrating play and nature will allow her opportunities to see growth from multiple perspectives and determine ways in which she can count and be capable herself.

Model for treatment

This will be a case of bringing nature to the child rather than taking the child into nature given the location of the home and therapy spaces. Jaylani's mother is eager to be involved in the therapeutic process as she would like to see her daughter both happy and developing well and wants to reduce stressful conflicts within the home. These conflicts were discussed as opportunities to determine power and capability, so her mother was encouraged to show Jaylani how necessary her help around the apartment was through her chores. Helping her to delineate her own role and function within the family without needing to fight to be seen would let the family enjoy their time at home together more often. This would also help with easing the burden of troubles at school. As Jaylani seemed to be begging for opportunities to be involved, her mother was asked to explore potential opportunities for her, such as getting involved in a school or church group, perhaps volunteering with something like a backpack program and seeking donations of food or helping to organize an outdoor workday at the church so she could see the need for various levels of involvement with larger projects. Her mother also discussed wanting to make time for the family to be together a few times a week. She was encouraged to let Jaylani pick the activity or game for one of these times. Her parents were encouraged to utilize outdoor spaces when possible, by taking a picnic lunch to a nearby park at least one Sunday a month and asking Jaylani to help plan the menus and activities.

In sessions, Jaylani was offered activities that incorporated nature and play at age-appropriate levels. She enjoyed artistic and creative activities, especially those that included physical activity. Puppets were offered to create a puppet show, and Jaylani was asked to help create props for a nature-based show including trees and other greenery as well as additional animal puppets out of paper bags and socks.

Outcomes

In developing her puppet show, Jaylani created multiple animal puppets and props, and her creativity and problem-solving skills were noticed and encouraged. She began to seek innovative ways to create her animals, such as gluing pine needles onto the back of a bag to create a baby hedgehog. She began to mutter comments like "I wonder if …" before she began to try a new technique for creating something. When an idea did not work out, she initially became aggravated and would crumble the bag she was using to throw it away. Over time, as her efforts were praised, her sense of resiliency and determination began to grow, and she could more easily recover from perceived failures and try new options. She would even begin to ask the therapist to seek out other nature-based supplies to have on hand for further creation, such as more acorn tops to use as eyes and various sizes of twigs for limbs. Jaylani began to see herself capable of creating these detailed toys and capable of sharing her needs, and worth enough to have them be met.

One activity that Jaylani particularly enjoyed during sessions stemmed from picture cards that were available in the office to create stories and utilize metaphors. Jaylani and her therapist would each pick three cards and create a story utilizing the three images. Jaylani became excited and animated as she developed her stories. She would often create detailed narratives weaving the three images together and through this process showed themes of protecting the smallest living creature in the images and detailing how actions by that creature created a ripple effect of impacts across all the images. For example, in one story she noticed an ant in the lower corner of an image. The other two images included a picture of the tops of trees in a forest from a bottom-up perspective and a garden of flowers. She wove a tale about this ant working to feed its family and the lengths it would go to in order to be sure all of the ants in the colony were well-fed as they went about their jobs in various parts of the colony. This ant brought back seeds from the flowers one by one until an entire section of the storage area of the colony was filled with seeds. It then worked on the leaves to bring a selection of healthy food to its colony and watched with pride as the colony grew and flourished. Jaylani was able to detail this ant's need to feel that it counted and had a role in its colony, and the lengths it would go to be capable of filling its role. Jaylani was able to listen to an interpretation of this story as potentially relating to her own life, and then shared a worry she had held onto about her brothers as not taking enough time to feed themselves well between school and running off to their jobs. She asked her mother if she could accompany her on grocery shopping trips to help choose some healthier foods that she could prepare for them and was so excited to report that her brothers loved her food and asked her to keep creating meals that were easy to pack for them. Jaylani and her mother also made plans to start a small container garden for vegetables on a section of their balcony, and she was eager to get started.

The family reported taking a picnic lunch to a nearby park once a month. Once there, they would eat, talk, and laugh, and then a football game would typically get started. This opportunity to run around and roughhouse appropriately with her brothers and father also helped meet a physical need for connection for Jaylani. In these afternoons, Jaylani was able to help her mother prepare the food for the outing and physically engage with her male relatives. Growing up with older brothers gave Jaylani frequent opportunities to engage in physical play as a young child, and as she grew and developed, her male relatives necessarily changed how they physically interacted with her. As she entered her teen years, Jaylani was missing these physical interactions and commented that she was glad to have the football matches as a way to continue engaging with them. She spoke about how she was able to maintain both the physical activity connection with her brothers and father, and the nurturing connection of feeding them with her mother, thus finding ways to connect, count, and be capable in multiple areas and relationships. While she did not end up getting active in volunteer activities, Jaylani mentioned that she was considering ways to become involved as she got a little older and would be able to get herself to different functions, but for now was happier and more content in her relationships within her family. "I see how I matter to them, and I see how important it is for me to be able to do stuff for and with them," she said. "I like how I can help them and that makes me feel really good, too."

Concluding thoughts

The examples that these children and families share highlight the importance of integrating nature and play therapy following case conceptualization by actively utilizing a theoretical orientation to understand the client and presenting strengths and challenges. Once this conceptualization has been completed, the therapeutic factors of nature and powers of play therapy stand out in terms of which can and should be facilitated during sessions. Only then should interventions be determined because only then does what the child need make sense! This conceptualization process is active on the part of the therapist and the more data that is included from intake and observations, the better. This process also allows for flexibility on the part of the therapist as the number of available toys or size of the available nature space does not matter as much as the intentionality behind utilizing each. Once the need for nature-based play is determined, then how to get that need met can be determined, as these examples have shown. In Chapter 9, I will highlight some ethical principles that should be considered as these determinations are made to again help therapists view cases from a completely holistic framework.

Chapter 9

Ethical and other considerations in nature-based play therapy

There are ethical codes, legal statutes, and regulations to guide every licensed mental health profession. More nuanced areas of practice, such as play therapy and nature-based therapies, do not have their own codes of ethical conduct under governing bodies. Thus, nature-based play therapists must follow the ethical principles of their professional affiliations, and legal statutes and regulations of their licensing boards. In this chapter, I outline specific considerations for ethical principles in nature-based play therapy that are universal in practice and encourage the clinician to consider individual cases from an ethical standpoint. This includes but is not limited to accessibility, cultural considerations (including race, ethnicity, ability, and more), and responsibility to the community. More specific recommendations will be described including obtaining appropriate consent from parents and clients, privacy and confidentiality, first aid training, and other considerations.

Ethical principles should always guide and determine therapeutic interactions, and nature-based play therapy requires general as well as some specific ethical considerations. I will assume that you have a general understanding of the ethical principles that govern your clinical profession and will spend time here outlining some suggestions for ethical considerations specific to nature-based play therapy. A limitation here is that I cannot cover every possible potential ethical dilemma, and a second limitation is that I am not a lawyer or licensing board reviewer. Please take these suggestions and considerations as "things to consider" rather than "must do" items, and always consult with your malpractice insurance provider and other professionals to discuss your specific considerations.

As a psychologist, I follow the American Psychological Association's ethical code. This code starts with outlining five general principles: Beneficence and Nonmaleficence, Fidelity and Responsibility, Integrity, Justice, and Respect for People's Rights and Dignity (American Psychological Association, 2017). Ethics codes are generally similar, with the National Association of Social Workers outlining principles of service, social justice, dignity and worth of the person, integrity, competence, and importance of human relationships (National Association

DOI: 10.4324/9781003332343-9

of Social Workers, 2017) and the BC Association of Clinical Counsellors delineating Respect for the Dignity of All Persons and Peoples, Responsible Caring, Integrity in Relationships, and Responsibility to Society (BC Association of Clinical Counsellors, 2014). The American Counseling Association is like these, including autonomy, nonmaleficence, beneficence, justice, fidelity, and veracity as their core principles for ethical considerations (American Counseling Association, 2014). The five principles from the American Psychological Association are a good place to start examining ethical considerations as the concepts include most of these categories. The principles do not stand alone, and thus, the discussion about each in relation to integrating nature into play therapy should not be taken individually either. These are general principles that should guide thinking about inclusion of nature in play therapy, as ethical issues are often fluid and require thinking through multiple areas of potential conflict and resolution. The Association for Play Therapy (2022) has published the Play Therapy Best Practices document which aligns well with these principles as it outlines guidelines for the best ethical practice of play therapy and will be discussed where appropriate herein.

Beneficence and nonmaleficence

The first general principle, Beneficence and Nonmaleficence, speaks to the need to benefit our clients and not do harm. When considering nature-based play therapy from this perspective, there are two major considerations: Will integrating nature benefit our clients, and how can it provide a harmful situation? As with any therapy-related question, the answer for both is "it depends." The early chapters of this book included discussions about why including nature can be incredibly powerful for clients. We also need to consider why it could not be beneficial. Some clients struggle with significant allergies or texture sensitivities, and thus, time in nature could cause more anxiety than help, at least without significant preparation. Perhaps integrating carefully selected natural materials into an enclosed play space, or choosing to not intentionally integrate nature at all, would make more sense for these clients. The nonmaleficence section is a good reminder to make sure that any nature-based play space we might use is as safe as we can make it. Just as a therapist would not include broken glass or other hazards in a playroom, it is important to check outdoor play spaces for potential hazards including but not limited to broken glass, garbage, animals, and plants that can cause negative reactions.

Developing our own competence in nature-based play therapy is important, too. If incorporating nature into play or taking play into nature is new to you, it would be well worth your time to seek training and consultation to ensure your own growth so that you can provide the best benefit to clients without doing harm. This includes not just the "how" of how to integrate the two fields safely and appropriately but also the "why" of why you are choosing to integrate the two modalities and understanding your choice from a theoretical and therapeutic factors perspective. This process will help you determine if you are truly choosing to utilize this modality for the client's benefit or are integrating nature and play for your own purposes.

Fidelity and responsibility

The second principle, Fidelity and Responsibility, speaks to developing a relationship of trust and covers our responsibility to society and community. The first part of this, developing a relationship of trust, really speaks to the therapist's need to explain the role of nature in play therapy sessions and get the client's express agreement should sessions take place outside. The client needs to be aware of what expectations are of both the client and the therapist, and where physical boundaries exist around the play space. This is also a reminder to discuss with the client and family what nature-based play therapy is and is not, so they can make an informed decision about whether they choose to engage in this service. Informed consent, while important in any type of therapy, must now include an additional element of describing the form of nature-based play therapy along with potential benefits and limitations. There are examples of informed consent documents available in other resources, and I would encourage you to discuss your version with both a lawyer and your malpractice insurance provider to be sure you have covered the necessary basics.

When working with minor clients, we have the added necessity of gaining assent from the child in addition to informed consent from the guardian. As this is often the child's therapy time and space, they should be given the opportunity to understand what they are agreeing to in terms of participation and services. This could be a simple conversation about what is being offered with nature-based play therapy and allowing the child the opportunity to agree with services or decline the option. Giving the child the option to choose which services in which they will participate allows them to develop trust and respect within the therapeutic relationship, which is the core of the fidelity and responsibility guideline.

The responsibility to society and community is particularly important when integrating nature into play therapy. Part of being a good steward of natural spaces is caretaking for the natural world so it can continue to grow and exist. This includes keeping spaces clean and using sustainable harvesting techniques. Going back to the conservation versus preservation mindsets, for example, it is not wise to take all of a plant when you are gathering leaves or plants to bring inside for activities. Making sure that there are plenty of plants left to continue propagating is vital for continued maintenance and growth of an area. In many cases, this means leaving at least seven to ten of a variety untouched so there is plenty of opportunity for the plant to continue to grow and thrive. When taking materials for use, only taking what one needs is another good concept. It is not likely that a client needs the entire tree to create a nature collage, but rather a few leaves or twigs. Picking up most of the fallen sticks in an area is one thing, but stripping an area bare of plant life is completely different! Leaving a space better than you found it is a responsible way to utilize natural resources. Many nature-based therapists utilize a "take nothing but pictures" framework, while other groups who work in the outdoors follow "leave no trace." I respectfully suggest that there can be a balance found in these views, and that responsible moderation in terms of utilizing natural resources can be found and utilized. Above all, the rules of the space you use must be followed. Some places have posted signs indicating whether natural materials may be harvested or must be left alone. It is your responsibility to be aware of these rules per space.

Integrity

Integrity, the third general principle, relates to a clinician's accuracy, honesty, and truthfulness. This principle reminds the therapist to not engage in deceitful activities, especially during therapy. Relating to nature-based play therapy, following this principle encourages the play therapist to be truthful about potential experiences and not make a commitment that cannot be reasonably kept. At a very basic level, this could include not telling a client that they will see a certain species of bird as a bribe to get them outside. It also includes not telling a client that an object or material will not harm them when in fact you are not certain or even telling them that they will not get hurt outside. You can, however, tell clients that you will do your best to keep them safe and protect them, but that they will have to make some considerations themselves as well. Nature can be fickle, and being open about how varying temperatures and weather might impact sessions can go a long way toward practicing integrity (as well as modeling how to make appropriate preparations, and that is another issue to consider!).

Justice

Justice is the fourth general principle and describes the need for equal access and opportunities for therapy services in general. When we consider integrating nature into play therapy sessions, making nature available for all clients becomes necessary. The way in which nature is offered may change, but the offering of nature should apply to all clients. For example, I would always have natural materials available in my playroom for all clients to utilize, but use of an outdoor space would depend upon availability, safety of the space, and need of the client. The play therapy session may be one of the only times a particular client gets to truly experience and explore a natural world, so understanding a client's "nature history" is also important here. Cultural and historical considerations must be considered through this process, including but not limited to experiences in nature from personal and collective pasts. This is a good time to think about understanding how each client defines "nature" or "outdoors" as well. Their definitions might not include "open green space" as you might hope they do. It is also possible that traumatic life events occurred in a nature-based setting, and that could be impacting their thoughts on going outside and exploring. Understanding what they have available and are familiar with is key to offering and suggesting equal access and opportunities within nature-based play therapy. This is also an important concept in terms of deciding what to suggest for outdoor time outside of sessions. If the family does not have easy access to a park or trail system, then encouraging open time outdoors as a family may take a different explanation and creativity. The Association for Play Therapy's Best Practices (2022) speaks to understanding the diverse cultural backgrounds with which clients present, and this is equally important in nature-based play therapy. Some cultures do not view time in nature as beneficial but instead a waste of time. Pushing for time spent outdoors without exploring this worldview would be highly disrespectful to clients at a minimum and demonstrate a complete lack of understanding of the client's world.

Respect for people's rights and dignity

The fifth principle is Respect for People's Rights and Dignity. This principle refers to aspects of service including privacy, confidentiality, self-determination, and a recognition of strengths and differences. Privacy and confidentiality are two of the biggest areas of concern clinicians tend to have. The question of how we can maintain privacy if play therapy sessions are held outside of a traditional office is common. Again, there is no one answer to this question. Some play therapists have private "backyards" that abut their office spaces and become an extension of the playroom, which allows for privacy and confidentiality. Other play therapists choose to take clients on nature walks in more public areas, play at a nearby playground, or utilize an open park space to get outside, all of which require the consent of the caregiver as well as the assent of the client. They should decide together if the risk of breaching privacy is worth the anticipated outcome of the session, and that decision lies solely with the client and caregivers. Making this an open and ongoing discussion is the job of the therapist, as is discussing how potential breaches of confidentiality will be handled, especially if you are working in a public or open outdoor space. I suggest that you discuss options like nodding an acknowledgment toward another acquaintance you pass and continue on in your work, or perhaps saying you are in a meeting and will connect with them another time. Your client may also see people they know so discussing how they might like to acknowledge (or ignore) such acquaintances is important.

Self-determination speaks to how a client should have the option to decide if they want to include nature in a session or not, just as they should be able to choose if they want to attend therapy or not. They should have the option to stay indoors if an outdoor play space is offered, just as they can choose to utilize natural materials inside the playroom or not. Encouraging freedom of choice is how the Association for Play Therapy (2022) describes this concept, and it is vitally important for children to feel they have a say in their own treatment and that their opinions will be respected. The rationale for your clinical judgment in offering nature-based play therapy should be presented in a developmentally appropriate manner for both clients and families, which goes back to obtaining assent from minor clients and informed consent from guardians. Your rationale should also be documented in your client's case file, as should a treatment plan. The model presented in this book can help you develop the rationale along with treatment goals and objectives needed for this treatment plan.

Recognizing the strengths and differences people have is an interesting aspect to consider in nature-based play therapy. Every person has a different experience of the natural world, influenced by their own experiences, societal expectations, and intergenerational influences from their own families. Within that, each person brings their own strengths and knowledge of the natural world to play therapy sessions. This is clear in my own family unit. My husband has a great knowledge of tree identification, and our boys have decided to learn their trees as well. On any hike we take, I will hear them teaching and quizzing their younger sister on tree identification! Our kids also love learning about amphibians we encounter along the way, while I tend toward birds and plants. Individually our knowledge is separate and unique, and when we put it together to explore a new area, we get a much broader understanding of our surroundings. The same thing happens when a therapist and a client interact in the natural world. Each brings their own experiences and knowledge and can learn and grow together. This brings in the idea of a clinician's nature-based competence. What do you know of the natural world around you? What can you recognize and point out? What are the common poisonous plants and venomous creatures around you, and are you capable of recognizing them? Do you have basic first aid training and a way to summon help quickly enough should there be an accident? A nature-based play therapist does not need to know everything there is to know about everything in nature. It is more important to know what you do know, and know it well, and know what you still need to know!

Therapeutic and other considerations

Personal biases

Understanding your own potential biases about nature as a nature-based play therapist is crucial. This is why the questions about your own experiences in nature and thoughts about how nature has impacted your own development were included in the introduction to this book. Combining your understanding of your own experiences and definition of nature, and learning what the individual client has experienced, is a big step toward being able to treat each person fairly and with full respect, while also respecting your own boundaries and limitations. Through this process of self-exploration, you might discover some areas that could benefit from growth through consultation or therapy. It is important to be aware of these areas so that you can provide sound treatment for your clients.

Developing competency and seeking consultation

One thing that is clear across ethical codes is that therapists should be competent in the treatment they are providing. Nature-based play therapy may be a new area of practice for you as a provider. It is worth seeking supervision or consultation, along with trainings in ecotherapy and nature-based play, to develop competency. There are multiple training institutes around the world that offer courses in ecotherapy and nature-based therapies, and many individuals providing nature-based therapies who can serve as experts for consultation. Along with all the considerations presented here, I encourage nature-based play therapists to know how far you are willing to go with your practice of ecotherapy. This will help you continue to provide ethically sound nature-based play therapy sessions.

Therapeutic frame and boundaries

During indoor play therapy sessions, the therapeutic frame and physical boundaries of the space are relatively clear. The therapist is an adult and holds some power in the relationship, regardless of theoretical orientation. The therapist determines the length of time the session will last, is aware of shifts and transitions during the session, and brings the session to a close and helps the client transition out of the office. The walls of the playroom define the physical boundaries of the therapy space. When bringing nature into a playroom, these frame markers and boundaries do not shift drastically. However, when nature-based play therapy occurs in an outdoor play space, all these dynamics shift, even if just barely. The therapist should be aware of and expect these changes so the impact (both positive and negative) can be monitored. At a very basic level, we all develop internalized frames of therapy and markers that alert us when the session is drawing to a close. Personally, I have always seen that my sense of the passage of time changes when I am outside. Thus, this is something I need to be extra aware of during outdoor play therapy sessions. I do not have one or more clocks positioned around an outdoor space to alert me to the passage of time and the end of the session. Checking a watch or phone feels more obtrusive to me but becomes something I need to manage during each outdoor play session.

Along with identifying the end of session time, therapists also need to adjust how they help a client transition out of an outdoor play space. Some therapists create markers that indicate an entrance or exit to the outdoor space and have a small ritual around approaching the marker. This could be as large as an archway that clients walk under to transition between indoor and outdoor spaces or as small as river stones to create a tiny pathway or a plant near the entrance that can be noticed on the way in and out of the space. No matter what the transition item is, it can be helpful to have something delineating the transition point.

Outdoor play spaces can also feel overwhelming at times without the physical boundary walls of an office create. Defining the physical boundaries of an outdoor play space can be quite useful, especially when introducing nature-based play therapy. This helps both the client and the therapist to create or recognize a container for the therapeutic work within such a dynamic and changing space. These physical boundaries do not need to be physical, as with a fence or a hedgerow. Children are often familiar with "invisible boundaries," such as staying on one side of a tree and imagining a boundary line between two physical objects. Touring the outer boundaries of an outdoor play space when introducing outdoor nature-based play therapy is a useful way to help create the sense of containment within the therapeutic work.

As I think about all these considerations, I also think about when it makes sense to suggest or encourage outdoor play time during therapy. Some therapists might start out a therapeutic relationship by always meeting outside. Others offer it as a potential avenue for treatment when the client requests to go outside. Most fall somewhere between these two. Determining at what point during a therapeutic relationship the idea is suggested does depend upon your modality, theoretical understanding of the importance of integrating nature for the specific client, and personal factors of the client. While I do believe that time in nature benefits everyone, the degree to which I will encourage clients to engage in outdoor nature-based play therapy or even outdoor activities outside of sessions differs. We as therapists strive to help clients achieve comfort during in-office sessions (even if this comfort comes after some degree of therapeutic distress!). This can look different in nature-based play therapy sessions. What is the client's comfort level with the outdoors? Are there fears that are not present in the office that we should be aware of (usually related to weather or animals)? What is the weather like right now? What role will the weather play in comfort? Choosing to run around and play in the rain and get soaking wet leads to a very different reaction than being caught in an unexpected downpour while wearing your favorite new outfit!

Allergies and sensitivities

Integrating nature into play therapy also means integrating knowledge of allergies and sensitivities in a way that could be easy to gloss over in traditional indoor play therapy sessions. Do your clients suffer seasonal allergies, or are they allergic to insect stings or poison ivy? What is your plan for handling a low-level allergic reaction all the way up to an anaphylactic reaction, and can you identify the warning signs of these? Where will the guardian be during sessions? Knowing how you plan to react when first aid is needed is also important.

When leaving an indoor play space to move to an outdoor environment, taking your own bag with a first aid kit and cell phone to call for help if needed is useful. Once a family agrees to outdoor play therapy sessions, discussing their preference for applying sunscreen to their child before session and using insect repellant during session can also be helpful.

Risky or adventurous play

Depending on your environment, children may engage in risky or adventurous play. It is important to understand both your outdoor space and your own thoughts on limits to these environments. As discussed previously, there are tremendous benefits to allowing a child to fully explore outdoor environments through climbing, racing, running, and navigating obstacles. These physical and cognitive benefits can line up nicely with therapeutic treatment goals. However, every adult has a different window of tolerance in terms of which aspects of this play they are comfortable with and how far they are willing to let children explore before intervening themselves. It is important to be aware of your own limits on these behaviors and explorations as well as the limits of the child's family members so that you are aware of what you might be activating within the family should you encourage these behaviors. If a parent has always stopped risky play due to risk of injury and the parent's own anxiety over what might happen, the child can be either too anxious to engage in the play or overly exuberant when it comes to the exploration because the parent is not watching and stopping the play. If the discussion about these boundaries is not held prior to sessions, there may be some repercussions you need to handle afterward when the child bounces home to share just how far they got on the edge of that huge rock!

Dirt and the weather

On a lighter note, another consideration is dirt. Nature comes with dirt. There is no getting around that. Given the opportunity, children will find the dirt, play in the dirt, and cover themselves in the dirt. Most children do not have a problem with this. Parents and other adults, however, often do. It is worth your time to warn caregivers about the certainty of getting dirty during nature-based play therapy sessions and encourage them to have children dress in play clothes they can get messy. It is also a good idea to keep some aprons or smocks available should parents or children request them.

Along with this consideration, being aware of weather and temperature changes is important if you will be going outside. Most children also love puddles and mud, and being prepared for these eventualities will help the session remain a positive experience. Changes in the weather impact outdoor nature-based play therapy sessions much differently than either traditional play therapy sessions or indoor nature-based play therapy. Things to consider here include what if plans need to change because of upcoming weather or what if the weather changes drastically during an outdoor session itself and requires flexibility on the part of the therapist and client? Would both the client and the therapist be prepared to make these adjustments, or should indoor sessions be considered as a primary modality?

Concluding thoughts

All in all, there are many ethical and other considerations present when engaging in nature-based play therapy. Some of these fall within the ethical scope of practice, while others are more therapeutic in nature. Many of them are specific to bringing clients into outdoor spaces for nature-based play. Being aware of ways to ethically practice and guidelines for best practices as well as your own understanding of nature and the multidimensional enrichment and challenges it can bring will help guide you to provide developmentally appropriate services that are inclusive of clients' needs and circumstances, creating the core components of nature-based play therapy.

References

American Counseling Association. (2014). *2014 ACA code of ethics.* https://www. counseling.org/docs/default-source/default-document-library/2014-code-of-ethics-finaladdress.pdf?sfvrsn=96b532c_8

American Psychological Association. (2017, January 1). *Ethical principles of psychologists and code of conduct.* https://www.apa.org/ethics/code

Association for Play Therapy. (2022). *Play therapy best practices: Clinical, professional & ethical issues.* https://cdn.ymaws.com/www.a4pt.org/resource/resmgr/publications/best_practices.pdf

BC Association of Clinical Counsellors. (2014). *Code of ethical conduct.* https://bcacc.ca/wp-content/uploads/2022/10/BCACC-Code-of-Ethical-Conduct-2014.pdf

National Association of Social Workers. (2017). *NASW code of ethics.* https://www.socialworkers.org/About/Ethics/Code-of-Ethics/Code-of-Ethics-English#principles

Chapter 10

Special adaptations of nature-based play therapy

Now that the rationale for utilizing nature-based play therapy with individuals and the importance of understanding theory and the therapeutic powers of nature and play have been thoroughly explored, adaptations to nature-based play therapy can be discussed. The adaptations that will be introduced here include using nature-based play therapy with families and groups, parent coaching specific to integrating nature and play, and nature-based play therapy supervision (bringing nature into supervision and bringing supervision into nature!). The parent coaching aspect is specifically designed to encourage families and individuals to get outside more frequently and will include some activities for families and parents to consider. The activities included here will be games and activities that can be adapted to outdoor play, fun nature-based activities, adventures to create and make happen, and so on. As always, understand why you are considering and choosing nature-based methods as you consider ways to adapt the method!

Using nature-based play therapy with families and groups

As we explored in Tommy's case study, including nature in play therapy can be powerful when working with families or groups! As with individual therapy, options include bringing nature in to the sessions and bringing the sessions out to nature. Families can also be guided in ways to include more nature time outside of session. In Tommy's example, the Summer family was encouraged to spend time together in nature outside of session as well as participated in outdoor sessions. Nature-based family play therapy sessions can be a wonderful opportunity to extend assessment of family dynamics and interactions. It is not uncommon for parents struggle a bit when asked to be part of sessions outdoors. They are more aware of safety issues that could emerge for their children and want to stop them from engaging in what could otherwise be considered age-appropriate explorations. As discussed previously, the tendency for society to trend toward risk-adverse outdoor play can become evident in family play therapy sessions held outdoors! At these times it is important for the therapist to be overt with the

DOI: 10.4324/9781003332343-10

parents in regard to explanations of what acceptable behavior is and what will be stopped for safety reasons. Knowing that the therapist will be closely watching but also that not every accident can be avoided is a powerfully therapeutic conversation for many parents. Watching how parents react after this type of conversation is also quite telling. Are they able to step back and trust the therapist or child to lead? Do they continue to hover? Did they need the conversation to happen at all, or were they already comfortable letting their children physically explore the environment with only support requested by the children? These real-life experiences can be priceless in the therapy setting, and nature-based play therapy is perfectly suited for this exploration.

An additional benefit of nature-based family play therapy sessions, when held outdoors, is the increase in space available for games to be played by the entire family and playful interactions to grow bigger than possible inside four walls. In my smaller offices, it has been hard to engage in family sessions at times because there simply is not enough room for everyone to be physically comfortable. When play is added in, the tension of the physical space limiting movements can be felt and can contribute to challenges in the family dynamics. This is one dynamic that is removed when outdoor spaces are used as the literal confines of the walls are removed. Even if the outdoor space was the same size as my indoor office, not having the physical limitations of the walls and ceilings makes the space seem much more useable and malleable.

As with individual sessions, nature-based play therapy with families should be grounded in theory and the therapeutic powers of nature and play therapy. Intake and assessments should include the family's comfort level with and exposure to nature, as well as allergies and potential negative reactions to plants, animals, and so on, and medical conditions that might be exacerbated by time outside. Presenting concerns of the identified client should be viewed in light of the family system including how the concerns impact and are maintained by the family unit. While some play therapy theoretical orientations more naturally tend toward inclusion of the family unit than others, the importance of the family and role of those relationships should never be discounted. Actively understanding the importance of the therapeutic powers of nature and play to guide initiation and facilitation of these powers during family nature-based play therapy, combined with understanding the role of the family unit in symptom presentation and maintenance, will help guide your case conceptualization and treatment planning process, which will help you focus on the necessary aspects of treatment.

The model presented in this book will be of use in family and group sessions alike. So long as conceptualization from a theoretical perspective is happening, the process of actually integrating nature and play becomes smooth and processes or interventions logically fall into place. In these outdoor nature-based play therapy sessions, the expectations that come with being within four walls are lessened or removed completely. For example, children are expected to physically behave differently outdoors compared to indoors. Moving family or group sessions outdoors removes the expectation to sit still and listen to the leader (in these cases, the therapist). This may be an unconscious expectation, while some families in particular make it more overt and expect the identified client to "behave" and "listen" to the therapeutic wisdom being offered. In nature-based sessions, nature becomes the co-therapist, and simply removing the walls as boundaries lessens this expectation as well. Children are allowed more freedoms outside, and this includes the freedoms to be more expressive, more exploratory, and more active in their own therapy process. This is particularly important for family sessions, but is also useful in a group setting.

In group sessions, the nature-based play therapist does not have just the individuals making up the group to consider but the interactions and relationships between them all as well as the interactions and relationships with nature! This brings a multitude of possibilities to the sessions, as well as a multitude of dynamics to observe and potentially utilize. There will likely be differing levels of comfort with nature. For some groups, the entire scope of treatment can occur in an outdoor space, while for others it makes more sense to either alternate being indoors or outdoors, or bring natural materials to the group indoors only. Any of these options can be utilized in nature-based play therapy so long as interventions are chosen based on the therapist's theoretical understanding of the presenting concerns and the therapeutic powers of play and nature they wish to activate. The traditional phases of group therapy (forming, storming, norming, and performing) occur in outdoor nature-based play therapy. The differences here include the changes in physical boundaries and the addition of relationships with nature. As each person in the group has a different relationship with nature, these additional relationships all come into the therapy group sessions. When boundaries are pushed within the group dynamics, the physical boundaries can also be pushed. This is something to consider when defining the group space and where it is safe or unsafe for group members to physically remove themselves from the group setting, but also important for developing team building or challenge interventions.

Groups can be tricky as often the therapist is not able to consistently pick and choose to create the perfect composition of clients, especially in a school setting. Again, so long as the therapist is grounded in a theoretical understanding of what the clients need and how the group can provide for those needs utilizing specific therapeutic powers of play and nature, success can be had. Within group work, it can be helpful to remember Yalom's (1985) therapeutic group factors. As with the therapeutic powers of play, some of these are particularly well suited to inclusion in nature-based play therapy. For example, the concept of universality is well understood in the nature-based factor of interconnectedness and expanding one's thinking to include more than the self. Seeing trees continue to grow healthy and strong around huge obstacles of rocks and stumps in their path can instill hope as a group relates this metaphor to their individual lives, and the catharsis involved with running, pounding the ground, and other natural outdoor activities can be quite healing within a group setting as well!

A specific consideration of group nature-based play therapy held outdoors is the potential inclusion of a second therapist. For example, consider the physical boundaries of the session and whether you might benefit from having a second group therapist or leader present to help keep clients within the prescribed space. This obviously depends upon the composition of the group and other factors, namely the available space, symptom presentations, and dynamics of the group, but is something to consider when planning to utilize outdoor spaces. A second therapist can also help with balancing and managing the dynamics of the group. For example, in a client-led group experience, having more than one therapist available can help make sure that therapeutic opportunities for exploration of material (metaphors and such) are not missed. The simple logistics of the matter are that once the space is expanded, your range of availability decreases! This makes it possible for certain therapeutic moments to happen outside your full awareness.

Bringing natural materials into an indoor group play therapy setting is another option. Sticks and some seed pods make great additions to music circles, and there are so many options for natural materials for creating sensory boards. Miniatures and pretend play toys can be created with natural materials in a group setting, and activities that encourage creative problem-solving or self-regulation are a lot of fun in a play therapy group. For example, clients can work together to create a natural bridge that dolls or toy cars must use to get from one side of a room to the other or a bridge made solely of twigs and sticky resin to hold increasing weights. Directing their breath to guide boats made of leaves, twigs, and acorn tops across a basin of water can guide proper breathing skills. Clients can have feather races in which they gently blow a feather across a designated racetrack or try to keep a feather in the air for a certain amount of time. There are many options for including natural materials into play therapy activities that routinely occur in groups, and allowing yourself the creativity to do so can be fun. As always, knowing WHY you are integrating nature allows you flexibility and creativity in the HOW.

Parent coaching

There are two main aspects of parent coaching to present here. One is to encourage parents or guardians to get outside together, and the other is to encourage the importance of individual time outdoors. Part of both is teaching parents about the importance of time spent outside. The information I share ranges from the mental health benefits outlined in previous chapters of this book to physical changes we are seeing as children spend more time indoors and on screens rather than outdoors running around. These physical changes include research results such as occupational therapists seeing increased problems in children's gross and fine motor skills, core body tone and strength, and challenges with navigating rough terrains, as well as ophthalmology findings that children are developing nearsightedness at ever-increasing rates (Mederios, 2022). As children spend more time focusing their gaze at objects directly in front of them rather than distant views, their eyes literally change shape and can grow too long, resulting in myopia. Spending an hour or two outdoors and in the sunshine can drastically impact the rate of this growth (Mederios, 2022). In terms of motor development, researchers have found that children who have access to more outdoor play time have better overall motor skills than children who are indoors more frequently (Sääkslahti & Niemistö, 2021). Often hearing these statistics is enough to encourage parents to find ways to integrate outdoor play time into their families' daily routines. Part of the parent coaching aspect will be helping them to figure out what this can look like. Taking homework outside is an easy first step, as is saying no to screens used for recreation or downtime until 20–60 minutes of outdoor time is achieved (depending on schedules, availability of outdoor space, and so on). There is an option that is possible for every family. The key piece is achieving the buy-in from the parents and helping them to make outdoor time a priority and achieve it consistently. Sometimes this means going outside with their children. A walk around the block after dinner and before bedtime routines can be a simple way to start integrating time outdoors together, no matter what the weather. Identifying and managing potential obstacles can be a helpful role for the nature-based play therapist.

When working with any client, I encourage special play time at home between sessions. The purpose of this is to connect families, or caregivers and children, and give the children a chance to be in control of the play time. The effects of this time are often wonderful, especially as time goes on and the play time continues. Families can use this time to decompress together, get to know each other better, and connect more strongly. I have found that encouraging time together outside has a similarly strong impact on family development and cohesion, as well as contributes to the family's overall health and well-being. Many times, parents are not sure how to go about adding nature time into their schedules and what exactly is supposed to happen during this time. In these situations, it is important to coach parents through this process.

I do believe that spending time outdoors, individually as well as together, simply soaking in the physical and mental benefits of nature, improves the overall health of the family. I have yet to see this in research (and it could be there, I just have not found it yet!), but it just makes sense, and I have seen it happen time and time again as well as experienced it ourselves. Family members get a chance to regulate their nervous systems, attitudes get readjusted naturally, and physical exercise happens along the way adding multiple health benefits. Being together outside allows for co-regulation to happen as well, and that dynamic benefit lasts well outside of the outdoor time. Educating parents about these benefits, and those described earlier in this book, allows for deeper understanding of the principles of nature-based play and the importance of carving out the time to be outside together. Encouraging parents to identify a comfortable place outside where their entire family can fit and enjoy the space is the first step. This might be a backyard, a local park, a spot next to a tree growing near the sidewalk, a beach, or any number of places. The important considerations include feeling safe as a family and having enough space to spread out yet be together.

The second step is doing it. Encourage families to get outside together at least twice a week for a minimum of 15 minutes. Research indicates that 120 minutes a week is the optimal amount of nature time to derive the full benefit especially for cognitive functioning (White et al., 2019), and that can be the end goal. For now, making basic time happen is key. Time outdoors should be screen-free for all participants and can include active engagement with the natural world or a more passive involvement. Ideas for passive involvement include forest bathing, sitting and feeling the sunshine, and sit spotting, which is the Forest School method of choosing a particular spot to sit in routinely to observe the world around that spot as time goes on (Walmsley & Westall, 2018). Ideas for more active engagement include child-led free play time outdoors, organized games like tag or hopscotch, nature walks, hiking, biking, and other activities. Turning traditional board games into life-size versions by using sidewalk chalk to draw the game board and a large die or spinner to determine the moves the players make is always fun.

Families can start off with simple activities to get used to being together outdoors if need be. Encourage them to designate an old blanket or tablecloth as their "outside rug," and throw it down outside to sit or lay on. Have a picnic once a month. Bring a board game outside. Read a story together on the outside rug. Identify other typically indoor activities that parents can bring outside to get comfortable doing things together. Encourage them to let the kids lead and just explore a space together. When you really look, there is so much to be found in a one-foot-square section of the ground! Let them take some cheap magnifying glasses outside and see if three of the blades of grass in one square foot are the same or different. Measure how long it takes for an ant to cover one foot of ground. Once the kids start to take over, and adults let them go, the sky is the limit! If the family needs more structure to start, choosing a topic to learn about such as trees, plants, or animals could help. Families can observe or collect samples and learn identification skills as they explore their environments. There are fun interactive field guidebooks that function as a combination of information-giving and data-gathering as they provide information for people to start observing and exploring in nature, and then tracking and detailing what was found with fill-in sections available (the Outdoor School series is one of my favorites, published by Odd Dot). Starting an activity like geocaching or joining a hiking challenge can also help encourage families to get outside, get exploring, and learn about their geographical areas.

As parents grow in their own comfort with the natural world, the children's experiences will encourage further growth. Whether or not a family intuitively takes to the family nature time is related to the family's view of nature and the importance (or lack thereof) of time spent in nature. Working through parents' expectations of time in nature, perceived importance of time spent out of doors as they were growing up, and role they want nature time to play in their children's development and future lives is well worth the discussion. If parents treat nature time as a chore, that is how children will view it as well. If it becomes a time to connect and grow together, even for five minutes at a time, then that will become the child's internal story.

Supervision

There are three major ways to consider including nature in play therapy supervision: Using nature yourself as a person, therapist, and supervisor; bringing nature into supervision; and bringing supervision out into nature. By learning, experiencing, and exploring nature yourself, you allow the value of nature to become part of your daily life. This helps you expand your comfort zone in terms of using and integrating nature in play therapy. Just like we should never try a play therapy technique with a client without trying it ourselves first, we should not try integrating nature without first developing some level of comfort in and understanding of nature ourselves.

Simply spending time in the natural world is a great way to work on using nature yourself. Find a spot outside that can become yours and use it on a regular basis for "sit spotting" (Walmsley & Westall, 2018). It does not have to be a large space. A step leading into an apartment building works, as does a mossy seat under a tree canopy. Sit in it. Relax in it. Observe it. See what it looks like throughout the year in different seasons. Learn what trees, plants, and critters live in that space. Explore it and make it your own. What matters is that you spend some time in the same spot on a regular basis so you can really get to know the space. As with developing any new habit, fitting quiet nature time into a daily schedule can be challenging, and quite easy to remove from the schedule as soon as you miss a day or two. I tend to take my morning coffee to the same chair on the back patio. On cold or rainy days, the kitchen table is an option that overlooks the same space. Over time I have added plants and feeders to attract my favorite hummingbirds during the spring and summer to add to my enjoyment of the space and to encourage me to get there more often! Building my own appreciation, knowledge, and experiences of nature lets me have more to share with supervisees and grounds me more regularly which makes me a stronger therapist and supervisor, because I have taken the time to deal with any of my own "stuff" regarding nature that could spill into and potentially disrupt sessions.

To bring nature into play therapy supervision sessions, there are three main dimensions to consider. These include professional development, instruction, and processing specific client factors. The role of nature in each of these should be considered and explored to realize the full potential of nature-based play therapy supervision. Developing these skills and habits yourself is important for being able to bring this knowledge to supervision. Teaching supervisees about the importance of integrating nature into play therapy sessions allows them to grow in their own comfort of using nature and gives them verbiage to share with reticent parents or caregivers. As they practice nature skills and develop nature habits, they begin to develop competence in understanding and utilizing nature in therapy. In terms of actively using nature in play therapy supervision, you can either bring nature to your supervisees or bring them into nature. These experiences can be similar to how nature is integrated into play therapy sessions, but often require a bit more verbal explanation about why it is important to learn about integrating and using nature.

Professional development includes developing competencies necessary for a solid play therapist: understanding and utilizing a theoretical orientation, learning the therapeutic powers of play, recognizing the role of self in the therapy process, making ethical decisions, working with various clientele, and the like. The integration of nature into this development can be specific (use nature as part of an intervention or learning experience) or general (explore and develop understanding of the natural world to influence therapy process and development as a play therapist). Part of professional development in the therapy world is understanding one's sense of self and becoming knowledgeable of your own strengths, areas to develop, views of the world and human development, and where you fit in the therapeutic relationship. Taking time to explore your own thoughts, biases, likes and dislikes regarding nature is incredibly important before bringing nature into play therapy or supervision. For instance, I do not like to interact with snakes. I like the role they play in an ecosystem and respect the need for snakes in the natural world. I just like that all to happen … over there. Not near me. Honestly, I do not even like fake snakes! Yet I have them in my playroom, and I have developed my own understanding of my personal reactions to snakes, and therefore what I need to be aware of if I encounter one while outside with a client. I can educate a client about the importance and role of snakes and have learned to manage my own reactions to remain in tune with the client's needs in the moment while respecting my own needs. We can enjoy watching a snake move from a decent distance away and admire the patterns on its skin, but do not need to be any closer to experience the moment.

Trainings on integrating nature into play therapy can be useful and an important part of the ongoing professional development growth of play therapists. As this is a relatively new field for training purposes, even though ecotherapists and other nature-based therapists have been utilizing nature in psychotherapy for many years, there are not a lot of trainings available that are specific to nature-based play therapy. I do see this as growing over the next few years, and more opportunities for professional growth will become available in this field. Until then, taking trainings in more general aspects of nature-based therapies and eco-therapy would be useful, especially as play therapists determine to what extent they want to include nature in their play therapy offerings. There are one-day events for training, all the way up to full graduate degree programs or postgraduate certification tracks. Wanting to include more natural items within an indoor playroom requires a very different skill set than wanting to take a play therapy group into an outdoor play space at a neighborhood park! Understanding these differences with respect to training is important.

Part of professional development in a nature-based play therapy setting that should be discussed during supervision, in addition to the therapist's knowledge of nature, is their knowledge of and comfort with basic first aid. Depending on the type of nature-based work the therapist will be doing, it can be important to learn to recognize potential dangers or negative interactions, such as learning to identify poisonous plants or those prone to activating allergic reactions. This is important when gathering materials to bring into a playroom as well. I strongly encourage therapists to have a basic first aid knowledge and a way to call for help especially if sessions will be taking place outside.

Instruction during supervision refers to learning how to specifically utilize the therapeutic powers of play and play itself within the play therapy process. A supervisor who utilizes nature-based play therapy should be able to guide a new play therapist into ways of integrating nature into play while following a specific theoretical orientation and understanding how the therapeutic powers of play and nature are activated, especially with the addition of natural materials. Supervisees can be taught nature-based activities to use with clients, such as using twigs, leaves, and lichens to create a family drawing on the ground or table. They can explore what it is like to use only natural materials to create a mandala and what the tactile experience and felt difference in creation is like. They can experience the difference in holding building blocks made out of wood rather than plastic. It is important to understand what an intervention truly does before offering it to the client, so providing instruction and practice in supervision sessions is key to fully utilizing nature-based play therapy. These experiences can give supervisees permission to try new things in their nature-based play therapy sessions and be more open to allowing clients to create what they need to heal.

Processing client-specific factors utilizing a nature-based play therapy approach would include using natural materials to process parts of therapy during supervision. This could include creating miniatures to complete supervision sandtrays, using natural materials to represent clients and family members to explore perceptions of relationships, and the like. Removing the previously held associations people have to manufactured miniatures by using sticks, moss, acorns, pinecones, leaves, and other natural materials seems to help open stuck thinking patterns as well. Changing the way we interact with miniatures in the sand can help unconsciously challenge how supervisees view clients and their stuck spots in therapy. The creativity that is required to make a miniature and create a sand scene out of unformed items can jumpstart new thinking about the case. Offering images of natural scenes and asking a supervisee to choose one to represent a challenging client can open the door to new understanding as well. Often activities like this allow for deeper levels of metaphorical meaning to be explored, and unconscious expectations and reactions to clients and their worlds can be accessed. There are many stock images available online that can be printed and laminated to create a stack of images to browse, or your own photographs could be used. Sometimes people enjoy creating miniature versions of these images and affixing them to sticks to use as part of sandtray creations to bring the metaphor directly into the sand.

Concluding thoughts

All in all, there are many ways to adapt individual nature-based play therapy to meet a variety of needs. From family and group psychotherapy to teaching and supporting families through the process of integrating more nature time and exposure into their daily lives, the impact of nature-based play therapy can be seen in a different way than with individual sessions alone. Integrating the use of nature into play therapy supervision or consultation sessions is another powerful way to expand and enhance the use of nature-based play therapy. Helping a supervisee become more comfortable in and with nature themselves, as well as exploring cases through the lens of nature-based play therapy activities, can continue to grow this field through exploration, instruction, and experience.

References

Mederios, S. (2022, September 16). Prescription for keeping children out of glasses: Sunshine. *American Academy of Ophthalmology*. https://www.aao.org/eye-health/news/prevent-childhood-myopia-sunshine-outdoors

Sääkslahti, A., & Niemistö, D. (2021). Outdoor activities and motor development in 2–7-year-old boys and girls. *Journal of Physical Education and Sport, 21*(SI1), 463–468. https://doi.org/10.7752/jpes.2021.s1047

Walmsley, N., & Westall, D. (2018). *Forest school adventure: Outdoor skills and play for children*. Guild of Master Craftsman Publications Ltd.

White, M. P., Alcock, I., Grellier, J., Wheeler, B. W., Hartig, T., Warber, S. L., Bone, A., Depledge, M. H., & Fleming, L. E. (2019). Spending at least 120 minutes a week in nature is associated with good health and wellbeing. *Scientific Reports, 9*, 7730. https://doi.org/10.1038/s41598-019-44097-3

Yalom, I. D. (1985). *Theory and practice of group psychotherapy* (3rd ed.). Basic Books, Inc.

Chapter 11

Concluding thoughts and reflections

This book turned into quite the whirlwind tour! From the history of nature and play in children's lives and the development of societies and communities, to the play therapy theories prominent today, to understanding how nature-based play therapy truly works and how to actively utilize these aspects in your practice of nature-based play therapy, there are multiple takeaways that stood out to me as I worked through this material that are worth summarizing here. It is also worth discussing some applications to our professional work.

Changes in perceived value of children's play

Throughout history, children's play time has meant different things in different cultures. Play has been considered something to keep children busy and out from under their parents' feet; a direct avenue for learning necessary skills for adulthood; an opportunity to learn, grow, develop, and explore through child-led activities; and every combination therein. As a play therapist, I hold that the value of play in and of itself is immeasurable. Through play, children have the opportunity to understand themselves and the world in which they live. Play is a vital aspect of not only childhood but the entire lifespan. As described throughout this book, research has now been done that supports the value of play as well as the therapeutic benefits. We, as play therapists, are uniquely positioned to teach and encourage caregivers and other professionals about the importance and value of all play, but especially child-led free play. While many people recognize some of the importance of play, there is still much work to be done in terms of educating the public about the true impact of children's play and how it impacts children's cognitive, emotional, and social development.

Changes in perceived value of nature

The perceived value of nature has changed drastically, especially in some cultures, over the years. Early populations depended fully on the natural world for their survival, and this was gradually replaced by valuing changes made by

DOI: 10.4324/9781003332343-11

society and the world of manufacturing in particular that eased many burdens people experienced in living off the land. In general, I do think we are swinging back toward understanding the importance that nature can and should play in our daily lives as well as for society as a whole and are developing a research base to support such efforts. People are encouraged to take time to experience and enjoy nature and are more open to sharing those times with others. Games like geocaching and letterboxing have been developed to blend outdoor activities with technological advances. People of all ages paint and hide rocks along trails to encourage discovery by others and building communities. More and more libraries and community centers host discussions about nature topics ranging from teaching information about specific animals to edible plants to ways to get involved in taking care of the natural world. Such a shift in community-based perspectives opens a door for nature-based play therapists to guide families into exploring how the natural world can support their growth and development.

Play therapy case conceptualization model

I hope that through the exploration of play therapy theories and the therapeutic powers of play, along with how nature can be woven into this thinking, you have more ideas about how to include these topics in your case conceptualizations. Theory should always guide our understanding of our cases, and the therapeutic powers of play and nature should guide our treatment planning and selection of interventions. While this process takes practice, it is well worth the effort and study. What I have found particularly useful about the model presented here is that it can be effectively utilized with any theoretical orientation to help guide treatment planning as well as to explain what happens in play therapy to caregivers and other professionals. You can completely follow one theoretical orientation and prescriptively apply the therapeutic powers of play and nature to your cases. Someone else can follow another theory, and the conceptualization process applies to both. This method helps frame your thinking about your clients and their needs, and thus helps you to consolidate your treatment goals and objectives in a logical way. Doing so will help you to provide play therapy in an efficient manner.

Concluding thoughts

Integrating nature into all aspects of your personal and professional lives can allow for deeper growth and understanding of your clients and their needs, as well as ways to better encourage their path toward optimal development. My hope is that through this process of exploration, you walk away with a deeper understanding of what needs to be considered from a theoretical perspective to be able to apply the foundational principles behind nature-based play treatments to guide your clients through comprehensive nature-based play therapy work.

Knowing why you are doing what you do will guide your decision on how the treatment should happen! Only after you work through conceptualization should you be choosing interventions. Through it all, the importance of play and nature should not be diminished.

This brings me back to some of the original questions I asked you to consider in Chapter 1. I wonder if any answers have changed for you now, so will ask some again and include some new ones to consider. Again, this process of self-exploration is for you and your own growth and development.

- What stands out to you as a reason to include nature in your life?
- Do you play? What value do you place on play in your own life?
- How can you integrate more time experiencing nature for what it is—from little things like removing ear buds with podcasts playing as you walk to and from the office, to taking up hiking with your family on weekends?
- What are your stumbling blocks to integrating nature in your everyday life? What about integrating play?
- What are some small ways to include nature in your play therapy sessions and treatment planning?
- What is stopping you from integrating nature into your play therapy space? What are potential obstacles to overcome?
- How can you get families on board with the importance of nature time as well as child-led free play?
- How does the availability of nature and natural spaces in your area impact your clients?
- How do you see yourself integrating the principles of nature-based play therapy into your regular practice?

The final questions are: What now? What is the next step for you to take in your nature-based play therapy journey? What do you need to get there, and to continue to grow this area of your practice?

The following appendices are intended to help you put all this information into practice and to support you in your nature-based play therapy journey, from utilizing and incorporating the case conceptualization and treatment planning model to ways to include nature in your indoor and outdoor sessions, and suggestions to help families explore nature on their own. Appendix 1 consists of a larger-scale flowchart or worksheet to help you practice and consistently apply the case conceptualization model with your own cases. Appendix 2 contains suggestions for you as a nature-based play therapist with lists of suggested nature-based items to include in every play therapy space, ways to bring nature inside to play therapy sessions, and ways to bring play therapy outside. Appendix 3 consists of potential outdoor activities to suggest to families. These range from simple, "five minutes or less" setup time to weekend or longer activities. There is something here for every family! I hope that this has been a useful journey for you and look forward to watching the field of nature-based play therapy continue to grow!

Appendix 1

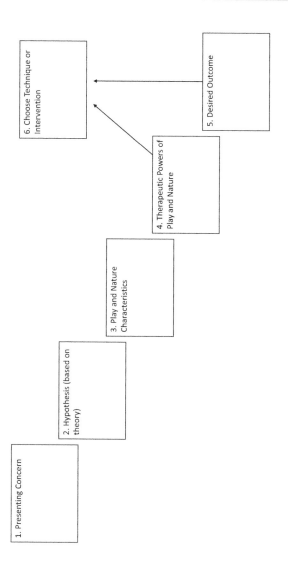

1. Presenting Concern

2. Hypothesis (based on theory)

3. Play and Nature Characteristics

4. Therapeutic Powers of Play and Nature

5. Desired Outcome

6. Choose Technique or Intervention

Appendix 2

Nature items to include in every play space

- Acorn tops
- Choose items made of wood over plastics (wooden blocks, furniture, doll furnishings)
- Feathers (from little songbirds up to large peacock)
- Ferns/fronds
- Games that support nature experiences (Ouisi and Get Wild are two of our favorites)
- Leaves (depending on the activity—they can crumble!)
- Moss/lichen
- Pictures of nature scenes—can be taken by you and printed inexpensively to hang on walls, use as miniatures, for collage supplies, or as part of card games
- Pine needles (to make brushes and for sensory experiences)
- Pinecones
- Potted plants or succulents in terrariums
- Rocks, stones, river rocks, polished "gems" or stones
- Sand
- Seashells
- Slices of small logs—ring patterns can be amazing!
- Sticks for building and play, driftwood
- Water (potentially in various forms. Snow in the winter)
- Woven baskets

Ways to bring nature inside to play therapy sessions

- Bird feeder on a window or outside of one
- Bring a pan of snow inside to sculpt or paint with spray bottles filled with water and food coloring, or watered down washable paints
- Encourage children to bring nature items they collect at home
- Have selections of natural materials ready to include in sandtray creations

- Make items to take home like bird feeders
- Make mud inside to create with
- Make natural brushes for paint or sand out of pine needles, twigs, bundle of leaves, and so forth
- Make nature dolls from pinecones and paper tubes
- Nature collages with leaves, sticks, rocks, wooden craft sticks, acorn tops
- Set up an observation station near a window with binoculars, field guides or specific pages, and journaling or drawing supplies
- Take a quick nature walk to collect items
- Use flowers and leaves to create stained glass images on clear sticky paper
- Use natural materials in crafts
- Use paints or stamps that you make together from natural materials (berries, mud, potatoes, apples, cut beets, etc.—just be aware that these can stain!)

Ways to bring play therapy sessions to the outdoor world

- Ask children to spend time playing outdoors when they go home, after school, and on weekends
- Create an outdoor play space, picnic table, and logs to climb
- Create stories based on cloud observations
- Find a sand or dirt patch outside to use for sandtray or just playing in the dirt!
- Have "nature kits" packed and ready to go on an adventure. Mine usually includes thick paper, colored pencils, a magnifying glass, water colors and a brush, a measuring tape, and paper bags
- Mark out one square foot of ground and spend time observing just within that square
- Meet at a public outdoor space for a nature walk or other activity
- Physical play whenever possible
- Scavenger hunts, color hunts, texture hunts, bingo games
- Use playgrounds or beaches to your benefit (sandtray at the beach!)
- Use your parking lot or driveway to draw with sidewalk chalk

Appendix 3

Activities to encourage families to engage with nature outside of sessions

- Borrow animal guides from the library and choose three animals to put on a "family watch list" to observe and learn about over time
- Camping (in the backyard counts!)
- Choose a spot outside to "claim" and visit it throughout the year to note changes
- Cloud watch. Spread a blanket on the ground and lay together, looking at the shapes in the sky
- Create a story about a tree or animal you can see out of a window
- Create obstacle courses
- Do a color hunt. Can you find something for every color of the rainbow? Or grab a handful of crayons on the way out the door and match each color to an object in nature
- Do a scavenger hunt together. Take it up a level by doing a sensory hunt and identify things related to each of the senses
- Do homework or read outside, maybe in a hammock
- Explore from the perspectives of different animals. Lay on the ground and look up to see the world from a worm's eye view. Crouch to see things from a rabbit's perspective. Stand tall and see what a bear might view
- Free play. Turn them loose!
- Geocaching
  - Explore www.geocaching.com for information. Must be 18 or older to create an account. These can include quick jaunts to a park and grab, a meetup event with other geocachers, cleanup days at specific locations, up to as much time and energy as families want to put in to exploring and walking!
- Have a responsible fire outdoors
- Hiking (start with short trails to explore the world)
- Hopscotch

- Learn about trees, plants, birds, bugs, flowers, and any other possible outdoor creation!
- Learn to jump rope
- Look into scouting groups and other outdoor group opportunities
- Nature journals
- Nature studies
- Observe the stars and night sky using binoculars and star charts from the library or other affordable source
- One-square-foot search. How many different plants, critters, or interesting things can you discover about one square foot of ground?
- Paint snow with spray bottles filled with water and food coloring
- Picnic
- Plant a garden
- Play in the puddles instead of walking around them
- Put up a bird feeder
- Ride bikes or scooters together. Create paths or obstacle courses with sidewalk chalk
- See what the local land trusts or other groups have available for open spaces for public use
- Sidewalk chalk to create games. Life-size Chutes and Ladders is a big hit!
- Skip stones
- Ten-minute walks after school or after dinner
  - Choose a sense to focus on—will they identify things they see, hear, smell, or can touch?
- Toss a baseball, basketball, or football around, or kick a soccer ball!
- Train for kid fun runs or 5ks
- Use a tent to create a fort (or just make a fort!)

Index

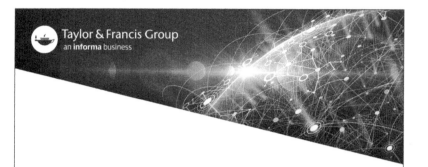